Essentials of Accounting

Fourth Edition

Robert N. Anthony
Ross Graham Walker Professor of Management Control, Emeritus
Harvard Business School

Addison-Wesley Publishing Company

Reading, Massachusetts • Menlo Park, California
New York • Don Mills, Ontario • Wokingham, England
Amsterdam • Bonn • Sydney • Singapore • Tokyo • Madrid • San Juan

Sponsoring Editor: Herbert Smith
Production Coordinator: Sarah Hallet
Editorial Coordinator: Mary Eagleson
Composition: Mona Zeftel; Jacqueline Davies; Sally Simpson
Text Design: Marie E. McAdam
Cover Designer: Marshall Henrichs
Technical Art Consultants: Joseph K. Vetere; Richard Morton
Illustrators: Phil Carver & Friends; Carol Flaherty
Manufacturing Supervisor: Roy Logan

Library of Congress Cataloging-in-Publication Data

Anthony, Robert Newton
Essentials of accounting / Robert N. Anthony.—4th ed.
p. cm.
ISBN 0-201-00017-2
1. Accounting. I. Title
HF5635.A6879 1988
657'.07—dc19 87-21944
CIP

Reprinted with corrections May, 1990.

10 AL 95949392

for Katherine

Acknowledgments

Dr. Matthew Israel developed the program for the First Edition.

Dr. Philip E. Meyers, Boston University, developed the Glossary.

Illustrations were developed by C. Stewart Anthony, Phil Carver, Jerrold E. Moore, and Carol Flaherty. Jerry Moore also made helpful comments on the substance.

Student testing and surveys were conducted by Prof. Julie H. Hertenstein, Harvard Business School; Prof. Susan Haas, Simmons College; Peter Yu and Lisa Martin, Harvard Extension Program, and Dr. Robert N. Anthony, Jr.

Frank J. Burns, Herbert Smith and Jane Tamlyn were my editors at Addison-Wesley. Others who participated in the editorial and production process at Addison-Wesley were Mary Eagleson, Sarah Hallet, Doris L. Machado, Linda O'Brien, and Mona Zeftel.

Nancy Anthony edited the manuscript.

My secretaries who worked on this project included Sandra Bardwell, Ann T. Carter, Judith Grady, Emily C. Hood, Elizabeth Keyes, and Patricia Lougee.

I am grateful for all this help and for the comments of many users whose ideas have led to improvements in this edition.

Contents

The following is in a separate booklet attached to the back of the book.

Introduction

This book is designed to help you teach yourself the basic concepts of accounting. It leads you to an understanding of what accounting statements can and cannot tell you about a business.

Accounting has been called the language of business and, like any language, it can never express ideas with perfect precision and clarity. The task of learning this language is complicated by the fact that many of the words used in accounting do not mean the same things as they mean in everyday life. You must learn to think of words in their accounting, rather than their popular, meaning. In this program, we have used a standard set of accounting terms. Frequent repetition and writing of these terms reinforces your basic grasp of the accounting language.

In any language there are some rules or principles that are *definite* and some others that are *not definite*. The latter are a matter of opinion or style. Accountants have different opinions, just as people speak in different dialects. In this program we have tried to describe the elements of good accounting practice, and to indicate some of the areas where there are differences of opinion as to what constitutes good practice. As language changes to meet the needs of communication in a society, so accounting changes to meet the needs of business. We have presented what is currently good practice in accounting.

How to Use This Program

General Instructions

1. Read each item or "frame" in the left-hand column, while covering the right-hand column with the mask provided.
2. *Write* your answer in the space provided or, where necessary, on a separate piece of scratch paper. (It is essential that you write rather than think your response.)
3. Check your response by moving the mask down the page to uncover the correct answer in the right-hand column.
4. If your answer is correct, go on to the next frame.
5. If your answer is *not* correct, read the frame again and try to understand why you were wrong.
6. Many of the frames refer to panel displays called *Exhibits*. These will be found in a separate booklet at the end of this book. When it becomes necessary to look at a given exhibit, tear it out along the perforation and place it beside your work, where you can refer to it as needed. Exhibits which have thus been removed and used should afterwards be clipped or otherwise secured to the inside cover of your book for further use.
7. Following the exhibits you will find a series of *Post Tests,* one for each part of the program. Do not look at any of these tests until you are instructed to do so. When you are ready to take a given test, tear it out along the perforation, then set aside the book and all exhibits (unless other instructions are given), and proceed as directed.

This programmed text has a proven format which involves a unique reversal of pages in the later chapters. This design allows the answer column always to appear in the right margin.

SEQUENCE

Each frame should be answered in turn. Do not skip frames unless directed to do so. If you have difficulty with a particular point, you should go back to the place where it first appeared and review those frames.

Avoid careless answers. If you begin to make mistakes because you are tired, take a rest.

TECHNICAL CONVENTIONS

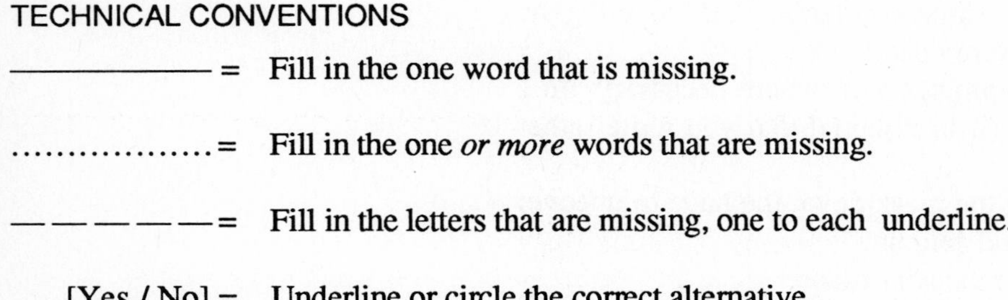

―――――― = Fill in the one word that is missing.

.... = Fill in the one *or more* words that are missing.

— — — — — = Fill in the letters that are missing, one to each underline.

. . . [Yes / No] = Underline or circle the correct alternative.

Part 1

Basic Concepts and the Balance Sheet

Learning Objectives

In this part you will learn:

- The accounting meaning of assets, liabilities, equities, and the balance sheet.
- The first three of the nine concepts that govern all accounting:
    - The dual-aspect concept.
    - The money-measurement concept.
    - The entity concept.

1-1. Accounting is a language. The purpose of any language is to provide information. Accounting information is provided by reports that are called **financial statements**. The objective of this program is to help you understand what the numbers in the financial statements mean and how they can be used. Please turn to Exhibit 1 (in the separate booklet) to see one of these financial statements. As indicated by the title at the top of the page, this report is called a _ _ _ _ _ _ _ **sheet**.

On an item like this, fill in one letter for each underline and then compare it with the correct answer, found here.

Balance

NOTE
Be sure to cover up the answers with the mask provided.

CONCLUDING NOTE

You now know the *essentials* of accounting. There is, of course, much more to the subject. Nevertheless, you now have a basic framework into which you can fit many other transactions when you encounter them. Moreover, notes are added to the financial statements which help explain them and give more detail than the statements themselves. You should always read these notes carefully.

We have used a common set of terms throughout this program. Unfortunately, there is no standard set of terms. Companies can use other terminology. Nevertheless, from your knowledge of the nature of the balance sheet and income statement, you can usually figure out what is meant by a term that is not used in this program.

Some transactions are governed by specific rules that are not described in this introductory treatment. For further study, see Robert N. Anthony and James S. Reece, *Accounting Principles*, 6th ed. (Homewood, Illinois: Richard D. Irwin, Inc., 1988).

ELEMENTS OF THE BALANCE SHEET

1-2. A balance sheet gives financial information about an **entity**. The name of the entity that this balance sheet refers to is Garsden _______.

Company

1-3. An entity is any organization or other unit for which financial statements are prepared. A business is an ______; so is a college, a government, a church, a synagogue or other nonprofit organization.

entity

1-4. The balance sheet reports the financial position of the entity as of one moment in time. As indicated by the heading in Exhibit 1, the balance sheet for Garsden Company reports its financial position as of December 31, ____.

1986

1-5. The date December 31, 1986, means [circle A or B]:

A. it was prepared on December 31, 1986.

B. it reports the entity's financial position as of December 31, 1986.

B
(probably it was prepared early in 1987)

1-6. Thus, the heading tells three things: (1) the fact that the report is a b_______ s_____, (2) the name of the entity, and (3) the date.

balance sheet

1-7. The balance sheet has two sides. The heading of the left side is called A_____, and the heading of the right side is L__________ and E________. We shall describe the meaning of each side.

Assets; Liabilities
Equities

ASSETS

1-8. An entity needs cash, equipment, and other resources in order to operate. These resources are its a_____. Assets are valuable resources owned by the entity. The balance sheet shows the amounts of these assets as of a certain date.

assets

KEY POINTS TO REMEMBER

- The Cash Flow Statement explains changes that have occurred in the Cash account during the accounting period. Usually, the largest source of additional cash is profitable operating activities. The amount of cash generated by operating activities is found by adjusting the net income amount for noncash changes. It is prepared by rearranging balance sheet and income statement items; it does not require additional accounts.
- Depreciation is not a source of working capital or cash. It is added to net income because it was an expense that did not represent the use of cash during the current period
- The financial statements do not tell the whole story about an entity because they report only past events, do not report market values, and are based on judgments and estimates. Nevertheless, they provide important information.
- Financial statements are analyzed by using ratios, rather than absolute dollar amounts. These ratios are compared with those for the same entity in the past, with those for similar entities, or with standards based on judgment.
- An overall measure of performance is Return on Equity (ROE). It takes into account both profitability and the capital used in generating profits. Another overall measure is Return on Permanent Capital, or Return on Investment, which is the ratio of profits (adjusted for interest) to total permanent capital.
- An entity with a low profit margin can provide a good return on equity investment if it has a sufficiently high capital turnover.
- In addition to information about profitability, financial statements provide information about the entity's liquidity and solvency.

You have completed Part 10 of this program. If you think you understand the material in this part, you should now take Post Test 10, which is in the separate booklet. If you are uncertain about your understanding, you should review Part 10.

The post test will serve both to test your comprehension and to review the highlights of Part 10. After taking the post test, you may find that you are unsure about certain points. You should review these points.

1-9. For example, the amount of Cash that Garsden Company owned on December 31, 1986 was $_ , _ _ _ , 000.

$1,449,000
(Note that numbers on this balance sheet omit 000.)

1-10. Assets are resources **owned** by Garsden Company. Its employees, although perhaps its most valuable resource, . . . [are / are not] accounting assets.

On an item like this, circle the answer of your choice.

are not
(No one owns humans since the abolition of slavery.)

LIABILITIES AND EQUITIES

1-11. The right side of the balance sheet shows the sources that provided the entity's assets. As the heading indicates, there are two general types of sources, L _ _ _ _ _ _ _ _ _ _ _ and E _ _ _ _ _ _ _ .

Liabilities; Equities

1-12. Liabilities are amounts provided by outside parties. These parties are generally called **creditors** because they have extended credit to the entity. As Exhibit 1 indicates, suppliers have extended credit in the amount of $5,602,000, as indicated by the item A _ _ _ _ _ _ _ p _ _ _ _ _ _ .

Accounts payable

1-13. Creditors have a **claim** against the assets in the amount shown as the liability. For example, a bank has loaned $1,000,000 to Garsden Company, and therefore has a claim of this amount, as indicated by the item, _ _ _ _ _ _ _ _ _ _ _ _ _ _ _.

Bank
loan payable

1-14. Because an entity will use its assets to pay off its claims, the claims are claims against _ _ _ _ _ _. They are claims against all the assets, not any particular asset.

assets

10-90. Ability to meet current obligations is called **liquidity**. The ratio of current assets to current liabilities, called the ________________ ratio, is a widely used measure of liquidity.

current

10-91. Ability to meet long-term obligations is called **solvency**. If a high proportion of permanent capital is obtained from debt, rather than from equities, this increases the danger of insolvency. The proportion of debt is indicated by the d _ _ _ r _ _ _ _ .

debt ratio

10-92. Any of dozens of other ratios may be used for various purposes in analyzing the profitability and financial condition of a business. Those described here are the ones in most general use. Others give a more detailed picture of the important relationships.

(No answer required.)

10-93. Financial analysts form their opinions about a company partly by studying ratios such as those we have presented. They also study the details of the financial statements, including the notes that accompany these statements. They obtain additional information by conversations and visits because they realize that the financial statements tell . . . [only part of the / the whole] story about the company.

only part of the

1-15. The other source of the funds that an entity uses to acquire its assets is called **Equities.** In Garsden Company, equity investors provided funds for which they received common stock. The total amount supplied by equity investors is called **Total paid-in capital**. In Garsden Company, it was $ _ _ , _ _ _ , 000. (We shall describe the details in a later part.)

$12,256,000

1-16. Equity funds also come from a second source, the profits or **earnings** generated by the entity. The amount of these earnings that has not been paid to equity investors is retained in the entity, and therefore is called _ _ _ _ _ _ _ _ Earnings. In Garsden Company, the amount was $ _ _ , _ _ _ ,000.

Retained

$13,640,000

1-17. Thus, there are two sources of equity funds: (1) the amount provided by equity investors, which is called _ _ _ _ -_ _ _ _ _ _ _ _ _ _ and (2) the amount retained from profits (or earnings), which is called _ _ _ _ _ _ _ _ _ _ _ _ _ _ _ _ _.

Paid-in capital

Retained

earnings

1-18. Creditors can sue the entity if the amounts due them are not paid. Equity investors have only a *residual claim*; if the entity is dissolved, they get whatever is left after the liabilities have been paid, which may be nothing. Liabilities therefore are a . . . [stronger/weaker] claim against the assets.

stronger

1-19. Thus, the right-hand side of the balance sheet reports two types of claims: (1) the claims of creditors, which are _ _ _ _ _ _ _ _ _ _ _ and (2) the residual claim of equity investors, which are _ _ _ _ _ _ _ _.

liabilities

equities

1-20. We have described the right-hand side of the balance sheet in two somewhat different ways: (1) as the amount of funds supplied by creditors and equity investors; and (2) as the claims of these parties against the assets. Use whichever of these is more meaningful to you.

(No answer required.)

The EBIT margin for the supermarket is only

$$\frac{\$\_\_\_\_}{\$\_\_\_\_} = \_\_\_\_ \%$$

$$\frac{400}{10{,}000} = 4\%$$

and for the department store, it is

$$\frac{\$\_\_\_\_}{\$\_\_\_\_} = \_\_\_\_ \% .$$

$$\frac{2{,}000}{10{,}000} = 20\%$$

The ratio for the department store is much . . . [lower / higher].

higher

10-87. However, the department store has more expensive fixtures, a larger inventory, and a lower inventory turnover than the supermarket, so its capital turnover is lower. Calculate the capital turnover of each.

	Sales	÷ Permanent Capital	= Capital turnover
Supermarket	$____	÷ $____	= ____ times
Deparment store	$____	÷ $____	= ____ times

$10,000 ÷ $1,000 = 10 times

$10,000 ÷ $5,000 = 2 times

10-88. The return on permanent capital is the same in both companies, as you can see for yourself in the following calculation.

	EBIT margin	x	Capital turnover	=	Return on permanent capital
Supermarket	0.____ %	x	$____ times	=	____ %
Department store	0.____ %	x	$____ times	=	____ %

0.04 x 10 = 40%

0.20 x 2 = 40%

TESTS OF FINANCIAL CONDITION

10-89. A business must be concerned with more than profitability. It must also maintain a sound financial condition. This means that it must be able to pay its debts when they come due.

(No answer required.)

DUAL-ASPECT CONCEPT

1-21. Whatever assets remain after the liabilities are taken into account will be claimed by the equity investors. Consider the case of an entity whose assets total $10,000, and whose liabilities total $4,000. Its equity must be $ ______________.

$6,000 (= $10,000 – $4,000)

A single blank indicates that the answer is one word or, when preceded by the dollar sign as it is here, one amount.

1-22. (1) Any assets not claimed by creditors will be claimed by equity investors, and (2) The total amount of claims (liabilities + equities) cannot exceed what there is to be claimed.

It follows from statements (1) and (2) that the total amount of assets will always be . . . [greater than / equal to / less than] the total amount of liabilities plus equities.

equal to

1-23. Here is the balance sheet of Garsden Company, greatly condensed so as to focus on the main elements, and disregarding thousands:

Garsden Company
Balance Sheet as of December 31, 1986

Assets		Liabilities & Equities	
Cash	$ 1,449	Liabilities	$12,343
Other assets	36,790	Equity	25,896
Total	$38,239	Total	$38,239

(1) $38,239 of funds were supplied to the entity from sources listed on the . . . [left / right] side.

right

(2) They are represented by assets listed on the . . .[left / right] side.

left

(3) The amount of assets can be neither more nor less than the amount of sources of these assets. The amount must be $38,239.

10-82. Another way of finding the return on permanent capital is to multiply the EBIT margin ratio by the capital turnover. Calculate this relationship.

EBIT margin x Capital turnover = Return on permanent capital
(Frame 10-77) (Frame 10-80)

[ ] % x [ ] = [ ] %

14% x 1.8 = 25%

10-83. This formula suggests two fundamental ways in which the profitability of a business can be improved:

1. . . . [increase / decrease] the EBIT margin ratio.
2. . . . [increase / decrease] the capital turnover.

increase

increase

(If you had difficulty in following these relationships, try out some numbers of your own.)

COMMENTS ON PROFITABILITY MEASUREMENT

10-84. In the analysis above, we used ratios, because absolute dollar amounts are . . . [rarely / often] useful in understanding what has happened in a business.

rarely

10-85. Also, we focused on *both* income and the capital used in earning that income. Focusing on just one of these elements can be . . . [just as good / misleading].

misleading

10-86. For example, consider the following results for a supermarket and a department store, each with $10 million of sales revenue.

	Supermarket	Department store
	(000 omitted)	
Sales revenue	$10,000	$10,000
EBIT	400	2,000
Permanent capital	1,000	5,000

1-24. This is another way of saying that total assets must always equal total ____________ plus _________ .

liabilities; equities

1-25. If the total assets are less than the total liabilities plus equities, the reason may be (circle one):

A. Assets have been lost or stolen.

B. The record keeper has made an error.

B
(When correctly done, the two sides are always equal.)

1-26. The fact that total assets must equal, or **balance**, total liabilities plus equities is why the statement we have been studying is called a _______ _____. This equality tells nothing about the entity's financial condition; it always exists unless the accountant has made a mistake.

balance
sheet

1-27. This fact leads to what is called the dual-aspect concept. Evidently the two aspects that this concept refers to are ____________ and ______________ plus ____________, and the concept states that these two aspects are always ______. (In what relation to each other?)

assets
liabilities; equities
equal

1-28. The dual-aspect concept is the first of nine fundamental accounting concepts we shall describe in this program. The concept can be written as an equation, that is, a statement that something is equal to something else. Write this equation, using just the words assets, liabilities, and equities:

__________ = ________________ + ____________

Assets
Liabilities + Equities

assets = liabilities + equities

1-29. This equation is fundamental. It governs all accounting. Write a similar equation in a form that emphasizes the fact that equity is a residual interest:

__________ – ________________ = Equities

Assets – Liabilities

10-78. The permanent capital as of December 31, 19x2, is the debt capital (i.e., noncurrent liabilities) of $______,000 plus the equity capital of $________,000, a total of $__________,000. The return on permanent capital is found by dividing EBIT by this total. Calculate the return on permanent capital.

$$\frac{\boxed{}}{\boxed{}} = \frac{\$\boxed{}}{\$\boxed{}} = \boxed{}\ \%$$

$40

$130; $170 ($40 + $30)

$$\frac{\text{EBIT}}{\text{Permanent capital}} = \frac{\$42}{\$170} = 25\%$$

10-79. Copy the numerator and denominator of the return on permanent capital on Line 4 of Exhibit 13.

Numerator: EBIT (Earnings before interest and taxes)
Denominator: Permanent capital

10-80. Another ratio shows how much sales revenue was generated by each dollar of permanent capital. This ratio is called the **capital turnover** ratio. Calculate it for Arlen Company.

$$\text{Capital turnover} = \frac{\text{Sales revenue}}{\text{Permanent capital}} = \frac{\$\boxed{}}{\$\boxed{}} = \_\_\_\_\_\_ \text{ times}$$

$$\frac{\$300}{\$170} = 1.8 \text{ times}$$

Copy the numerator and denominator of this ratio on Line 12 of Exhibit 13.

Numerator: Sales revenue
Denominator: Permanent capital

10-81. The typical American manufacturing company has a capital turnover ratio of roughly two times. A company that has a large capital investment in relation to its sales revenue is called a **capital-intensive** company. A capital-intensive company, such as a steel manufacturing company or a public utility, has a relatively . . . [high / low] capital turnover.

low

1-30. The liabilities of Violet Company total $3,000. Its equities total $16,000. The company must have assets that total $__________.

$19,000 (= $3,000 + $16,000)

1-31. Suppose a business has assets totaling $20,000 and liabilities totaling $18,000. Evidently, its equities are $____________.

$2,000 = ($20,000 - $18,000)

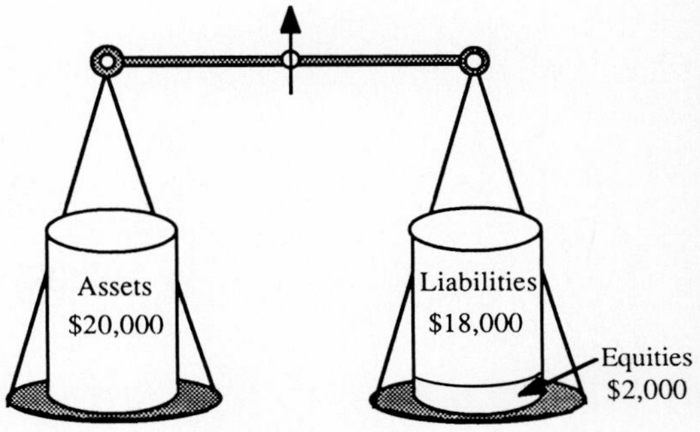

1-32. Suppose a business has $30,000 in assets. Between the claims of the creditors (the______________) and those of equity investors, which have priority—that is, which have the first claim? ____________________.

liabilities
Creditors (liabilities)

1-33. As a review of terms we have discussed so far, here is a list of ordinary terms. In the right-hand column, write the accounting term for each.

Ordinary term	Accounting term	
things of value	______________	assets
one who lends money	______________	creditor
creditors' claim	______________	liabilities
investors' claim	______________	equities

10-72. On line 3 of Exhibit 13, enter the numerator and denominator of the price-earnings ratio.

Numerator: Average market price
Denominator: Earnings per share

10-73. Price-earnings ratios of many companies are published daily in the financial page of newspapers. Typically, the ratio is roughly 8 to 1, but it varies greatly depending on market conditions. If investors think that earnings per share will increase, this ratio could be much higher. Apparently, investors are willing to pay . . . [more /less] per dollar of earnings in a growing company.

more

10-74. We have focused on return on equities (ROE) as an overall measure of performance. Another useful measure is the **return on permanent capital**. This shows how well the entity used its capital, without considering how much of its permanent capital came from each of the two sources: d _ _ _ and e _ _ _ _ _ . This ratio is also called **return on investment (ROI)**.

debt; equity

10-75. The *return* portion of this ratio is *not* net income. Net income includes a deduction for interest expense, but interest expense *is* the return on debt capital. Therefore, net income . . . [understates / overstates] the return earned on all permanent capital. Also, income tax expense often is disregarded so as to focus on purely operating activities.

understates

10-76. The return used in this calculation is **Earnings Before** the deduction of **Interest** and **Taxes** on income. It is abbreviated by the first letters of the words in boldface, that is, _ _ _ _ .

EBIT

10-77. As with other income statement numbers, EBIT is calculated as the percentage of sales revenue. This gives the **EBIT margin.** Calculate it for Arlen Company.

$$\frac{\text{EBIT}}{\text{Sales revenue}} = \frac{\$\ \_\_\_\_}{\$\ \_\_\_\_} = \_\_\_\_\%\ \text{EBIT margin}$$

$$\frac{\$42}{\$300} = 14\%$$

Enter the numerator and denominator of the EBIT margin ratio on Line 7 of Exhibit 13.

Numerator: EBIT
Denominator: Sales revenue

1-34. The amount of cash owned by a business is likely to . . . [remain constant / change] from day to day.

change

1-35. Do you think that the amounts of the other assets and of liabilities will change from day to day? [Yes / No.]

Yes

1-36. You may surmise, therefore, that any given balance sheet reports the amounts of A________________, L________________, and E________________ . . . [over an extended period of time / at one point in time].

Assets
Liabilities; Equities
at one point in time

1-37. Because a balance sheet reports amounts for a . . . [period of / point in] time, the balance sheet must be dated. From here on we shall use the term "19x1" to refer to the first year, "19x2" for the next year, and so on. Thus, a balance sheet as of December 31 of the first year is dated "as of December 31, _ _ _ _ ."

point in

19x1

1-38. At the close of business on December 31, 19x1, Dowling Company had $2,000 in its bank account. It owned other assets totaling $24,000. The company owed $10,000 to creditors. Its equities were $16,000. Complete the balance sheet for Dowling Company:

DOWLING COMPANY

Balance Sheet as of ________________

Assets		Liabilities and Equities	
Cash	$	Liabilities .	$
Other assets ..	$	Equities	$
Total		Total	

DOWLING COMPANY

Balance Sheet as of December 31, 19x1

Assets		Liabilities and Equities	
Cash	$ 2,000	Liabilities	$ 10,000
Other assets	24,000	Equities	16,000
Total	$26,000	Total	$26,000

10-66. In the calculations above, we used balance sheet amounts taken from the ending balance sheet. For some purposes, it is more informative to use an **average** of beginning and ending balance sheet amounts. Arlen Company had $130,000 of equities at the end of 19x2. If it had $110,000 at the beginning of 19x2, its aver*age* *e*quity during 19x2 was $__________. Since its net income in 19x2 was $24,000, its return on *average* equity investment was ________ %.

$120,000

20% (= $24,000 ÷ $120,000)

10-67. The return on equity (ROE) in typical American corporations is roughly 15%. Arlen Company's performance in 19x2 was . . . [above average / below average].

above average

OTHER MEASURES OF PERFORMANCE

10-68. Another measure of performance is **earnings per share**. As the name suggests, the ratio is simply the total __________ for a given period, divided by the number of ________ of common stock outstanding.

earnings (*or* net income)

shares

10-69. The earnings (i.e., net income) of Arlen Company during 19x2 was $__________. Exhibit 12 shows that the number of shares outstanding during 19x2 was __________. Therefore, earnings per share was ________.

$24,000

4,800

$5 (= $24,000 ÷ 4,800)

10-70. On line 2 of Exhibit 13 enter the numerator and denominator of the earnings-per-share ratio.

Numerator: Net income
Denominator: Number of shares outstanding

10-71. Earnings per share is used in calculating another ratio—the **price-earnings ratio.** It is obtained by dividing the average market price of the stock by the earnings per share. If the average market price for Arlen Company stock during 19x2 was $35, then the price-earnings ratio is the ratio of $35 to $5 or ____ to 1.

7 (= $35 ÷ $5)

1-39. One year later, on December 31, 19x2, Dowling Company owed $8,000 to creditors and had $3,000 in its bank account. Other properties of value totaled $25,000.

One item is missing. Calculate the amount of this item so that the balance sheet will balance. Prepare a balance sheet as of December 31, 19x2 on a separate piece of paper.

DOWLING COMPANY

Balance Sheet as of December 31, 19x2

Assets		Liabilities and Equities	
Cash	$ 3,000	Liabilities	.$ 8,000
Other assets	25,000	Equities.................	20,000
Total	$ 28,000	Total	$28,000

1-40. If Dowling Company prepared a balance sheet as of the beginning of business the next day, January 1, 19x3, would it be different from the one you prepared above? . . . [Yes / No]

No (because nothing changes between the close of business on one day and the beginning of business on the next day.)

MONEY MEASUREMENT CONCEPT

1-41. If a fruit store owned $200 of cash, 100 dozen oranges, and 20 dozen apples, could you add up its total assets from this information? . . . [Yes / No]

No (because you can't add apples and oranges.)

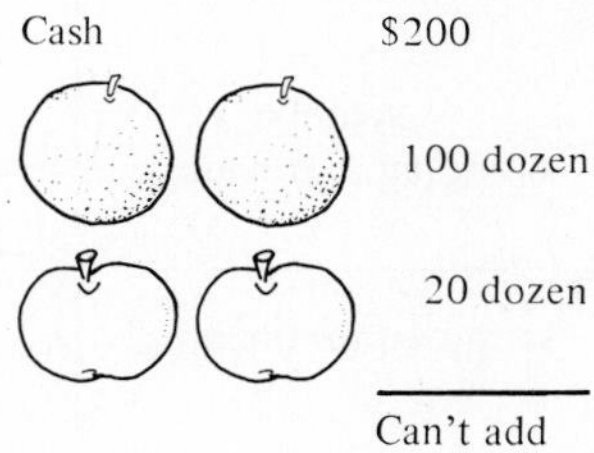

1-42. If you knew that the 100 dozen oranges cost $3 a dozen and the 20 dozen apples cost $2 a dozen, you could then add these amounts to the $200 cash, and find the total assets to be $__________ .

$540
[= ($3 x 100) + ($2 x 20) + $200]

Cash $200
300
40
$540

1-43. You can't add together objects as different as apples, oranges, automobiles, shoes, cash, supplies, etc., unless they are expressed in . . . [different / similar] units.

similar

10-60. Copy the numerator and the denominator of the current ratio on Line 10 of Exhibit 13.

Numerator: Current assets
Denominator: Current liabilities

10-61. If Arlen Company decreased its current ratio to 1.5, this would . . . [increase / decrease] its ROE. However, such a low current ratio would . . .[increase / decrease] the possibility that Arlen would not be able to pay its current liabilities when they come due.

increase
increase

10-62. The final ratio we shall use in examining capitalization is the **debt ratio**. As explained in Part 9, this is the ratio of debt capital to total permanent capital. Noncurrent liabilities are d _ _ _ capital, and noncurrent liabilities plus equities are t _ _ _ _ p _ _ _ _ _ _ _ _ capital. Calculate the debt ratio for Arlen Company.

debt
total permanent

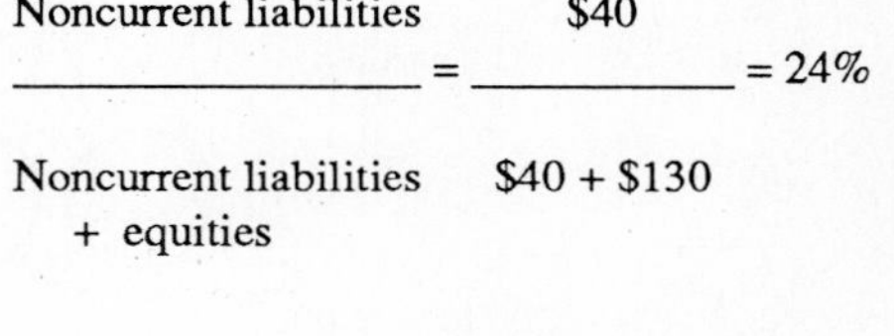

$$\frac{\text{Noncurrent liabilities}}{\text{Noncurrent liabilities + equities}} = \frac{\$40}{\$40 + \$130} = 24\%$$

10-63. Copy the numerator and denominator of the debt ratio on Line 11 of Exhibit 13.

Numerator: Noncurrent liabilities
Denominator: Noncurrent liabilities + equities

10-64. The larger the proportion of permanent capital that is obtained from debt, the smaller is the amount of equity capital that is needed. If Arlen had obtained $85,000 of its $170,000 permanent capital from debt, its debt ratio would have been ________ %, and its ROE would have been . . . [higher / lower] than the 18.5% shown in Exhibit 13.

50%
higher

10-65. However, as you learned in Part 9, a high debt ratio results in a . . .[more / less] risky capital structure than does a low debt ratio.

more

1-44. Can you add the amounts of apples and oranges if they are stated in terms of money? . . . [Yes / No]

Yes. (You could also add them to get "pieces of fruit" but this is not a useful number.)

1-45. The facts that appear in an accounting report are stated in units of money, that is, dollars and cents. This is the **money-measurement** concept. By converting different facts to monetary amounts, we can deal with them . . . [verbally / arithmetically]; that is, we can add one item to another, or we can subtract one item from another.

arithmetically

1-46. If facts cannot be expressed in monetary terms, they cannot be reported on a balance sheet. Which of the following facts could be found out by reading a balance sheet of Able Company?

(a) How much cash Able Company has.
(b) The health of the president of Able Company.
(c) How much money Able Company owes.
(d) A strike is beginning at Able Company.
(e) How many automobiles Able Company owns.
(f) Able Company is about to sign a very profitable contract with Charlie Company.

(a) and (c)
(Not (e) because the *number* of automobiles is not a monetary amount.)

1-47. Because accounting reports include only facts that can be stated in monetary amounts, accounting is necessarily a(n) . . . [complete / incomplete] record of the status of a business and . . . [does / does not] always give the most important facts about a business.

incomplete
does not

1-48. Some people believe that accounting reports tell everything important that one needs to know about a business. Such a belief is . . . [correct / wrong].

wrong

1-49. The **money-measurement concept** is the second of the nine major accounting concepts to be explained in this program. The first one was the **dual-aspect concept**. What is the meaning of each of these concepts? (Write your answer on a separate piece of paper.)

Dual-aspect concept:
Assets = Liabilities + Equities

Money-measurement concept:
Accounting reports only facts that can be expressed in monetary amounts.

10-55. The amount of capital tied up in inventory can be examined by calculating the **inventory turnover ratio.** Since inventory is recorded at cost, this ratio is calculated in relation to cost of sales, rather than to sales revenue.

Calculate the inventory turnover ratio for Arlen Company (refer to Exhibit 13 if necessary).

$$\frac{\qquad}{\qquad} = \frac{\$\qquad}{\$\qquad} = \square \text{ times}$$

$$\frac{\text{Cost of sales}}{\text{Inventory}} = \frac{\$180}{\$60} = 3 \text{ times}$$

10-56. Copy the numerator and the denominator of the inventory turnover ratio on Line 9 of Exhibit 13.

Numerator: Cost of sales
Denominator: Inventory

10-57. If Arlen Company had maintained an inventory of $90,000 to support $180,000 cost of sales, its inventory turnover would have been ______ (how many?) times, rather than 3 times. If other items were unchanged, its ROE would have been . . . [higher / lower] than the amounts shown in Exhibit 13.

2

lower

10-58. The **current ratio** is another way of examining the current section of the balance sheet. In an earlier part we pointed out that if the ratio of current assets to current liabilities is too low, the company might not be able to pay its bills. However, if the current ratio is too high, the company would not be taking advantage of the opportunity to finance current assets with current l _ _ _ _ _ _ _ _ _ s. Additional current liabilities would . . . [increase / decrease] its ROE.

liabilities; increase

10-59. Calculate the current ratio for Arlen Company, referring to Exhibit 13 if necessary.

$$\frac{\qquad}{\qquad} = \frac{\$\qquad}{\$\qquad} = \square$$

$$\frac{\text{Current assets}}{\text{Current liabilities}} = \frac{\$140}{\$60} = 2.3$$

ENTITY CONCEPT

1-50. Accounts are kept for **entities**, rather than for the persons who own, operate, or otherwise are associated with those entities. For example, suppose Green Company is a business entity, and Sue Smith is its owner. Sue Smith withdraws $100 from the business. In preparing financial accounts for Green Company, we should record the effect of this withdrawal on the accounts of . . . [Sue Smith / the entity].

the entity

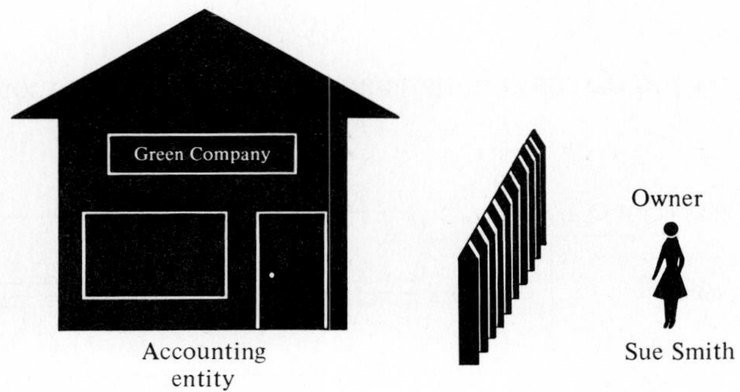

1-51. Sue Smith withdraws $100 from Green Company, of which she is the sole owner. Smith now has $100 more cash, but she has $100 less equity in Green Company.

Smith is . . . [better off / worse off / no better or worse off] than she was before.

no better or worse off

1-52. If Smith withdraws $100 from Green Company, of which she is the sole owner, she is just as well off after this withdrawal as before. What about Green Company? It now has . . . [$100 more / the same amount / $100 less] in assets.

$100 less

1-53. Events such as this can affect the owner in one way and the entity in another way. Financial statements of Green Company report the effect that the event has:

A. only on the owner.
B. only on the entity.
C. on both the owner and the entity.

B
(Sue Green can, of course, have her own personal financial statements.)

10-50. Thus, in examining how well an entity used its capital, we need to ask two questions:

(1) Were assets kept reasonably . . . [high / low]?

(2) Were liabilities kept reasonably . . . [high / low]?

low

high

10-51. CAUTION: Our focus here is solely on factors that affect return on equity (ROE). Later, we shall discuss other factors that must be taken into account in judging how well the entity managed its assets and liabilities. The final appraisal must consider these factors as well as the impact on ROE.

(No answer required.)

10-52. Let's start with the current assets. If current assets are reasonably low in relation to sales volume, this has a(n) . . . [favorable / unfavorable] effect on ROE.

favorable

10-53. In earlier parts, two ratios for measuring current assets were described. One related to accounts receivable and was called the **days' receivables ratio.** It shows how many days of sales revenue are tied up in accounts receivable.

Calculate days' receivables for Arlen Company.

$$\frac{\square}{\square \div 365} = \frac{\$\square}{\$\square \div 365} = \square \text{ days' receivables}$$

$$\frac{\text{Accounts receivable}}{\text{Sales revenue} \div 365} = \frac{\$40}{\$300 \div 365} = 49 \text{ days}$$

(If you do not recall this ratio, the calculation is shown in Exhibit 13.)

10-54. Copy the numerator and the denominator of the days' receivable ratio on Line 8 of Exhibit 13.

Numerator: Accounts receivable
Denominator: Sales revenue ÷ 365

1-54. The fact that accounts are kept for entities as distinguished from the persons associated with those entities is called the e_ _ _ _ _ concept.

entity

1-55. Owners of some small retail stores (called "mom and pop" stores) do not identify the cost of merchandise they withdraw for personal use, personal telephone calls, and the like. They do not apply the ________________ concept. Consequently, the financial statements of these stores are inaccurate.

entity

1-56. A business may be organized under any one of several legal forms: a corporation, a partnership (two or more owners), or a proprietorship (a single owner). The entity concept applies regardless of the legal status.

(No answer required.)

1-57. John and Bob own the John and Bob Laundry, a partnership. Each takes $1,000 cash from the partnership entity and puts it into his personal bank account. An accounting report of the financial position of the John and Bob Laundry would show that:

A. the net change in the entity's equity is zero.

B. the entity has $2,000 less cash.

C. John and Bob each have $1,000 more cash.

B

(John's and Bob's *personal* statements would show that each had $1,000 more cash.)

1-58. Municipalities, hospitals, religious organizations, colleges, and other nonbusiness organizations are also accounting entities. Although in this program we focus on businesses, the accounting for nonbusiness entities is similar.

(No answer required.)

1-59. The entity concept is the third of the nine fundamental accounting concepts. The three we have discussed so far are:

Dual-aspect concept

Money-measurement concept

Entity concept

What is the meaning of each? (Be sure to write your answer.)

Dual-aspect concept:
Assets = Liabilities + Equities

Money-measurement concept:
Accounting reports show only facts that can be expressed in monetary amounts.

Entity concept:
Accounts are kept for entities as distinguished from the persons who own those entitites.

10-45. As background for this analysis, let's examine some relationships in Camden Company, which has the following condensed balance sheet:

Assets		Liabilities and Equities	
		Total liabilities	400,000
		Total equities	600,000
Total	$1,000,000	Total	$1,000,000

If net income was $60,000, Camden Company's return on equity (ROE) was Net income ÷ Equities, or __________ %.

10% (= $60,000 ÷ $600,000)

10-46. If Camden Company could reduce its equities to $500,000, still maintaining its net income of $60,000, its ROE would become __________ %.

12% (= $60,000 ÷ $500,000)

10-47. Evidently, with net income held constant, Camden Company can increase its ROE by . . . [increasing / decreasing] its equities.

decreasing

10-48. Since total assets always equal liabilities plus equities, equity can be decreased only (1) if assets are . . . [increased / decreased], (2) if liabilities are . . . [increased / decreased], or (3) if there is some combination of these two types of changes.

decreased

increased

10-49. For example, equities would be decreased by $100,000 (to $500,000) if assets were decreased by $40,000 (to $960,000) and liabilities were . . . [increased / decreased] by $__________ (to $__________). If equity was $500,000 and net income was $60,000, ROE would be

$$\frac{\$\ \_\_\_\_\_\_}{\$\ \_\_\_\_\_\_} = \_\_\_\ \%$$

increased; $60,000 (= $100,000 – $40,000)

$460,000 (= $400,000 + $60,000)

$$\frac{\$60{,}000}{\$500{,}000} = 12\%$$

KEY POINTS TO REMEMBER

- The assets of an entity are the things of value that it owns.
- The sources of funds used to acquire assets are

  (1) liabilities and

  (2) equities.
- Liabilities are sources from creditors.
- Equities are (1) funds obtained from equity investors, who are owners, and (2) retained earnings resulting from the entity's profitable operation.
- Creditors have a strong claim on the assets. They can sue if the amounts due them are not paid. Equity investors have only a residual claim.
- The total assets equals the total of liabilities plus equities. This is the dual-aspect concept.
- Assets, liabilities and equities as of one point in time are reported on the entity's balance sheet.
- The money-measurement concept: accounting reports only those facts that can be stated in money amounts.
- The entity concept: accounts are kept for entities, rather than for the persons who own, operate, or otherwise are associated with those entities.

You have completed Part 1 of this program. If you think you understand the material in this Part, you should now take Post Test 1, which is in the separate booklet. If you are uncertain about your understanding, you should review Part 1.

The post test will serve both to test your comprehension and to review the highlights of Part 1. After taking the post test, you may find that you are unsure about certain points. You should review these points before continuing with Part 2.

10-39. Gross margin percentages vary widely. A profitable supermarket may have a gross margin of only 15%. Many manufacturing companies have gross margins of about 35%. Compared with these numbers, the gross margin of Arlen Company is . . . [low / high].

high

10-40. A high gross margin does not necessarily lead to a high net income. Net income is what remains after expenses have been deducted from the gross margin, and the higher the expenses, the . . . [higher / lower] the net income.

lower

10-41. The **profit margin percentage** is a useful number for analyzing net income. You calculated it in an earlier part. Calculate it for Arlen Company.

$$\frac{\qquad}{\qquad} = \frac{\$\qquad}{\$\qquad} = \boxed{\quad} \text{ \% profit margin}$$

$$\frac{\text{Net income}}{\text{Sales revenue}} = \frac{\$\ 24}{\$300} = 8\ \%$$

10-42. Copy the numerator and denominator of the profit margin percentage on Line 6 of Exhibit 13.

Numerator: Net income
Denominator: Sales revenue

10-43. Statistics on the average profit margin percentage in various industries are published and can be used by Arlen Company as a basis for comparison. Statistics on the average *dollar* amount of net income are not published. Such statistics . . . [are / are not] useful because sheer size is not a good indication of profitability.

are not

TESTS OF CAPITAL UTILIZATION

10-44. The bottom section of the diagram in Exhibit 13 shows the main components of Arlen Company's capital. The information is taken from its . . . [income statement / balance sheet]. We shall examine ratios useful in understanding these components.

balance sheet

Part 2

More About the Balance Sheet

Learning Objectives

In this part you will learn:

- Two more of the nine basic accounting concepts:
    - The going-concern concept.
    - The cost concept.
- The meaning of the principal items reported on a balance sheet.

GOING-CONCERN CONCEPT

2-1. Every year some entities go bankrupt or cease to operate for other reasons. Most entities, however, keep on going from one year to the next. Accounting must assume either that (a) entities are about to cease operations, or (b) they are likely to keep on going. The more realistic assumption is . . . [(a) / (b)].

(b)

2-2. Accounting assumes that an entity, or **concern,** will normally keep on going from one year to the next. This assumption is called the g _ _ _ _– **concern concept.**

going

FACTORS AFFECTING RETURN ON EQUITY

10-36. Ratios help explain the factors that influenced return on equity. Some of these were explained in earlier parts. We shall review these ratios and introduce others, using the financial statements of Arlen Company in Exhibit 12 and the diagram of these factors at the top of Exhibit 13. These ratios are to be summarized in the bottom section of Exhibit 13. We have already described the Return on Equity ratio, which is:

$$\frac{\text{(numerator) Net income}}{\text{(denominator) Equity}} = \text{ROE}$$

Copy the numerator and denominator of this ratio on Line 1 of the bottom part of Exhibit 13.

Numerator: Net income
Denominator: Equity

10-37. Several factors affect net income. One is gross margin. In an earlier part you calculated the **gross margin percentage.** Calculate it for Arlen Company.

$$\frac{\text{\_\_\_\_\_\_\_\_}}{\text{\_\_\_\_\_\_\_\_}} = \frac{\$\text{\_\_\_\_\_\_}^{*}}{\$\text{\_\_\_\_\_\_}} = \text{\_\_\_\_}\ \%\ \text{gross margin}$$

$$\frac{\text{Gross margin}}{\text{Sales revenue}} = \frac{\$120}{\$300} = \%\ \text{gross margin}$$

*From here on, when calculating these ratios, omit the three zeros to reduce pencil work; that is, write 120 instead of 120,000.

(If you have difficulty with this or other calculations, refer to Exhibit 13, where the amounts are calculated.)

10-38. On Line 5 of the bottom part of Exhibit 13, write the name of the numerator and of the denominator of the gross margin percentage.

Numerator: Gross margin
Denominator: Sales revenue

2-3. More specifically, the g _ _ _ _-c _ _ _ _ _ _ concept is that accounting assumes that an entity will continue to operate indefinitely unless there is evidence to the contrary. (If the entity is not a going concern, special accounting rules apply; they are not discussed in this introductory program.)

going-concern

2-4. Because of the going-concern concept, accounting ... [does / does not] report what the assets could be sold for if the entity ceased to exist.

does not

2-5. On December 31, 19x1, the balance sheet of Hamel Company reported total assets of $50,000. If Hamel Company ceased to operate,

A. its assets could be sold for $50,000.

B. we do not know what its assets could be sold for.

B

COST CONCEPT

2-6. When an entity buys an asset, it records the amount of the asset at its cost. Thus, if Mondale Company bought a plot of land for $10,000 in 19x1, it would show on its December 31, 19x1, balance sheet the item: Land, $____________. This amount was the c _ _ _ of the land.

$10,000; cost

2-7. The amount for which an asset can be sold in the marketplace is called its m _ _ _ _ _ value. If you bought a pair of shoes a year ago for $75 and find that today you can sell them for $15, their cost was $__________, and their market value is $__________.

market

$75

$15

2-8. Some assets wear out. Inflation affects the value of some assets. For these and other reasons, the market value of assets ... [remains the same / changes] as time goes on. Therefore, on December 31, 19x6, the market value of Mondale Company's land was probably ... [$10,000 / different from $10,000].

changes

different from $10,000

10-31. Finally, if from our experience we *judge* that a company like Arlen should have earned an ROE of 20%, we conclude that Arlen's ROE was . . . [better / worse] than this **judgmental standard.**

worse

10-32. Most comparisons are made in one or more of the three ways described above. Give the meaning of each.

(1) **Historical**: comparing the entity with ....

its own performance in the past

(2) **External**: comparing the entity with ....

another entity's performance or industry averages

(3) **Judgmental**: comparing the entity with ....

a standard based on our judgment

10-33. Arlen Company's net income in 19x2 was $24,000. Baker Company's net income in 19x2 was $50,000. From this information we cannot tell which company performed better. Why not? ....

Because we do not know Baker Company's equity.

10-34. Baker Company's equity was $1,000,000. Its net income in 19x2 was $50,000. Its ROE was therefore

$$\frac{\$\,\boxed{}}{\$\,\boxed{}} = \_\_\_\_\_\%.$$

$$\frac{\$50,000}{\$1,000,000} = 5\%$$

Arlen Company with an ROE of 18.5% performed . . . [better / worse] than Baker Company.

better

10-35. The comparison of Arlen Company and Baker Company illustrates an important point. Most comparisons require the use of *percentages* or *ratios* rather than dollar amounts.

(No answer required.)

2-9. Accounting, however, does not attempt to trace changes in the market value of most assets. Instead, accounting focuses on their cost. Thus, on its December 31, 19x6, balance sheet, Mondale Company would report the land at its c _ _ _ of $______________ .

cost; $10,000

2-10. The cost concept is that accounting focuses on the . . . [cost / market value] of assets, rather than on their . . . [cost / market value].

cost

market value

2-11. Many people think that the balance sheet shows what assets are *worth*, that is, their market value. This belief is . . . [true / false].

false

2-12. One reason why accounting is based on the cost concept is that the market value of an asset is difficult to estimate. If you bought a pair of shoes for $75, the cost was clearly $________ . However, if a few months later you asked two friends to tell you the market value of these used shoes, they probably would . . . [agree / disagree] as to the amount.

$75

Cost $75
Market value???

disagree

2-13. Estimating the market value of each asset every time a balance sheet is prepared would be . . . [difficult / easy]. Furthermore, the estimates would be a matter of opinion and therefore . . . [objective / subjective].

difficult

subjective
(that is, affected by personal feelings, rather than by facts)

2-14. A second reason for using the cost concept is that the entity will not sell many of its assets immediately. Instead, it will keep them to use in its operations. The entity therefore . . . [does / does not] need to know their market value. This reason stems from the previous concept, the g _ _ _ _– c _ _ _ _ _ _ concept.

does not

going-concern

2-15. To summarize, the two reasons why accounting focuses on costs rather than on market values are that:

(1) market values are difficult to estimate, that is, they are . . . [objective / subjective], whereas costs are . . . [objective / subjective]; and

(2) the_________ - _____________ concept makes it unnecessary to know the market value of many assets; the assets will be used in future operations rather than being sold immediately.

subjective; objective

going-concern

10-26. Equity investors (e.g., shareholders) invest money in a business in order to earn a profit, or **return**, on that equity. Thus, from the viewpoint of the shareholders, the best overall measure of the entity's performance is the r _ _ _ _ _ that was earned *on* e _ _ _ _ _ . (This is abbreviated as ROE.)

return; equity

10-27. The accounting name for the profit or return earned in a year is n _ _ i _ _ _ _ _ .

net income

Return on equity is the percentage obtained by dividing n _ _ i _ _ _ _ _ by e _ _ _ _ _ .

net income
equity

10-28. In 19x2 Arlen Company had net income of $24,000, and its equity on December 31, 19x2 was $130,000. Calculate its ROE for 19x2.

$$\frac{\boxed{}}{\boxed{}} = \frac{\$\ \boxed{}}{\$\ \boxed{}} = \boxed{}^{*}\ \%\ \text{ROE}$$

$$\frac{\text{Net income}}{\text{Equity}} = \frac{\$\ 24{,}000}{\$\ 130{,}000} = 18.5\ \%\ \text{ROE}$$

* one decimal place

10-29. In order to judge how well Arlen Company performed, its 18.5% ROE must be compared with something. If in 19x1 Arlen Company had an ROE of 20%, we can say that its performance in 19x2 was . . . [better / worse] than in 19x1. This is the **historical** basis of comparison.

worse

10-30. If in 19x2 another company had an ROE of 15%, Arlen's ROE was . . . [better / worse] than the other company's. Or if in 19x2 the average ROE of companies in the same industry as Arlen was 15%, Arlen's ROE was . . . [better / worse] than the industry average. This is the **external** basis of comparison.

better

better

2-16. Accounting . . . [does / does not] report what many of the individual assets are worth, that is, their m _ _ _ _ _ v _ _ _ _ . Accounting therefore . . . [does / does not] report what the whole entity is worth. Those who criticize accounting for its failure to report an entity's "worth" do not appreciate that this task would be difficult, subjective, and unnecessary.

does not

market value

does not

2-17. An entity bought land in 19x1 for $10,000. On December 31, 19x6, the entity received an offer of $20,000 for the land. This meant that the ____________ ____________ of the land was $20,000. At what amount should this land be reported on the balance sheet of December 31, 19x6? $____________

market value

$10,000

2-18. A shoe store purchased shoes for $1,000. It had every expectation of selling these shoes to customers for $1,500. At what amount should these shoes be reported on the balance sheet? $____________

$1,000

2-19. The cost concept is the fifth of the nine fundamental accounting concepts. The first five are:

Dual-aspect concept

Money-measurement concept

Entity concept

Going-concern concept

Cost concept

What is the meaning of each?

Dual-aspect concept:
Assets = liabilities + equities

Money-measurement concept:
Accounting records show only facts that can be expressed in monetary amounts.

Entity concept:
Accounts are kept for entities, as distinguished from the persons associated with those entitites.

Going-concern concept:
Accounting assumes that an entity will continue to operate indefinitely.

Cost concept:
Accounting focuses on the cost of assets, rather than on their market value.

10-21. A second limitation is that financial statements report only events that . . . [have happened / will happen], whereas we are also interested in estimating events that . . . [have happened / will happen]. The fact that an entity earned $1,000,000 last year . . . [definitely predicts / is not necessarily an indication of] what it will earn next year.

have happened
will happen
is not necessarily an indication of

10-22. Third, the balance sheet does not show the . . . [cost / market value] of most assets. In accordance with the c _ _ _ concept, plant assets are reported at their . . . [unexpired cost / market value].

market value
cost
unexpired cost

Also, depreciation is a writeoff of . . . [cost / market value]. It is NOT an indication of changes in the real value of plant assets. The balance sheet does not show the entity's "net worth."

cost

10-23. Fourth, the accountant and management have some latitude in choosing among alternative ways of recording an event in the accounts. An example of flexibility in accounting is that in determining inventory values and cost of sales, the entity may use the L _ _ _ , F _ _ _ , or average cost method.

LIFO, FIFO

10-24. Fifth, many accounting amounts are estimates. In calculating the depreciation expense of a plant asset, for example, one must estimate its s _ _ _ _ _ _ l _ _ _ and its r _ _ _ _ _ _ _ v _ _ _ _ .

service life; residual value

OVERALL MEASURES OF PERFORMANCE

10-25. Although they have limitations, financial statements usually are the most useful source of information about an entity. We shall focus first on what they tell about its overall **performance.**

(No answer required.)

BALANCE SHEET ITEMS

2-20. Refer to Exhibit 1 in your booklet. This is the balance sheet we introduced in Part 1. It reports the amounts of a_ _ _ _ _, l_ _ _ _ _ _ _ _ _ _ _, and e_ _ _ _ _ _ _ of Garsden Company as of ______________________________ .

assets
liabilities; equities
December 31, 1986

2-21. Remember that the note "(000 omitted)" means that the numbers are reported in thousands of dollars. For example, the number reported for Cash, $1,449, means that the amount of cash was $______________. This is common practice; it is done in order to make the numbers easier to read.

$1,449,000

2-22. Recall also that the total of the assets always equals the total of the liabilities plus equities. Total assets were $______________ and total liabilities plus equities were $______________ .

$38,239,000
$38,239,000

2-23. Most items on a balance sheet are summaries of more detailed accounts. For example, the cash is probably located in a number of separate bank accounts, in cash registers, and in petty cash boxes. The total of all the cash is $____________, rounded to the nearest thousand dollars.

$1,449,000
(NOT $1,449)

2-24. In the remainder of this part, we explain the meaning of some of the items on this balance sheet. Those not covered here will be explained in later parts.

(No answer required.)

ASSETS

2-25. In Part 1 we referred to assets as "th_ _ _ _ of v_ _ _ _." We now make this idea more specific. In order to count as an asset in accounting, an item must pass three tests.

things; value

10-15. The letter says that the auditors . . . [prepared / examined] the financial statements.

examined
(The company, not the auditor, is responsible for *preparing* the statements.)

10-16. The letter says that the financial statements . . . [accurately / fairly] present the financial results.

fairly
(Because judgments and estimates are involved, no one can say that the financial statements are entirely *accurate*.)

10-17. In the last paragraph of the letter, the auditors assure the reader that the statements were prepared in conformity with g__________ a__________ a__________ p__________ that were applied on a c _ _ _ _ _ _ _ _ _ basis.

generally
accepted accounting principles
consistent

10-18. If any of the statements above cannot be made, the auditors call attention to the exceptions.

(No answer required.)

LIMITATIONS ON FINANCIAL STATEMENT ANALYSIS

10-19. In the remainder of this part, we shall describe how information in financial statements is used. Before doing this, let's review the reasons why accounting cannot provide a complete picture of the status or performance of an entity.

(No answer required.)

10-20. One limitation is suggested by the word **financial**; that is, financial statements report only events that can be measured in m _ _ _ _ _ _ y amounts.

monetary

2-26. The first requirement is that the item must be **controlled** by the entity. Usually this means that the entity must **own** the item.* If Able Company rents a building owned by Baker Company, this building . . . [is / is not] an asset of Able Company. The building . . . [is / is not] an asset of Baker Company.

is not
is

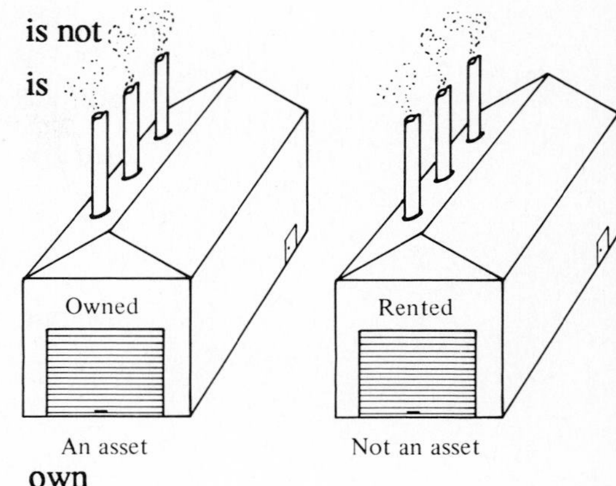

An asset   Not an asset

---

*As an exception to this rule, certain leased items, called capital leases, are assets. These are described in Part 8.

2-27. In accounting, the employees of an entity are *not* assets because the entity does not ______ them. However, if a baseball club has a contract in which the player agrees to provide his services, the contract . . . [is / is not] an asset.

own

is (The asset is the *contract*, not the player, and it is an asset only if it passes the third test, in frame 2–29.)

2-28. The second requirement is that the item must be **valuable** to the entity. Which of these would qualify as assets of a company that sells dresses?

A. The company's right to collect amounts owed by customers.
B. Regular dresses held for sale.
C. Dresses that no one wants because they have gone out of style.
D. A cash register in working condition.
E. A cash register that doesn't work and can't be repaired.

A, B, and D

2-29. The third requirement is that the item must have been acquired at a **measurable cost**. If Jones Company bought a trademark from another company for $1 million, this trademark . . . [would / would not] be an asset of Jones Company.

would

2-30. By contrast, if Jones Company has built up an excellent reputation because of the consistently high quality of its products, this repu–tation . . . [would / would not] count as an asset in accounting.

would not

10-9. The third operating adjustment, "Change in receivables, inventory and payables," converts revenues and cost of sales from an accrual basis to a cash receipts and cash payments basis. Since the amount is added to net income, we know that cash generated by operating activities was $1,174,000 . . . [lower / higher] than the difference between revenues and cost of sales.

higher

10-10. The second section of the cash flow statement is headed "Cash flows from financing activities." It shows the increases and decreases in cash arising from financing transactions. For example, Garsden Company paid off some long-term debt, which . . . [increased / decreased] cash by $500,000; and it borrowed money from a bank, which . . . [increased / decreased] cash by $1,000,000.

decreased

increased

10-11. The third section shows the investments made during the period that used cash. The largest was the acquisition of new plant and equipment, which . . . [increased / decreased] cash by $2,433,000.

decreased

10-12. The cash flow statement is prepared by rearranging information collected in the accounts for the main purpose of preparing the balance sheet and income statement. It does not require additional accounts or journal entries.

(No answer required.)

AUDITING

10-13. All large companies and many smaller ones have their accounting records reviewed by independent, certified public accountants. This process is call **auditing,** and the independent accountants are called _ _ _ _ tors.

auditors

10-14. Ordinarily, after completing their examination, the _ _ _ _ _ _ _ s write a letter giving their opinion. This o _ _ _ _ _ _ letter is reproduced in the company's annual report. A typical opinion letter is shown in Exhibit 11.

auditors

opinion

2-31. "Coke" and "7•Up" are well known and valuable trademarks for soft drinks. The Coca-Cola Company developed the value of its trademark through its own efforts over many years. "Coke" . . . [is / is not] an asset in accounting. Philip Morris Inc. purchased the Seven-Up Company, and included in the purchase was an item called "Trademarks, patents, and goodwill," valued at $390 million. In accounting, "7•Up" . . . [is / is not] an asset of Philip Morris, Inc.

is not an asset

is an asset

2-32. To summarize, an item that is listed as an asset must meet three requirements:

(1) It must be _ _ _ ed or c _ _ _ _ _ _ _ ed by the entity.

(2) It must be v _ _ _ _ _ _ _ to the entity.

(3) It must have been acquired at a m ______________________ c ________.

owned; controlled

valuable

measurable

cost

2-33. Which of the following items of Homes Incorporated, a builder of houses, are its assets?

A. Telephones it rents from the telephone company, worth $5,000.

B. Lumber in good condition purchased for $50,000.

C. Scrap lumber purchased for $2,000, but now worthless.

D. Its reputation for building fine houses, said to be worth $100,000.

E. Its truck, in good condition, purchased for $30,000 five years ago.

B and E
Not A: not owned
Not C: not valuable
Not D: not measurable cost

CURRENT ASSETS

2-34. Current assets are cash and assets that are expected to be converted into cash or used up in the near future, usually within one year. Groceries on the shelves of a grocery store . . . [are / are not] current assets. The store building . . . [is / is not] a c _ _ _ _ _ _ a _ _ _ _. On a balance sheet, current assets are usually reported separately from other assets.

are

is not; current asset

PLEASE DON'T PEEK

If you look at the answer before **writing** *your response, you will lose much of the educational value.*

10-3. In most businesses the principal source of cash during a period is the profitable operation of the business. Thus, the first section of the statement is headed C___f____ from o________ a__________.

Cash flows from operating activities

10-4. Because the accrual accounting system often does not provide a separate record of the cash generated by operations, this section arrives at the amount by adjusting the N__I_____ for the noncash items that entered into the calculation of net income.

Net Income

10-5. For example, most of the plant assets used in the current year were acquired in previous years. When these assets were acquired, cash or its equivalent was paid for them, but the depreciation expense for these plant assets during the current year . . . [did / did not] involve a cash payment during the current year.

did not

10-6. Therefore, as shown in Exhibit 10, the $864,000 of depreciation expense, is . . . [added to / subtracted from] net income as one adjustment to convert net income to a cash basis.

added to

10-7. Because depreciation expense is added to net income, some people think that depreciation is a source of cash. Actually, the source of cash is the profitable operation of the business, so this belief is . . . [approximately correct / dead wrong]. The depreciation item merely adjusts net income to a cash basis.

dead wrong

10-8. As you learned in Part 8, income tax expense reported on the income statement may include an element called deferred income taxes. This item . . . [did / did not] involve a cash payment during the current year, so it is another of the . . . [additions to / subtractions from] net income, made to adjust net income to a cash basis.

did not
additions to

2-35. Cash is money on hand and money in bank accounts that can be withdrawn at any time. On January 8, Jones Company had $843 in its cash register and $12,012 in its checking account at the bank. Its cash was $____________.

$12,855 (= $12,012 + $843)

2-36. On the evening of January 8, Jones Company deposited in its checking account $743 of the money in the cash register. After it had done this, its cash still totaled $____________.

$12,855

2-37. When an entity writes a check, the amount of its cash is not actually reduced until the check has been cashed. Nevertheless, the usual practice is to record a decrease in cash on the day the check is mailed.

(No answer required).

2-38. Securities are stocks and bonds. They give valuable rights to the entity that owns them. The U.S. Treasury promises to pay stated amounts of money to entities that own its bonds. Therefore, U.S. Treasury Bonds owned by Garsden Company . . . [are / are not] assets of Garsden Company.

are

2-39. Marketable securities are securities that are expected to be converted into cash within a year. An entity owns these securities so as to earn a return on funds that otherwise would be idle. Marketable Securities are . . . [current / noncurrent] assets.

current

2-40. In Exhibit 1, note that on the **marketable securities** line the . . . [cost / market value] is given in parentheses as $__________. The amount of $246,000 listed as the asset amount must therefore be the . . . [cost / market value].

market value; $248,000

cost

Part 10

Analysis of Financial Statements

Learning Objectives

In this final part you will learn:

- The nature of the Cash Flow Statement.
- Auditing.
- The limitations of financial statement information.
- An approach to analyzing financial statements.
- Overall measures of performance.
- Other ratios used in financial statement analysis.

CASH FLOW STATEMENT

10-1. So far we have focused on two financial statements: (1) a statement reporting on the flows of revenues and expenses during an accounting period, called the I________________ S____________________; and (2) a statement showing the entity's financial status as of the end of the period, called the B________________ S______________.

Income Statement

Balance Sheet

10-2. Entities are required to prepare a third financial statement. It reports on the flow of cash during an accounting period and is called a C _ _ _ F _ _ _ S _ _ _ _ _ _ _ _ _. Please refer to Exhibit 10 in your booklet which shows a cash flow statement for Garsden Company.

Cash
Flow Statement

2-41. An **account receivable** is an amount that is owed to the business, usually by one of its customers, as a result of the ordinary extension of a credit. A customer's monthly bill from the electric company would be an a______ r__________ of the electric company until the customer paid the bill.

account receivable

2-42. The word "net" on the Accounts Receivable line means that the amount is less than the amount that customers actually owe. The reason for this is given in Part 5.

(No answer required.)

2-43. If the customer signs a written **promissory note** agreeing to pay what is owed, the amount would be listed as **N___ Receivable,** rather than as an ______________ Receivable. An example is given below. Evidently, Garsden Company . . . [did / did not] have any Notes Receivable.

Note

Account

did not

CONSUMER NOTE

$ 400 xx July 1, 1982

FOR VALUE RECEIVED, I, Fred Cochran, promise to pay to Ryan Lougee or order the sum of Four hundred Dollars

in one year from this date with interest to be paid monthly at the rate of 12 per centum per annum during said term, and for such further time as the said principal sum, or any part thereof shall remain unpaid.

Witness

Michael J. Vitine Fred Cochran

Secured by a Security Agreement (Chattel Mortgage) and / or a Financing Statement to be recorded in the Recording Office of the
☐ Secretary of State
☐ City or Town Clerk of County
☐ Register of Deeds in the County of

FORM 306 REVISED 1959 HOBBS & WARREN, INC. PUBLISHERS, BOSTON
REVISED 1961 . CHAPTER 535

2-44. Inventories are goods being held for sale, as well as supplies, raw materials, and partially finished products that will be sold upon completion. For example, a truck owned by an automobile dealer for resale to its customers . . . [is / is not] inventory. A truck owned by an entity and used to transport its own goods . . . [is / is not] inventory.

is

is not

You have completed Part 9 of this program. If you think you understand the material in this part, you should now take Post Test 9, which is in the separate booklet. If you are uncertain about your understanding, you should review Part 9.

The post test will serve both to test your comprehension and to review the highlights of Part 9. After taking the post test, you may find that you are unsure about certain points. You should review these points before continuing with Part 10.

2-45. In Exhibit 1 the inventories of Garsden Company are reported as $____________________.

$10,623,000

2-46. An entity's burglar alarm system is valuable because it provides security and protection against loss. The burglar alarm system is an asset. Would a fire insurance policy that protects the entity against losses caused by fire damage also be an asset? . . . [Yes / No]

Yes

2-47. Entities buy insurance protection ahead of the period that the insurance policy covers. When they buy the insurance policy, they have acquired an a____. Since the policy covers only a short period of time, the asset is a . . . [current / noncurrent] asset. Insurance protection can't be seen or touched. It is an **intangible** asset.

asset

current

(Some insurance policies provide protection for more than one year; even so, they are usually listed as current assets.)

2-48. Prepaid Expenses is the name for intangible assets that will be used up in the near future, that is, intangible . . . [current / noncurrent] assets. (The reason for using the word "expense" will be explained in Part 6.) Exhibit 1 shows that Garsden Company had $__________ of Prepaid Expenses on December 31, 1986.

current

$389,000

2-49. Current assets consist of c________ and of assets that are expected to be converted into c________ or used up within a short period, usually within______ __________ (how long?).

cash

cash

one year

NONCURRENT ASSETS

2-50. As the name suggests, assets that are expected to be useful for longer than one year are called . . . [current / noncurrent] assets.

noncurrent

9-96. In an entity with dozens of subsidiaries, some of which have their own subsidiaries, eliminating the intercompany transactions is a complicated task. Only the general principles have been described here.

(No answer required.)

KEY POINTS TO REMEMBER

- A company obtains its permanent capital from two sources: (1) debt (noncurrent liabilities) and (2) equity. It uses this capital to finance (1) working capital (current assets – current liabilities) and (2) noncurrent assets.

- Most debt capital is obtained by issuing bonds. Bonds obligate the company to pay interest and to repay the principal when it is due.

- Equity capital is obtained by (1) issuing shares of stock and (2) retaining earnings.

- The amount of capital obtained from preferred and common shareholders is the amount they paid in. The par, or stated, value of common stock is not an important number today but is still reported on the balance sheet.

- Cash dividends decrease the amount of equity captial. Stock dividends or stock splits do not affect the total equity.

- Retained earnings are total earnings (i.e., net income) since the entity began operations, less total dividends.

- Although sometimes called "net worth," the amount of owners' equity does *not* show what the equity is worth.

- In deciding on its permanent capital structure, a company attempts to strike the right balance between risky but low-cost debt capital and less risky but high-cost equity capital. The balance in a given company is indicated by its debt ratio.

- Most companies have subsidiaries. The economic entity is a family consisting of the parent and the subsidiaries in which it owns more than 50% of the stock. Consolidated financial statements are prepared for such an economic entity by combining their separate financial statements, and eliminating transactions among members of the family.

- The consolidated balance sheet reports all the assets owned by the consolidated entity and all the claims of parties outside the family.

- The consolidated income statement reports only revenues from sales to outside parties and expenses resulting from costs incurred with outside parties. Intercompany revenues and expenses are eliminated.

2-51. Tangible assets are assets that can be seen or touched; they have physical substance. Buildings, trucks, and machines are t _ _ _ _ _ _ _ assets. | tangible

2-52. As indicated by the first term under noncurrent assets in Exhibit 1, the usual name for tangible, noncurrent assets is __________, __________, and ______________. Because they are noncurrent, we know that these assets are expected to be used in the entity for more than ______ ____________ (how long?). | Property Plant; Equipment; one year

2-53. Exhibit 1 shows the . . . [cost / market value] of property, plant and equipment to be $26,946,000. It shows that a portion of the cost of this asset has been subtracted from the original cost because it has been "used up." This "used-up" portion is called ______________ ______________ and totals $____________. | cost; accumulated depreciation; $13,534,000

2-54. After this amount is subtracted, the asset amount is shown as $____________. (In Part 8, we shall explain what this amount means. For now, do not be concerned about it.) | $13,412,000

2-55. The other noncurrent asset items are intangible assets; that is, they have no physical substance, except as pieces of paper. The investments are securities. Evidently Garsden Company does not intend to turn these investments into cash within ______ ____________ (how long?). If these securities were expected to be turned into cash within that period, they would be listed as a current asset, M _ _ _ _ _ _ _ _ _ S _ _ _ _ _ _ _ _ _ . | one year; Marketable Securities

2-56. The next noncurrent asset reported is **Patents and Trademarks.** These are rights to use patents and rights to valuable product names (such as "7•Up"). Because they are assets, we know that

(1) they are v _ _ _ _ _ _ _ , | valuable

(2) they are o _ _ _ _ by Garsden Company, and | owned

(3) they were acquired at a measurable c _ _ _ . | cost

9-90. Palm Company owns 40% of Gray Company stock. This asset is listed on Palm Company's balance sheet at $100,000. This asset would NOT be eliminated from the consolidated balance sheet. Why not? ....
....
....

Because only companies in which the parent owns more than 50% are consolidated.

9-91. Palm Company owns 60% of the stock of Sand Company. This stock was reported on the balance sheet of Palm Company as an asset, Investment in Subsidiaries, at $60,000. The equity of Sand Corporation is $100,000. On the consolidated balance sheet, the $60,000 asset would be eliminated, and because debits must equal credits, . . . [$60,000 / $100,000] of Sand Company's equity also would be eliminated.

$60,000

9-92. Palm Company owns 60% of Sand company's stock, which is a . . . [majority / minority] of the stock. Other shareholders own the other 40% of Sand Company stock; they are . . . [majority / minority] shareholders. They have an interest in the consolidated entity, and this interest is reported in the . . . [assets / liabilities and equities] side of the consolidated balance sheet. It is labeled **minority interest**.

majority
minority
liabilities and equities

9-93. The consolidated income statement reports revenues from . . . [all sales / sales to outside parties only] and expenses resulting from . . . [all costs incurred / costs incurred with outside parties]. Intercompany revenues and expenses are e _ _ _ _ _ _ _ _ d.

sales to outside parties only
costs incurred with outside parties
eliminated

9-94. The consolidated financial statements report on the entity "Palm Company and Subsidiaries." This family of corporations . . . [is / is not] an economic entity, but it . . . [is / is not] a legal entity.

is
is not

9-95. Most corporations have subsidiaries. Since the consolidated financial statements give the best information about the economic entity, most published financial statements are c _ _ _ _ _ _ _ _ _ _ d financial statements.

consolidated

2-57. Goodwill, the final item on the asset side, has a special meaning in accounting. It arises when one company buys another company and pays more than the value of its assets. If Garsden Company bought Baker Company for $1,663,000, and Baker Company's assets (after subtracting its liabilities) had a value of $1,000,000, Garsden Company would record the asset G _ _ _ _ _ _ _, at $______________.

Goodwill $663,000

2-58. Remember that some assets, such as automobiles, are a property, which is ... [tangible / intangible] and others, such as insurance protection, are a property right, which is ... [tangible / intangible].

tangible

intangible (You can't touch or see an intangible asset, but it is still valuable.)

CURRENT LIABILITIES

2-59. The right-hand side of the Garsden Company balance sheet lists the company's liabilities and equities. As explained in Part 1, these can be regarded either as c _ _ _ _ _ against the assets or as the s _ _ _ _ _ _ used to acquire the assets. The claims of creditors and other outside parties are called l _ _ _ _ _ _ _ _ _ _ .

claims; sources

liabilities

2-60. In Exhibit 1, the first category of liabilities is ___________ liabilities. As we might expect from the discussion of current assets, current liabilities are claims that become due within a ... [short / long] time, usually within _____ __________ (how long?).

current

short

one year

2-61. The first current liability listed in Exhibit 1 is ______________ ____________________. These are the opposite of Accounts Receivable; that is, they are amounts that ... [the company owes to its suppliers / are owed to the company by its customers].

Accounts

Payable

the company owes to its suppliers

2-62. In December 19x1, Smith Company sold a personal computer to Brown Company for $3,000. Brown Company agreed to pay for it within 60 days. On the December 31, 19x1, balance sheet, Smith Company would report the $3,000 as Accounts ... [Receivable / Payable] and Brown Company would report the $3,000 as Accounts ... [Receivable / Payable].

Receivable

Payable

9-85. For example, if Palm Company has $10,000 cash, Sea Company has $5,000 cash, and Sand Company has $4,000 cash, the whole family has $________ cash, and this amount would be reported on the c______________ balance sheet.

$19,000
consolidated

9-86. An entity earns income by making sales to outside customers. It cannot earn income by dealing with itself. Corporations in the consolidated family may buy from and sell to one another. Transactions between members of the family . . . [do / do not] earn income for the consolidated entity. The effect of these **intercompany transactions** therefore must be eliminated from the consolidated statements.

do not

9-87. In 19x1, Palm Company had sales revenue of $1,000,000, Sea Company had sales revenue of $200,000, and Sand company had sales revenue of $400,000. Palm Company sold $30,000 of products to Sea Company. All other sales were to outside customers. On the consolidated income statement, the amount of sales reported would be $______________.

$1,570,000
(Total sales = $1,000,000 + $200,000 + $400,000 = $1,600,000. Intercompany sales = $30,000. Consolidated sales = $1,600,000 − 30,000 = $1,570,000)

9-88. Intercompany transactions are also eliminated from the consolidated balance sheet. For example, if Sand Company owed Palm Company $10,000, this amount would appear as Accounts . . . [Receivable / Payable] on the balance sheet of Palm Company and as Accounts . . . [Receivable / Payable] on the balance sheet of Sand Company. On the consolidated balance sheet, the Accounts Receivable and Accounts Payable would each be $10,000 . . . [more / less] than the sum of these amounts on the balance sheets of the three family members.

Receivable
Payable
less

9-89. The balance sheet of Palm Company reports as an asset the Sand Company and Sea Company stock that it owns. This asset . . . [remains unchanged / must be eliminated] from the consolidated balance sheet. On the balance sheets of the subsidiaries, the corresponding amounts are reported as . . . [noncurrent liabilities / equity], and these amounts are also eliminated.

must be eliminated
equity

2-63. The next item, **Bank Loan Payable,** corresponds to the asset, Notes Receivable. It is reported separately from Accounts Payable because the debt is evidenced by a promissory n _ _ _.

note

2-64. Amounts owed to employees and others for services they have provided but for which they have not been paid are listed as **Accrued Liabilities.** They will be described in Part 6.

(No answer required.)

2-65. Estimated Tax Liability is the amount owed to the government for taxes. It is shown separately from other liabilities, both because the amount is large and also because the exact amount owed may not be known as of the date of the balance sheet. In Exhibit 1 this amount is shown as $__________ . It is a current liability because the amount is due within ______ __________ (how long?).

$1,541,000

one year

2-66. Two items of **Long-term Debt** are shown as liabilities. One, labelled "current portion" amounts to $__________. The other, listed under non-current liabilities, amounts to $__________. Evidently, the total amount of long-term debt is the sum of these two amounts, that is, $__________.

$500,000

$2,000,000

$2,500,000

2-67. The $500,000 is shown separately as a current liability because it is due within _____ ________ (how soon?), that is, before December 31, 198__. The remaining $2,000,000 does not become due until sometime later on, that is, after December 31, 198__.

one year

1987

1987

CURRENT RATIO

2-68. The current assets and current liabilities are shown separately from noncurrent assets and noncurrent liabilities because they indicate the entity's ability to meet its current obligations. A measure of this ability is the **current ratio,** which is the ratio of current assets to current liabilities. For Garsden Company, the current ratio is:

9-80. Most industrial companies have a debt ratio of less than 50%. Lougee Company . . . [is / is not] in this category.

is

CONSOLIDATED FINANCIAL STATEMENTS

9-81. If one corporation owns more than 50% of the stock in another corporation, it can control the affairs of that corporation because it can outvote any other owners. Many businesses consist of a number of corporations that are legally separate entities but, because they are controlled by one corporation, are part of a single "family."

(No answer required.)

9-82. A corporation which controls one or more other corporations is called the **parent**, and the controlled corporations are called **subsidiaries**.

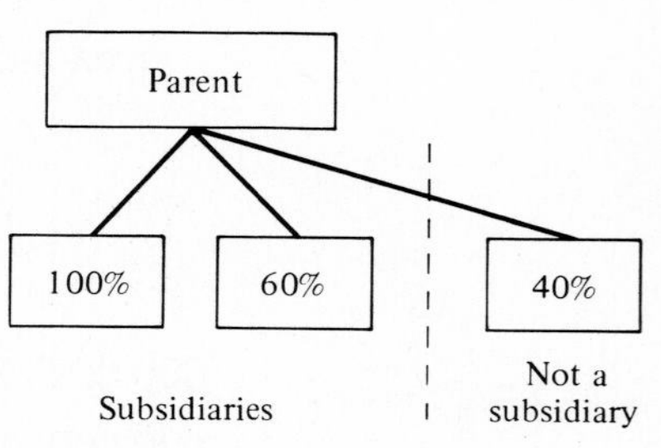

Palm Company owns 100% of the stock of Sea Company, 60% of the stock of Sand Company, and 40% of the stock of Gray Company. The **parent** company is ____________ ____________. The **subsidiaries** are ....

Palm Company
Sea Company and Sand Company

9-83. Since the management of the parent, Palm Company, controls the activities of the subsidiaries, Sea Company and Sand Company, these three companies operate as a single entity. The e _ _ _ _ _ concept requires that a set of financial statements be prepared for this family.

entity

9-84. Each corporation is a legal entity with its own financial statements. The set of financial statements for the whole family brings together, or **consolidates**, these separate statements. The set for the whole family is therefore called a set of c _ _ _ _ _ _ _ _ _ _ d financial statements.

consolidated

current assets	=	$	=	* to 1
current liabilities		$		

$22,651,000 / $ 9,519,000 = 2.4 to 1

* Carry this amount to one decimal place.

2-69. As a rough rule of thumb, a current ratio of at least 2 to 1 is desirable. Garsden Company . . . [does / does not] pass this test.

does

NONCURRENT LIABILITIES

2-70. As we have seen, Garsden Company has obtained funds by borrowing, and $______________ of this debt is not due to be repaid until after December 31, 198___. This amount is therefore a . . . [current / noncurrent] liability.

$2,000,000

1987; noncurrent

2-71. Suppose the $500,000 current portion was paid in 1987, and an additional $500,000 of debt became due in 1988. On the balance sheet as of December 31, 1987, the current portion of long-term debt would be reported as $______________, and the noncurrent liability would be reduced to $______________.

$500,000

$1,500,000

(Note: Although a single **liability** may have both a current portion and a noncurrent portion, a single **asset** is not so divided. Prepaid Insurance of $2,000 covering protection for two future years is reported as a current asset of $2,000.)

2-72. The other noncurrent liability, Deferred Income Taxes, will be described in Part 8.

(No answer required.)

2-73. Liabilities are claims against all the assets. The $5,602,000 of accounts payable on the Garsden Company balance sheet is a claim against . . . [the cash of $1,449,000 / the total assets of $38,239,000].

the total assets of $38,239,000

9-75. A company runs the risk of going bankrupt if it has too high a proportion of . . . [debt / equity] capital. A company pays an unnecessarily high cost for its permanent capital if it has too high a proportion of . . . [debt / equity] capital.

debt

equity

9-76. A company that obtains a high proportion of its permanent capital from debt is said to be **highly leveraged.** If such a company does not get into financial difficulty, it will earn a high return for its equity investors, because each dollar of debt capital takes the place of a . . . [more / less] expensive dollar of equity capital.

more

9-77. However, highly leveraged companies are risky because the high proportion of debt capital and the associated requirement to pay interest . . . [increases / decreases] the chance that the company will not be able to meet its obligations.

increases

9-78. A common way of measuring the relative amount of debt and equity capital is the **debt ratio,** which is the ratio of debt capital to total permanent capital. Recall that **debt capital** is another name for . . . [total / current / noncurrent] liabilities. Equity capital consists of Paid-in Capital plus R_ _ _ _ _ _ _ E_ _ _ _ _ _ _ _.

noncurrent

Retained Earnings

9-79. Earlier you worked with the following permanent capital structure.

LOUGEE COMPANY
Sources and Uses of Permanent Capital
As of December 31, 19x1

Uses of Capital		Sources of Capital	
Working capital	$ 6,000	Noncurrent liabilities	$9,000
Noncurrent assets	20,000	Equity	17,000
Total uses	$26,000	Total sources	$26,000

Calculate the debt ratio for Lougee Company.

$$\frac{\text{Debt capital (noncurrent liabilities)}}{\text{Debt capital + equity capital}} = \frac{\$\square}{\$\square} = \square\ \%$$

$$\frac{\$\,9{,}000}{\$26{,}000} = \boxed{35}\ \%$$

EQUITIES

2-74. Equities consist of capital obtained from sources other than creditors and other liabilities. As Exhibit 1 indicates, there are two sources of equity capital: (1) $12,256,000, which is labelled Total ________ - ____ ________________; and (2) $13,640,000, which is labelled ________________ ________________ .

Paid-in
Capital
Retained Earnings

2-75. Paid-in Capital is the amount of capital supplied by equity investors. They own the entity. The details of how this item is reported depends on the type of organization. Garsden Company is a corporation, and its owners receive *shares* of common ____________ as evidence of their ownership. They are therefore called s _ _ _ _ holders. Other forms of ownership will be discussed in Part 9.

stock
shareholders (or stockholders)

2-76. The Paid-in Capital is reported as two separate amounts: $1,000,000, which is labelled ______________ ______________ , and $11,256,000, labelled Other __________ - ___ ______________ . The reasons for this distinction are described in Part 9. The important number is the total amount paid in by the shareholders, which is $ ________________ .

Common Stock
Paid-in Capital

$12,256,000

2-77. Thus, one type of equity in a corporation is the amount that was originally contributed by the s________________ .

shareholders

2-78. Individual shareholders may later sell their stock to someone else, but this has no effect on the balance sheet of the corporation. The market price of shares of General Motors Corporation stock changes practically every day; the amount of Paid-in Capital reported on the General Motors balance sheet . . . [does / does not] reflect these changes. This is consistent with the e____________ concept; transactions between individuals do not affect the entity.

does not
entity

2-79. The other equity item, $13,640,000, shows the amount of equity that has been *earned* by the profitable operations of the company and that has been *retained* in the entity; hence the name, R _ _ _ _ _ _ _ E _ _ _ _ _ _ _ .

Retained
Earnings

9-70. Since bonds are an obligation and stocks are not an obligation, *investors* have more risk if they invest in a company's stock than if they invest in the bonds of the same company. They are not sure of getting either an annual payment (dividends) or repayment of their investment. Investors therefore expect a . . . [higher / lower] return from an investment in stock than from an investment in bonds in the same company.

higher

9-71. For example, if a company's bonds had an interest rate of 12%, investors would invest in its stock only if they expected that the return on stock would be . . . [at least 12% / considerably more than 12%]. (The expected return on stock consists of both expected dividends and an expected increase in the market value of the stock.)

considerably more than 12%

9-72. Thus, from the viewpoint of the issuing company, stock, which is . . . [debt / equity] capital, is a . . . [more / less] expensive source of capital than bonds, which are . . . [debt / equity] capital.

equity; more
debt

9-73. Circle the correct words in the following table, which shows the principal differences between debt capital and equity capital.

	Bonds (Debt)	Stock (Equity)	
Annual payments required	[Yes / No]	[Yes / No]	Yes; No
Principal payments required	[Yes / No]	[Yes / No]	Yes; No
Risk to the entity is	[High / Low]	[High / Low]	High; Low
But its cost is relatively	[High / Low]	[High / Low]	Low; High

9-74. In deciding on its permanent capital structure, a company must decide on the proper balance between debt capital, which has a relatively . . . [high / low] risk and a relatively . . . [high / low] cost, and equity capital, which has a relatively . . . [high / low] risk and a relatively [high / low] cost.

high
low
low; high

2-80. Retained Earnings represents those amounts that have been retained in the entity after part of the company's earnings (i.e., profits) have been paid to shareholders in the form of dividends. Thus, we might write the equation:

Retained Earnings = [ ] – [ ] .

Earnings – Dividends

2-81. Retained Earnings are additions to capital that have accumulated since the entity began, not those of a single year. Therefore, unless Garsden Company has been in business only one year, the $13,640,000 shown as Retained Earnings as of December 31, 1986, reflects . . . [one / all previous] year(s) of operations.

all previous

2-82. The amount of Retained Earnings shows the amount of capital generated by operating activities. It is **not** cash. Cash is an asset. On December 31, 1986, the amount of Cash was $ ____________. The amount of Retained Earnings was $ ____________.

$1,449,000

$13,640,000

2-83. In summary, the equities section of the balance sheet reports the amount of capital obtained from two sources:

(1) The amount provided directly by equity investors (i.e. shareholders in a corporation), which is called __________ - ______ ____________.

(2) The amount generated by profitable operations and retained in the entity, which is called __________ ____________.

Paid-in

Capital

Retained Earnings

2-84. The Equities section is often labelled "Shareholders' Equity" or "Owners' Equity."

(No answer required.)

9-64. In summary, the equities section of a corporation's balance sheet has these main items:

(1) Paid-in Capital from stock that has preference, called ______________ stock.

(2) Paid-in Capital from common stock, which consists of (a) the . . . [par or stated value / market value] of the number of shares . . . [authorized / issued / outstanding], plus (b) the additional amount paid for the stock, called Other P _ _ _-in C _ _ _ _ _ _.

(3) Retained Earnings, which is the cumulative difference between __________ ______________ and ______________.

preferred

par or stated value

outstanding

Other Paid-in Capital

net income; dividends

9-65. These items . . . [are / are not] related to the market value of the stock.

are not

BALANCE BETWEEN DEBT AND EQUITY CAPITAL

9-66. A corporation obtains some capital from retained earnings. In addition, it obtains capital from the issuance of stock, which is . . . [debt / equity] capital, and from the issuance of bonds, which is . . . [debt / equity] capital.

equity

debt

9-67. A corporation has no fixed obligations to its shareholders; that is, the company . . . [must / need not] declare dividends each year, and . . . [must / need not] repay the amount the shareholders have invested.

need not

need not

9-68. A company has two fixed obligations to its bondholders, however:

(1) ....

(2) ....

(1) payment of interest

(2) repayment of principal

9-69. If the company fails to pay either the interest or the principal when due, the bondholders may force the company into bankruptcy.

Evidently bonds are a . . . [less / more] risky method of raising capital than stock; that is, debt capital is a . . . [less / more] risky source of capital than equity capital.

more

more

2-85. Keep in mind the fundamental accounting equation:

	=		+	

Assets = Liabilities + Equities

The right-hand side of the balance sheet shows the *sources* of capital. The capital itself exists in the form of assets which are reported on the left-hand side.

KEY POINTS TO REMEMBER

- The going-concern concept: Accounting assumes that an entity will continue to operate indefinitely.
- The cost concept: Accounting focuses on the cost of assets, rather than on their market value.
- Assets are valuable items that are owned or controlled by the entity and that were acquired at a measurable cost. Goodwill is not an asset unless it was purchased.
- Current assets are cash and assets that are expected to be converted into cash or used up in the near future, usually within one year.
- Current liabilities are obligations due in the near future, usually within one year.
- The current ratio is the ratio of current assets to current liabilities.
- Marketable securities are current assets; investments are noncurrent assets.
- A single liability may have both a current portion and a noncurrent portion.
- Equities consist of paid-in capital (which in a corporation is represented by stock) plus earnings retained since the entity began. It has nothing to do with the market value of the stock. Retained earnings is not cash; it is part of the owners' claim.

You have completed Part 2 of this program. If you think you understand the material in this part, you should now take Post Test 2, which is in the separate booklet. If you are uncertain about your understanding, you should review Part 2.

The post test will serve both to test your comprehension and to review the highlights of Part 2. After taking the post test, you may find that you are unsure about certain points. You should review these points before continuing with Part 3.

9-59. In a common stock dividend, the Retained Earnings account decreases by an amount equal to the increase in the Other Paid-in Capital account; therefore the total amount of equity . . . [increases / does not change / decreases].

does not change

9-60. Complete the following table by writing in each box the word "increases," "decreases," or "unchanged."

	Total amount of equity	Total number of shares outstanding
Cash dividend	decreases	unchanged
Stock dividend		

unchanged; increases

STOCK SPLIT

9-61. A corporation may decide to exchange the number of shares outstanding for other shares, often two or more times the number. The process is called a **stock split**. In a three-for-one stock split, for example, each shareholder receives three new shares for each old share held. This causes the total number of shares outstanding to . . . [decrease / stay the same / increase].

increase

9-62. A stock split does not affect the total amount of equity or the percentage of stock held by each shareholder. A shareholder who owns 1% of the stock before a stock split owns ____ %, of it afterwards, and owns . . . [fewer / the same amount of / more] shares.

1%

more

9-63. Complete the following table by writing in each box the word "increases," "decreases," or "unchanged."

	Total amount of equity	Total number of shares outstanding
Cash dividend	decreases	unchanged
Stock dividend	unchanged	increases
Stock split		

unchanged; increases

Part 3

Balance Sheet Changes

Learning Objectives

In this part you will learn:

- How various types of transactions change the amounts reported on the balance sheet.
- The nature of income and the income statement.

3-1. The amounts of assets, liabilities and equities of an entity . . . [remain constant / change] from day to day. Therefore the amounts shown on its balance sheet also . . . [remain constant / change].	change change
3-2. Although a balance sheet must be prepared at the end of each year, it can be prepared more often. In this part you will be asked to prepare a balance sheet at the end of each day. We shall consider a business named Glendale Market owned by a proprietor, John Smith. The **entity** here is . . . [John Smith / Glendale Market].	Glendale Market
3-3. On January 2, Smith started Glendale Market by opening a bank account in its name and depositing $10,000 of his money in it.	

9-54. In the table below, record the effects of a cash dividend on equity and the number of shares outstanding by writing in each box the word "increases," "decreases," or "unchanged."

	Total amount of equity	Total number of shares outstanding
Cash dividend		

decreases; unchanged

STOCK DIVIDEND

9-55. Dividends are usually paid in the form of cash. Sometimes, however, the dividend consists of shares of stock in the corporation. The latter is called a . . . [cash / stock] dividend.

stock

9-56. In a typical stock dividend, shareholders are issued additional shares amounting to 5% or 10% of the total they currently own. In a 10% stock dividend, for example, the holder of 900 shares would receive ______ additional shares of stock.

90 (= 0.10 x 900)

9-57. Since the number of shares received by each shareholder in a stock dividend is proportional to the number of shares that each shareholder currently owns, the percentage of the total equity owned by each stockholder . . . [increases / stays the same / decreases] as a result of a stock dividend.

stays the same

9-58. When a dividend of common stock is declared, Retained Earnings is decreased and Other Paid-in Capital is increased by the amount of the dividend.

Write a journal entry to record a dividend of $10,000 of common stock.

Dr. __________ __________ .... __________

Cr. __________ ________ ____ __________ ...... ________

Dr. Retained Earnings 10,000

Cr. Other Paid-in Capital .. 10,000

In the assets column of the following balance, enter the name of the asset that Glendale Market possessed at the close of business on January 2, and the appropriate amount.

GLENDALE MARKET

Balance sheet as of January 2

Assets	Liabilities and Equities
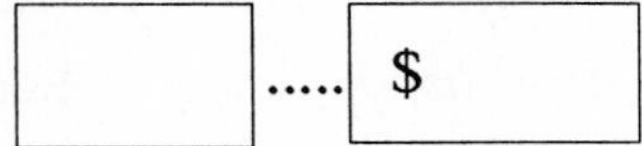	

GLENDALE MARKET

Balance Sheet as of January 2

Assets	Liabilities and Equities
Cash $10,000	

3-4. Recall that a name for equity capital is "Paid-in Capital."

In the space below, record the amount of paid-in capital as of the close of business on January 2.

GLENDALE MARKET

Balance sheet as of January 2

Assets	Liabilities and Equities
Cash $10,000	[ ] ..... $ [ ]

Paid-in capital $10,000

3-5. This balance sheet tells us how much cash . . . [Glendale Market / John Smith] had on January 2. The separation of Glendale Market from John Smith, the person, is an illustration of the e _ _ _ _ _ concept.

Glendale Market

entity

3-6. An entity owned by one person, such as Glendale Market, is called a **proprietorship**. In some proprietorships, the equities item is labelled with the proprietor's name: "John Smith, Capital." This is a variation in terminology, not a difference in concepts from those described in Part 2.

(No answer required.)

9-48. As the examples above show, **net income** refers to the increase in equity . . . [in one year / over the life of the corporation to date], whereas **retained earnings** refers to the net increases (after deduction of dividends) . . . [in one year / over the life of the corporation to date].

in one year

over the life of the corporation to date

9-49. Retained earnings reports the capital made available to the entity because part of net income was retained in the entity rather than being distributed as d _ _ _ _ _ _ _ s.

dividends

9-50. Retained earnings is one **source** of capital. It is reported on the . . . [left / right] side of the balance sheet. The capital is in the form of assets, and assets are reported on the . . . [left / right] side of the balance sheet.

right

left

(Note: Many people think that retained earnings are assets. Retained earnings are *not* assets.)

9-51. Equity is sometimes called net worth. This term suggests that the amount shows what the owners' claim on the assets is *worth.* Because the amounts reported on the assets side of the balance sheet . . . [do / do not] represent the real worth of these assets, this suggestion is . . . [absolutely right / dead wrong].

do not

dead wrong

9-52. The **worth** of a company's stock is what people will pay for it. This is the market price of the stock, which . . . [does / does not] appear anywhere on the balance sheet.

does not

TYPES OF DIVIDENDS

9-53. Suppose that a dividend of $5,000 is declared and paid in cash. Write the journal entry necessary to record the effect of this transaction on the Cash and Retained Earnings accounts.

Dr. ____________ ____________ .... ________

Cr. ____________ .... ________

Dr. Retained Earnings 5,000

Cr. Cash 5,000

3-7. On January 2, Glendale Market received $10,000 cash from John Smith. To record the effect of this event on the financial condition of the entity, you made __________ (how many?) changes in the balance sheet. After you made these changes, the balance sheet . . . [did / did not] balance. This is an illustration of the d _ _ _-a _ _ _ _ _ concept.

two

did

dual-aspect

3-8. A total should always be given for each side of a balance sheet, regardless of the number of items to be totaled. Complete the following balance sheet.

BROWN COMPANY

Balance Sheet as of June 30, 19x1

Assets		Liabilities and Equities	
Cash	$50,000	Accounts Payable .	$10,000
		Paid-in Capital	40,000
[ ]	$	[ ]	$

BROWN COMPANY

Balance Sheet as of June 30, 19x1

Assets		Liabilities and Equities	
Cash	$50,000	Accounts Payable .	$10,000
		Paid-in Capital	40,000
Total	$50,000	Total	$50,000

3-9. Amounts on a balance sheet are generally listed with the most current items first. Correct the following list to make it accord with this practice.

Liabilities (as of December 31, 19x1)

Bank loan payable (due next October)
Accounts payable (due in 60 days)
Long-term debt

Accounts payable
Bank loan payable
Long-term debt

9-42. Preferred shareholders usually have preference to a stated amount of annual dividends. Pemi Corporation has issued $100,000 of 9% preferred stock. No dividend can be paid to common shareholders until the preferred shareholders have received their full dividend of 9% of $100,000, amounting to $__________ a year.

$9,000

RETAINED EARNINGS AND DIVIDENDS

9-43. The net income of a period increases e _ _ _ _ _ _ _. The directors may vote to distribute money to the shareholders in the form of **dividends**. Dividends decrease e _ _ _ _ _ _ _.

equities

equities

9-44. Earnings means the same as net income. If earnings are not distributed as dividends, they are **retained** in the corporation. This amount is reported on the balance sheet as R _ _ _ _ _ _ _ E _ _ _ _ _ _ s.

Retained Earnings

9-45. The Retained Earnings account . . . [decreases / increases] by the amount of net income each period and . . . [decreases / increases] by the amount of dividends. Thus, if Retained Earnings are $100,000 at the start of a period during which a dividend of $20,000 is declared and during which net income is $30,000, Retained Earnings will be $__________ at the close of the period.

increases

decreases

$110,000
(= $100,000 – $20,000 + $30,000)

9-46. Levy Corporation started business in 19x1. Its net income was $100,000 in 19x1, $100,000 in 19x2, and $100,000 in 19x3. During this period, it paid no dividends. On the December 31, 19x3, balance sheet of Levy Corporation, the amount reported as Retained Earnings would be $__________.

$300,000
(= $100,000 + $100,000 + $100,000)

9-47. Frese Corporation also started business in 19x1 and had net income of $100,000 in each of its first three years. It paid dividends equal to its net income. On the December 31, 19x3, balance sheet of Frese Corporation, the amount reported as Retained Earnings would be $__________.

$0 (That is zero.)

3-10. When an entity borrows money, it may sign a written promise to repay. Such a written promise is termed a **note**. For example, if Business *A* borrows money from Business *B*, signing a note, Business *A* will record a . . . [note receivable / note payable] on its balance sheet, and Business *B* will record a . . . [note receivable /note payable].	note payable note receivable
3-11. On January 3, Glendale Market borrowed $5,000 cash from a bank, giving a note therefor. Change the following January 2 balance sheet as required in order to make it show the financial condition on January 3. In making your changes, cross out any material to be changed and write the corrections like this: 15,000 ~~10,000~~	

GLENDALE MARKET

Balance Sheet as of January 2

Assets		Liabilities and Equities	
		[ ] ..	$
Cash	$10,000	Paid-in Capital	$10,000
Total	$10,000	Total	$10,000

GLENDALE MARKET

Balance Sheet as of January ~~2~~ 3

Assets		Liabilities and Equities	
		Note payable	$5,000
Cash	~~$10,000~~ 15,000	Paid-in Capital	$10,000
Total	~~$10,000~~ 15,000	Total	~~$10,000~~ 15,000

3-12. To record the effect of the event of January 3, ________ (how many?) change(s) in the balance sheet (not counting the new totals and the new date) were necessary. The change(s) . . . [did / did not] affect the equality that had existed between assets and liabilities + equities.	two did not

9-36. When shareholders sell their stock to other investors, the price at which the sale takes place is determined in the **marketplace**. The value at which a stock is sold in such a transaction is called the . . . [market / par / stated] value.

market

9-37. The market value of a company's stock has no necessary relation to its par value, its stated value, or the amount of paid-in capital. If the par value of a certain stock is $1, the market value . . . [will be $1 / can be any value whatsoever]. If the stated value of another stock is $10, the market value . . . [will be $10 / can be any value whatsoever]. If paid-in capital is $12 per share, the market value . . . [will be $12 / can be any value whatsover].

can be any value whatsoever

can be any value whatsoever

can be any value whatsoever

9-38. The total equities are equal to total assets less total liabilities. This is not likely to be equal to the total market value of all stock outstanding. Evidently accounting . . . [is a way of measuring / does not attempt to measure] the market value of the shareholders' equity.

does not attempt to measure

PREFERRED STOCK

9-39. Some corporations issue stock that gives its owners preferential treatment over the common shareholders. As the word "preferential" suggests, such stock is called p _ _ _ _ _ _ ed stock.

preferred

9-40. Usually preferred shareholders have a preferential claim over the common shareholders for the par value of their stock if the corporation should be liquidated. Thus, if the corporation were liquidated, the owner of 500 shares of $100 preferred stock would get $__________ before the common shareholders got anything.

$50,000 (= 500 x $100)

9-41. As you learned earlier, par value of common stock has . . . [some / practically no] significance. Because preferred stock usually does have a preferential claim on assets equal to its par value, its par value has . . . [some / practically no] significance.

practically no

some

3-13. On January 4, Glendale Market purchased inventory costing $2,000, paying cash.

Change the following January 3 balance sheet as required to make it show the financial condition on January 4. Strike out any items that must be changed, and write the corrections above (or below) them.

GLENDALE MARKET

Balance Sheet as of January 3

Assets		Liabilities and Equities	
Cash	$15,000	Note payable	$ 5,000
		Paid-in capital	10,000
Total	$15,000	Total	$15,000

GLENDALE MARKET

Balance Sheet as of January ~~3~~ 4

Assets		Liabilities and Equities	
Cash	~~$15,000~~ 13,000	Note payable	$ 5,000
Inventory..........	2,000	Paid-in capital	10,000
Total	$15,000	Total	$15,000

3-14. The event of January 4 required two changes on the balance sheet, even though . . . [only one / both] side(s) of the balance sheet was (were) affected.

only one

3-15. Each event that is recorded in the accounting records is called a **transaction**. When Glendale Market received $10,000 from John Smith and deposited it in its bank account, this qualified as a ____________under the definition given above, because it was "an event that ____ ____."

transaction

was recorded in the accounting records

3-16. Each transaction you have recorded has caused at least _____ (how many?) change(s) on the balance sheet (not counting the changes in the totals and in the date), even when only one side of the balance sheet was affected. This is true of all transactions, and this is why accounting is called a . . . [single / double / triple]-entry system.

two

double

9-31. When a corporation is formed, its directors vote to **authorize** a certain number of shares of stock and to **issue** some of this authorized stock to investors. Thus, at any given time the amount of stock authorized is generally . . . [larger than / the same as / smaller than] the amount issued.

larger than

9-32. A corporation may buy back some of the stock that it had previously issued. Such stock is then called **treasury stock**. The **outstanding stock** consists of the issued stock less the treasury stock.

If a company issues 100,000 shares and buys back 15,000 shares, its treasury stock is ______________ shares, and its outstanding stock is ______________ shares.

15,000
85,000 (= 100,000 – 15,000)

9-33. The balance sheet amount for common stock is the amount for the number of shares of stock outstanding.

Maxim Company has authorized 100,000 shares of stock. It has issued 60,000 shares, for which it received the stated value of $10 per share. As of December 31, 19x1, it has bought back 10,000 shares, paying $10 per share. These shares are in its treasury stock. The balance sheet amount for common stock is $______________ .

$500,000 [= (60,000 x $10) – (10,000 x $10)]

9-34. On the balance sheet, both the amount of common stock and the amount of treasury stock are reported. This section of the balance sheet for Maxim Company would read:

Common stock	$600,000
Less [ ]	______
Paid-in capital	______

Treasury stock 100,000
500,000

9-35. Shareholders may sell their stock to other investors. Such sales . . . [do / do not] affect the balance sheet of the corporation.

do not

3-17. Earlier we described the fundamental accounting equation, assets = liabilities + equities. If we were to record only *one* aspect of a transaction, this equation . . . [would / would not] continue to describe an equality.

would not

3-18. The fundamental accounting equation, which is ___________ = _____________ + ___________ was also referred to in Part 1 as the d _ _ _ -aspect concept.

assets = liabilities + equities
dual

3-19. When a business sells merchandise for $150 that had cost it $100, the profit of $50 represents an increase of $50 in equity. As we saw in Part 2, the item Retained Earnings is used to record changes in equity arising from the operation of the business. These facts will help you in analyzing the transactions that follow.

(No answer required)

3-20. On January 5, Glendale Market sold merchandise for $300, receiving cash. The merchandise had cost $200.

Change the following January 4 balance sheet so that it reports the financial condition on January 5. (If you cannot do this frame, skip to the next without looking at the answer to this one.)

GLENDALE MARKET

Balance Sheet as of January 4

Assets		Liabilities and Equities	
Cash	$13,000	Note payable	$ 5,000
Inventory	2,000	Paid-in capital	10,000
Total	$15,000	Total	$15,000

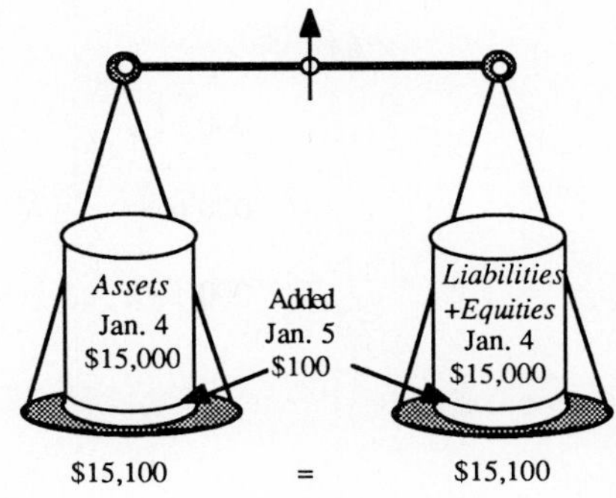

GLENDALE MARKET

Balance Sheet as of January ~~4~~ 5

Assets		Liabilities and Equities	
Cash	~~$13,000~~ 13,300	Note payable	$ 5,000
Inventory	~~2,000~~ 1,800	Paid-in capital	10,000
		Retained earnings	100
Total	$15,100	Total	$15,100

(If you answered this frame correctly, skip to frame 3-27.)

9-27. The amount that the shareholders paid the corporation in exchange for their stock is **paid-in capital.** The difference between par value and the total paid-in capital is called **other paid-in capital.**

Jones paid $10,000 cash to Marple Company and received 1,000 shares of its $1 par-value common stock. Complete the journal entry that Marple Company would make for this transaction.

Dr. Cash .... ________		10,000
Cr. Common stock	________	1,000
Cr. Other paid-in capital	________	9,000

9-28. If Jones's payment of $10,000 were the only equity transaction, this section of the Marple Company balance sheet would appear as follows:

Common stock	$________	$ 1,000
Other paid-in capital	________	9,000
Total paid-in capital	________	$ 10,000

9-29. Not all stocks have a par value. For these **no-par-value stocks,** the directors state a value. This value, called the s _ _ _ _ d value, is usually set close to the amount that the corporation actually receives from the issuance of the stock.

stated

9-30. No-par-value stock is recorded at its stated value. The difference between this amount and cash received is Other Paid-in Capital, just as in the case of par-value stock.

Medoc Corporation received $100,000 cash from the issuance of 10,000 shares of stock with a stated value of $9 per share. Give the journal entry for this transaction.

Dr. ________________ .... ________

Cr. ____________ ____________......... ________

Cr. __________ __________ __________.. ________

Dr. Cash	100,000	
Cr. Common stock.		90,000
Cr. Other paid-in capital		10,000

3-21. On January 5, Glendale Market sold merchandise for $300 cash that cost $200. To record this transaction, let us handle its individual parts separately. Change the date. Then, record only the amount of cash after the receipt of the $300. (Disregard, for the moment, any other changes, including changes in totals.)

GLENDALE MARKET

Balance Sheet as of January 4

Assets		Liabilities and Equities	
Cash	$13,000	Note payable	$ 5,000
Inventory	2,000	Paid-in capital	10,000
Total	$15,000	Total	$15,000

GLENDALE MARKET

Balance Sheet as of January ~~4~~ 5

Assets		Liabilities and Equities	
Cash	~~$13,000~~ 13,300	Note payable	$ 5,000
Inventory	2,000	Paid-in capital	10,000
Total	$15,000	Total	$15,000

3-22. On January 5, Glendale Market sold merchandise for $300 cash that cost $200. Next, record only the amount of inventory after this transaction.

GLENDALE MARKET

Balance Sheet as of January ~~4~~ 5

Assets		Liabilities and Equities	
Cash	~~$13,000~~ 13,300	Note payable	$ 5,000
Inventory	2,000	Paid-in capital	10,000
Total	$15,000	Total	$15,000

GLENDALE MARKET

Balance Sheet as of January ~~4~~ 5

Assets		Liabilities and Equities	
Cash	~~$13,000~~ 13,300	Note payable	$ 5,000
Inventory	~~2,000~~ 1,800	Paid-in capital	10,000
Total	$15,000	Total	$15,000

9-23. Owners of a corporation are called **shareholders** because they hold shares of the corporation's stock. The equities section of a corporation's balance sheet is therefore labeled s _ _ _ _ _ _ _ _ _ _ e _ _ _ _ _ _ s.

shareholder equities

9-24. There are two types of shareholders: **common shareholders** and **preferred shareholders**. The stock held by the former is called ________________ stock, and that held by the latter is called ________________ stock. We shall first describe accounting for common stock.

common

preferred

COMMON STOCK

9-25. Sometimes stock is issued with a specific amount printed on the face of each certificate. This amount is called the **par value**. In the stock certificate shown below, for example, the par value is $ ______________.

$1

No. 701

COMMON STOCK
$1 PAR VALUE

INSTRON
ENGINEERING CORPORATION
INCORPORATED UNDER THE LAWS OF THE COMMONWEALTH OF MASSACHUSETTS

COMMON STOCK
$1 PAR VALUE

THIS CERTIFIES THAT ** ROBERT N. ANTHONY AND GRETCHEN L. ANTHONY as tenants in common, is the owner of

—FIFTY—

FULLY-PAID AND NON-ASSESSABLE SHARES OF THE COMMON STOCK OF THE PAR VALUE OF $1 EACH OF INSTRON ENGINEERING CORPORATION transferable upon the books of the corporation upon surrender of this certificate duly indorsed or assigned. This certificate and the shares represented hereby are subject to the laws of the Commonwealth of Massachusetts and to the Articles of Organization and By-laws of the corporation and amendments thereto. This certificate is not valid until countersigned by the Transfer Agent and registered by the Registrar.

WITNESS the facsimile seal of INSTRON ENGINEERING CORPORATION and the facsimile signatures of its duly authorized officers.

Dated: JAN 1 0 1953

TREASURER

PRESIDENT

9-26. Strangely enough, the par value of stock has practically no significance. It is a holdover from the days when shareholders were liable if they purchased stock for less than its par value. In order to avoid this liability, stock today is always issued for much more than its par value. Nevertheless, the par value of stock continues to be reported on the balance sheet.

(No answer required.)

3-23. On January 5, Glendale Market sold merchandise for $300 cash that cost $200. Now total the assets as of the close of business on January 5, and show the new total.

GLENDALE MARKET

Balance Sheet as of January 4

Assets		Liabilities and Equities	
Cash	$13,000	Note payable	$ 5,000
Inventory	2,000	Paid-in capital	10,000
Total	$15,000	Total	$15,000

GLENDALE MARKET

Balance Sheet as of January 4

Assets		Liabilities and Equities	
Cash	$13,000	Note payable	$ 5,000
Inventory	2,000	Paid-in capital	10,000
Total	$15,000	Total	$15,000

3-24. On January 5, Glendale Market sold merchandise for $300 cash that cost $200.

GLENDALE MARKET

Balance Sheet as of January 4

Assets		Liabilities and Equities	
Cash	$13,000	Note payable	$ 5,000
Inventory	2,000	Paid-in capital	10,000
Total	$15,000	Total	$15,000

Evidently the transaction of January 5 caused a net . . . [decrease / increase] of $________ in the assets of Glendale Market from what they had been at the close of business on January 4.

increase; $100

3-25. On January 5, Glendale Market sold merchandise for $300 that cost $200. The assets of the entity increased by $100. The increase was the result of selling merchandise at a profit. As we learned in Part 2, profitable operations result in an increase in equity, specifically in the item R______________ E______________.

Retained Earnings

9-19. As noted in earlier parts, there are two sources of equity capital:

(1) Amounts paid in by equity investors, who are the entity's owners. This amount is called . . . [Paid-in Capital / Retained Earnings].

(2) Amounts generated by the profitable operation of the entity. This amount is called . . . [Paid-in Capital / Retained Earnings].

Paid-in Capital

Retained Earnings

9-20. Some entities do not report these two sources separately. An unincorporated business owned by a single person is called a proprietorship. The equity item in a proprietorship is often reported by giving the proprietor's name, followed by the word Capital.

Suppose Mary Green, proprietor of Green's Market, has an equity of $10,000 in her business. Show how the owner's equity item would look by filling in the boxes.

[ ] .... [$]

Mary Green, Capital $10,000

9-21. A partnership is an unincorporated business owned by two or more persons jointly. If there are only a few partners, the equity of each might be shown separately.

John Black and Henry Green are equal partners in a laundry business. On December 31, 19x1, the equities in the business total $100,000. The equities might be reported on that date as follows:

________________	, Capital	$ ________
________________	, Capital	________
	Total equities	$ ________

John Black, Capital	$ 50,000
Henry Green, Capital	50,000
Total equities	$ 100,000

9-22. Equity consists of capital paid-in by owners, plus earnings retained in the business. Thus the item "John Black, Capital, $50,000" means (circle the correct answer):

(A) John Black contributed $50,000 cash to the entity.

(B) The entity owes John Black $50,000.

(C) John Black's ownership interest in the assets is $50,000.

(C)
Not (A): We don't know the amount of the original contribution.
Not (B): The entity does not "owe' its owners.

3-26. On January 5, Glendale Market sold merchandise for $300 that cost $200. Add $100 of Retained Earnings and show the new total of the right-hand side.

GLENDALE MARKET

Balance Sheet as of January ~~4~~ 5

Assets		Liabilities and Equities	
Cash	~~$13,000~~ 13,300	Note payable	$ 5,000
Inventory	~~2,000~~ 1,800	Paid-in capital	10,000
Total	~~$15,000~~ 15,100	Total	$15,000

3-27. On January 6, Glendale Market purchased merchandise for $2,000 and added it to its inventory. It agreed to pay the vendor within 30 days.

Change the following January 5 balance sheet so that it reports the financial condition on January 6. Recall that an obligation to pay a vendor is called an "Account Payable."

GLENDALE MARKET

Balance Sheet as of January 5

Assets		Liabilities and Equities	
Cash	$13,300		
Inventory	1,800	Note payable	$ 5,000
		Paid-in capital	10,000
		Retained earnings	100
Total	$15,100	Total	$15,100

GLENDALE MARKET

Balance Sheet as of January ~~4~~ 5

Assets		Liabilities and Equities	
Cash	~~$13,000~~ 13,300	Note payable	$ 5,000
Inventory	~~2,000~~ 1,800	Paid-in capital	10,000
		Retained earnings	100
Total	~~$15,000~~ 15,100	Total	~~$15,000~~ 15,100

GLENDALE MARKET

Balance Sheet as of January ~~5~~ 6

Assets		Liabilities and Equities	
Cash	$13,300	Accounts Payable	2,000
Inventory	~~1,800~~ 3,800	Note payable	$ 5,000
		Paid-in capital	10,000
		Retained earnings	100
Total	~~$15,100~~ 17,100	Total	~~$15,100~~ 17,100

9-13. When an entity issues bonds, it assumes two obligations. It is obligated (1) to repay the face amount, the **principal**, on the due date; and (2) to pay **interest**, usually at semiannual intervals (that is, twice a year). The obligations to pay the principal is usually a . . . [current / noncurrent] liability. The liability for interest is a . . . [current / noncurrent] liability.

noncurrent
current

9-14. Interest on bonds is an expense and should be recognized in the accounting period to which the interest applies. Thus, if in January 19x2 an entity makes a semiannual interest payment of $3,000 to cover the last six months of 19x1, this interest expense should be recognized in 19x__. This is required by the m _ _ _ _ _ _ g concept.

19x1
matching

9-15. The $3,000 of unpaid interest that was an expense in 19x1 would be recorded in 19x1 by the following entry.

Dr. I__________ E__________ 3,000

Cr. I__________ P__________ 3,000

Dr. Interest Expense 3,000

Cr. Interest Payable 3,000

9-16. In 19x2, when this interest was paid to the bondholders, the following entry would be made.

Dr. __________ __________ 3,000

Cr. __________ 3,000

Dr. Interest Payable 3,000

Cr. Cash 3,000

EQUITIES: PAID-IN CAPITAL

9-17. Capital obtained from bonds is called . . . [debt / equity] capital. The other source of permanent capital is equity, which is called . . . [debt / equity] capital.

debt

equity

9-18. A bond is a promise to pay. Such an obligation is a liability. By contrast, equity is an ownership interest in the entity, and the entity does not promise to pay equity investors anything. Equity, therefore, . . . [is / is not] a liability.

is not

3-28. On January 7, merchandise costing $500 was sold for $800, which was received in cash. Change the following January 6 balance sheet so that it reports the financial condition on January 7.

GLENDALE MARKET

Balance Sheet as of January 6

Assets		Liabilities and Equities	
Cash	$13,300	Accounts payable	$ 2,000
Inventory	3,800	Note payable	5,000
		Paid-in capital	10,000
		Retained earnings	100
Total	$17,100	Total	$17,100

3-29. On January 8, merchandise costing $600 was sold for $900. The customer agreed to pay $900 within 30 days. (Recall that when customers buy on credit, the entity has an asset called "Accounts Receivable.")

Change the following January 7 balance sheet so that it reports the financial condition on January 8.

GLENDALE MARKET

Balance Sheet as of January 7

Assets		Liabilities and Equities	
Cash	$14,100	Accounts payable	$ 2,000
		Note payable	5,000
Inventory	3,300	Paid-in capital	10,000
		Retained earnings	400
Total	$17,400	Total	$17,400

GLENDALE MARKET

Balance Sheet as of January ~~6~~ 7

Assets		Liabilities and Equities	
Cash	$~~13,300~~ 14,100	Accounts payable	$ 2,000
Inventory	~~3,800~~ 3,300	Note payable	5,000
		Paid-in capital	10,000
		Retained earnings	~~100~~ 400
Total	$~~17,100~~ 17,400	Total	$~~17,100~~ 17,400

GLENDALE MARKET

Balance Sheet as of January ~~7~~ 8

Assets		Liabilities and Equities	
Cash	$14,100	Accounts payable	$ 2,000
Accounts Receivable	900	Note payable	5,000
Inventory	~~3,300~~ 2,700	Paid-in capital	10,000
		Retained earnings	~~400~~ 700
Total	$~~17,400~~ 17,700	Total	$~~17,400~~ 17,700

DEBT CAPITAL

9-8. Although most liabilities are debts, the term **debt capital** refers only to noncurrent liabilities. Debt capital therefore refers to liabilities that come due . . .[within one year / sometime after one year].

sometime after one year

9-9. Debt capital is usually obtained by the issuance of **bonds**. A bond is a written promise to pay someone who lends money to the entity. Since a bond usually is a noncurrent liability, the payment is due . . .[within one year / sometime after one year].

sometime after one year

9-10. The total amount of loan that must be repaid is specified on the face of a bond and is termed the **face amount**.

If Green Company issues ten-year bonds whose face amounts total $100,000, Green Company has a liability, Bonds Payable, of $__________.

$100,000

9-11. If the entity does not receive cash equal to the face amount of the bonds, there are accounting complications not discussed in this introductory program. Suppose that Green Company does receive $100,000 cash from the issuance of bonds that have a face amount of $100,000. Write the jounal entry necessary to record the effect of this transaction on the Cash and Bonds Payable accounts.

Dr. ____________________..................... ________

Cr. ______________ ____________...... ________

Dr. Cash 100,000

Cr. Bonds payable 100,000

9-12. When they are issued, the bonds are . . . [current / noncurrent] liabilities. However, as time passes and the due date becomes less than one year, the bonds become a . . . [current/noncurrent] liability. In 19x1, a bond that is due on January 1, 19x3 would be a . . . [current/noncurrent] liability. In 19x2 the same bond would be a . . . [current / noncurrent] liability.

noncurrent

current

noncurrent

current

3-30. On January 9, Glendale Market purchased a one-year insurance policy for $200, paying cash. (Recall that the right to insurance protection is an asset. For this asset, use the term "Prepaid insurance.")

Change the following January 8 balance sheet so that it reports the financial condition on January 9.

GLENDALE MARKET

Balance Sheet as of January 8

Assets		Liabilities and Equities	
Cash	$14,100	Accounts payable	$ 2,000
Accounts receivable	900	Note payable	5,000
Inventory	2,700	Paid-in capital	10,000
		Retained earnings	700
Total	$17,700	Total	$17,700

GLENDALE MARKET

Balance Sheet as of January ~~8~~ 9

Assets		Liabilities and Equities	
Cash	~~$14,100~~ 13,900	Accounts payable	$ 2,000
Accounts receivable	900	Note payable	5,000
Inventory	2,700	Paid-in capital	10,000
Prepaid insurance	200	Retained earnings	700
Total	$17,700	Total	$17,700

3-31. On January 10, Glendale Market puchased two lots of land of equal size for a total of $10,000. It thereby acquired an asset, Land. It paid $2,000 in cash and gave a ten-year mortgage for the balance of $8,000. (Use the term "Mortgage payable" for the liability.)

Change the following January 9 balance sheet so that it reports the financial condition on January 10.

GLENDALE MARKET

Balance Sheet as of January 9

Assets		Liabilities and Equities	
Cash	$13,900	Accounts payable	$ 2,000
Accounts receivable	900	Note payable	5,000
Inventory	2,700		
Prepaid insurance .	200	Paid-in capital	10,000
		Retained earnings	700
Total	$17,700	Total	$17,700

GLENDALE MARKET

Balance Sheet as of January ~~9~~ 10

Assets		Liabilities and Equities	
Cash	~~$13,900~~ 11,900	Accounts payable	$ 2,000
Accounts receivable	900	Note payable	5,000
Inventory	2,700	Mortgage payable	8,000
Prepaid insurance .	200	Paid-in capital	10,000
Land	10,000	Retained earnings	700
Total	~~$17,700~~ 25,700	Total	~~$17,700~~ 25,700

SOURCES OF CAPITAL

9-5. To highlight how working capital and the noncurrent assets were financed, we can rearrange the items on the balance sheet as follows:

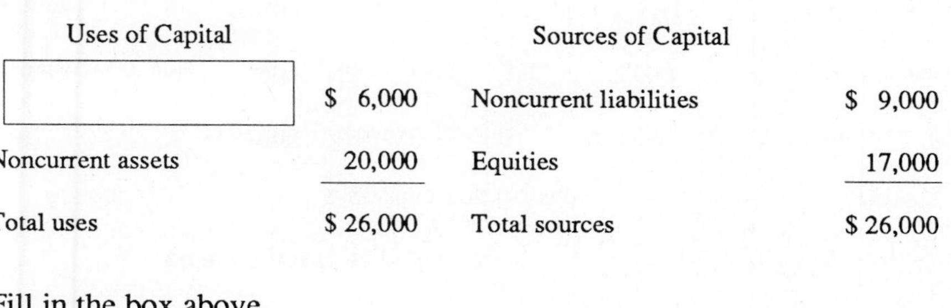

LOUGEE COMPANY
Sources and Uses of Permanent Capital
As of December 31, 19x1

Uses of Capital		Sources of Capital	
[ ]	$ 6,000	Noncurrent liabilities	$ 9,000
Noncurrent assets	20,000	Equities	17,000
Total uses	$ 26,000	Total sources	$ 26,000

Fill in the box above.

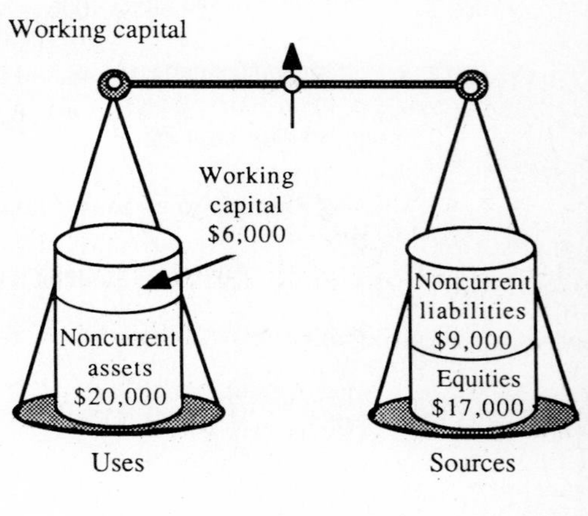

9-6. The right-hand side of the balance sheet given above shows the sources of capital used to finance the working capital and the noncurrent assets. Collectively, these sources are called **permanent capital**. As the balance sheet indicates, there are two types of permanent capital: (1) N _ _ _ _ _ _ _ _ t l _ _ _ _ _ _ _ _ _ s, and (2) E _ _ _ _ _ _ s. The total of these two sources is $__________, and they are used to finance assets that also total $__________.

Noncurrent liabilities; Equities
$26,000
$26,000

9-7. In this part we shall describe the two types of permanent c________ and the ways they are recorded in the accounts.

capital
(Note: although these items are called "capital," they are more accurately labelled "sources of capital.")

3-32. On January 11, Glendale Market sold one of the two lots of land for $5,000. The buyer paid $1,000 cash and assumed $4,000 of the mortgage; that is, Glendale Market was no longer responsible for this half of the mortgage payable.

Change the following January 10 balance sheet so that it reports the financial condition on January 11.

GLENDALE MARKET

Balance Sheet as of January 10

Assets		Liabilities and Equities	
Cash	$11,900	Accounts payable	$ 2,000
Accounts receivable	900	Note payable	5,000
Inventory	2,700	Mortgage payable	8,000
Prepaid insurance .	200	Paid-in capital	10,000
Land	10,000	Retained earnings	700
Total	$25,700	Total	$25,700

GLENDALE MARKET

Balance Sheet as of January ~~10~~ 11

Assets		Liabilities and Equities	
Cash	~~$11,900~~ 12,900	Accounts payable	$ 2,000
Accounts receivable	900	Note payable	5,000
Inventory	2,700	Mortgage payable	~~8,000~~ 4,000
Prepaid insurance .	200	Paid-in capital	10,000
Land	~~10,000~~ 5,000	Retained earnings	700
Total	~~$25,700~~ 21,700	Total	~~$25,700~~ 21,700

3-33. On January 12, Smith received an offer of $15,000 for his equity in Glendale Market. Although his equity was then only $10,700, he rejected the offer. It was evident that the store had already acquired goodwill of $4,300.

What change should be made in the following January 11 balance sheet so that it reports the financial condition on January 12?

GLENDALE MARKET

Balance Sheet as of January 11

Assets		Liabilities and Equities	
Cash	$12,900	Accounts payable	$ 2,000
Accounts receivable	900	Note payable	5,000
Inventory	2,700	Mortgage payable	4,000
Prepaid insurance .	200	Paid-in capital	10,000
Land	5,000	Retained earnings	700
Total	$21,700	Total	$21,700

The balance sheet is unchanged from that of January 11, except for the date. In accordance with the cost concept, goodwill is an asset only when it has been paid for. The balance sheet does not show the *market value* of the entity.

LOUGEE COMPANY
Balance Sheet as of December 31, 19x1

	[ ]		[ ]	
Current [ ]	$10,000	Current [ ]	$ 4,000	
Noncurrent [ ]	20,000	Noncurrent [ ]	9,000	
		Paid-in capital	7,000	
		Retained earnings	10,000	
Total [ ]	$30,000	Total [ ]	$30,000	

Assets; Liabilities and Equities

Assets; Liabilities

Assets; Liabilities

Assets: Liabilities and Equities

9-2. Current assets are assets that are expected to be turned into cash within ....(what period of time?). Current liabilities are obligations that come due within ....(what period of time?).

one year

one year

9-3. For Lougee Company, we can say that of the $10,000 current assets, $4,000 was financed by the c _ _ _ _ _ _ liabilities. The remaining $6,000 of current assets and the $20,000 of noncurrent assets were financed by the $9,000 of noncurrent liabilities and the $17,000 of equities.

current

9-4. That part of the current assets not financed by the current liabilities is called **working capital.** Working capital is therefore the difference between c____________ a____________ and c____________ l____________. In the example given above, working capital is:

$ ________ – $________ = $ ________ .

current assets

current liabilities

$10,000 – $4,000 = $6,000

3-34. On January 13, Smith withdrew for his personal use $200 cash from the Glendale Market bank account, and he also withdrew merchandise costing $400.

Change the following January 12 balance sheet so that it shows the financial condition on January 13.

GLENDALE MARKET

Balance Sheet as of January 12

Assets		Liabilities and Equities	
Cash	$12,900	Accounts payable	$ 2,000
Accounts receivable	900	Note payable	5,000
Inventory	2,700	Mortgage payable	4,000
Prepaid insurance .	200	Paid-in capital	10,000
Land	5,000	Retained earnings	700
Total	$21,700	Total	$21,700

GLENDALE MARKET

Balance Sheet as of January ~~12~~ 13

Assets		Liabilities and Equities	
Cash	~~$12,900~~ 12,700	Accounts payable	$ 2,000
Accounts receivable	900	Note payable	5,000
Inventory	~~2,700~~ 2,300	Mortgage payable	4,000
Prepaid insurance .	200	Paid-in capital	10,000
Land	5,000	Retained earnings	~~700~~ 100
Total	~~$21,700~~ 21,100	Total	~~$21,700~~ 21,100

3-35. On January 14, Smith learned that the person who purchased the land on January 11 for $5,000 sold it for $8,000. The lot still owned by Glendale Market was identical in value with this other plot.

What changes should be made in the following January 13 balance sheet so that it reports the financial condition on January 14?

GLENDALE MARKET

Balance Sheet as of January 13

Assets		Liabilities and Equities	
Cash	$12,700	Accounts payable	$ 2,000
Accounts receivable	900	Note payable	5,000
Inventory	2,300	Mortgage payable	4,000
Prepaid insurance .	200	Paid-in capital	10,000
Land	5,000	Retained earnings	100
Total	$21,100	Total	$21,100

The balance sheet is identical to that of January 13, except for the date. As required by the cost concept, the land continues to be shown at its cost.

Part 9

Liabilities and Equities

Learning Objectives

In this part, you will learn:

- The nature of working capital.
- Types of permanent capital: debt and equity.
- How to account for debt capital.
- How to account for equity capital.
  - Paid-in capital: common and preferred stock.
  - Retained earnings and dividends.
- The debt / equity ratio.
- The nature of consolidated financial statements.

WORKING CAPITAL

9-1. In earlier parts you learned that the balance sheet has two sides with equal totals. Fill in the two missing names in the boxes in the simplified balance sheet given on the following page.

3-36. On January 15, Glendale Market paid off $2,000 of its bank loan, giving cash (disregard interest).

Change the following January 14 balance sheet so that it reports the financial condition on January 15.

GLENDALE MARKET

Balance Sheet as of January 14

Assets		Liabilities and Equities	
Cash	$12,700	Accounts payable	$ 2,000
Accounts receivable	900	Note payable	5,000
Inventory	2,300	Mortgage payable.....	4,000
Prepaid insurance .	200	Paid-in capital	10,000
Land	5,000	Retained earnings	100
Total	$21,100	Total	$21,100

GLENDALE MARKET

Balance Sheet as of January ~~14~~ 15

Assets		Liabilities and Equities	
Cash	~~$12,700~~ 10,700	Accounts payable	$ 2,000
Accounts receivable	900	Note payable	~~5,000~~ 3,000
Inventory	2,300	Mortgage payable.....	4,000
Prepaid insurance .	200	Paid-in capital	10,000
Land	5,000	Retained earnings	100
Total	~~$21,100~~ 19,100	Total	~~$21,100~~ 19,100

3-37. On January 16, Glendale Market was changed to a corporation. John Smith received 100 shares of common stock in exchange for his $10,100 equity in the business. He immediately sold 25 of these shares for $4,000 cash.

Change the following January 15 balance sheet so that it reports the financial condition on January 16.

GLENDALE MARKET

Balance Sheet as of January 15

Assets		Liabilities and Equities	
Cash	$10,700	Accounts payable	$ 2,000
Accounts receivable	900	Note payable	3,000
Inventory	2,300	Mortgage payable.....	4,000
Prepaid insurance .	200	Paid-in capital	10,000
Land	5,000	Retained earnings	100
Total	$19,100	Total	$19,100

There is no change, except for the date. Changing the organization to a corporation did not affect any amount on the balance sheet. (Perhaps the name of the entity was changed to, say, Glendale Market Corporation, but this does not affect the numbers.) John Smith's sale of the stock did not affect the entity, Glendale Market.

You have completed Part 8 of this program. If you think you understand the material in this part, you should now take Post Test 8 which is in the separate booklet. If you are uncertain about your understanding, you should review Part 8.

The post test will serve both to test your comprehension and to review the highlights of Part 8. After taking the post test, you may find that you are unsure about certain points. You should review these points before continuing with Part 9.

3-38. Any conceivable transaction can be recorded in terms of its effect on the balance sheet, just as you have done in this section. Although we shall describe techniques, refinements, and shortcuts in later parts, none of them changes this basic fact.

(No answer required.)

EQUITIES AND INCOME

3-39. Please turn to Exhibit 2 in your booklet. It is a summary of the transactions for Glendale Market that you analyzed in Frames 3–3 to 3–29. We shall focus on those that affect Equities.

(No answer required.)

3-40. As explained in Part 1, an entity's equity increases for either of two reasons. One is the receipt of capital from owners. On January 2, Glendale Market received $10,000 from John Smith, its owner. You recorded this as an increase in Cash and an increase in the equities item, P______ - ____ C________________.

Paid-in
Capital

3-41. The other source of an increase in equity is the profitable operation of the entity. Transactions that increase profit also increase the equities item, R____________ E____________. Refer to the transactions for January 3–8. In the table on the following page, show the dollar amount of the change in Retained Earnings, if any, that resulted from each transaction. If the transaction had no effect on Retained Earnings, put an X in the "No effect" column.

Retained Earnings

8-97. The difference between actual income taxes paid and income tax expense is called Deferred Income Taxes. It is a liability account on the balance sheet. Refer to Exhibit 1 in your booklet. Garsden Company reported deferred income taxes as a . . . [current / noncurrent] liability of $____________. This is not to be confused with the Estimated Tax Liability, which is a . . . [current / noncurrent] liability of $____________. The latter amount is the amount it actually owed the government as of December 31, 1986, for its 1986 taxes.

noncurrent
$824,000
current
$1,541,000

KEY POINTS TO REMEMBER

- When acquired, a plant asset is recorded at its cost, including installation and other costs of making the asset ready for its intended use.
- Land has an unlimited life and is rarely depreciated.
- Plant assets are depreciated over their service life. A fraction of their cost is debited to Depreciation Expense each year and credited to Accumulated Depreciation.
- Depreciation Expense is an estimate. We do not know how long the service life will be, nor the asset's residual value.
- The book value of a plant asset is the difference between its cost and its accumulated depreciation. When book value reaches zero, no more depreciation expense is recorded.
- Book value does NOT report what the asset is worth.
- When an asset is sold, the difference between the sale price and book value is a gain or loss and is so reported on the income statement.
- For financial statements, depreciation expense is usually calculated on a straight-line basis. The depreciation rate, which is one unit divided by the service life, is applied to the depreciable cost, which is original cost less the residual value.
- Depletion is the process of writing off wasting assets, and amortization is the process of writing off intangible assets. The process is similar to depreciation, except that the credit is made directly to the asset account.
- Accelerated depreciation is often used for income tax purposes because it decreases the amount of taxable income in the early years.
- Taxable income may differ from pretax income reported on the income statement. If so, the reported income tax expense is calculated on the basis of accounting pretax income. The difference between this amount and the amount of tax paid is a balance sheet item, Deferred Income Taxes.

Retained Earnings

Date	Nature	Increased by	No effect
3	Borrowing		
4	Purchase		
5	Sale		
6	Purchase		
7	Sale		
8	Sale		
	Total	$	

Retained Earnings

Date	Nature	Increased by	No effect
3	Borrowing	$	X
4	Purchase		X
5	Sale	100	
6	Purchase		X
7	Sale	300	
8	Sale	300	
	Total	$ 700	

3-42. As can be seen from the table above, three of these transactions did not affect Retained Earnings: Borrowing money . . . [does / does not] affect Retained Earnings. The purchase of merchandise . . . [does / does not] affect Retained Earnings. The sale of that merchandise, however, . . . [does /does not] affect Retained Earnings.

does not
does not
does

3-43. The amount by which equity increased as a result of operations during a period of time is called the **income** of that period. You have just calculated that the total increase during the period January 2 through 8 was $__________, so Glendale Market's i_ _ _ _ _ for that period was $__________.

$700; income
$700

3-44. The amount of income and how it was earned is usually the most important information about a business entity. An accounting report called the **income statement** explains the income of a period. Note that the income statement is for a . . . [period of time / point in time], in contrast with the other statement, the b_ _ _ _ _ _ s_ _ _ _, which is for a . . . [period of time / moment in time].

period of time
balance sheet
moment in time

3-45. The $700 increase in Retained Earnings during the period is reported on the i_ _ _ _ _ s_ _ _ _ _ _ _ _ _. This statement explains *why* this increase occurred.

income statement

8-92. Taxable income and accounting income . . . [are always identical / may differ]. The tax regulations . . . [govern / do not govern] the way financial statements are prepared. Conversely, the way income is reported on a financial statement . . . [governs / does not govern] the way income is reported for tax purposes.

may differ do not govern

does not govern

(There is one exception: If LIFO is used in tax accounting, LIFO must also be used on the financial statements.)

DEFERRED INCOME TAXES

8-93. If a company uses accelerated depreciation in calculating its taxable income but uses straight-line depreciation in calculating its accounting income, its taxable income in the early years will be . . . [higher / lower] than its accounting income.

lower

8-94. Manley Corporation has accounting income in 19x1 of $2,000,000 but taxable income of only $1,100,000. If the income tax rate is 35%, it will pay an income tax of $__________. If the income tax had been calculated as 35% of its accounting income, the amount of tax would be $__________.

$385,000 (= $1,100,000 x 0.35)

$700,000 (= $2,000,000 x 0.35)

8-95. Manley Corporation's actual tax payment of $385,000 is lower than the tax calculated on its accounting income. The $385,000 does not **match** the accounting income. It is not consistent with the m __________ ing concept.

matching

8-96. As required by the matching concept, the amount of income tax expense reported on the income statement is the amount of income tax calculated on the basis of accounting income, not the amount actually paid. Thus, if its accounting income was $2,000,000 and its tax rate 35 percent, Manley Corporation would report income tax expense of $__________. If it actually paid only $385,000 income tax, it would somehow have to account for the difference of $__________.

$700,000

$315,000 (= $700,000 – $385,000)

3-46. To understand how the income statement does this, let's look at the January 5 transaction for Glendale Market. On January 5, Glendale Market sold for $300 cash some merchandise that had cost $200. This caused equities (Retained Earnings) to . . . [increase / decrease] by $______.

increase; $100

3-47. On January 5, Glendale Market sold merchandise for $300 cash that had cost $200. This transaction consists of two separate events: (1) the sale, which, taken by itself, . . . [increased / decreased] Retained Earnings by $300, and (2) the decrease in inventory, which, taken by itself, . . . [increased / decreased] Retained Earnings by $200.

increased

decreased

3-48. Taken by itself, the increase in Retained Earnings resulting from operations is called a **revenue**. When Glendale Market sold merchandise for $300, the transaction resulted in $300 of __________.

revenue

3-49. And taken by itself, the associated decrease in Retained Earnings is called an **expense**. When Glendale Market transferred merchandise to the customer, the transaction reduced inventory and resulted in $200 of __________ .

expense

3-50. Thus, when Glendale Market sold merchandise for $300 that cost $200, the effect of the transaction on Retained Earnings can be separated into two parts: a(n)________ of $______ and a(n)________ of $______.

revenue; $300; expense $200

3-51. In accounting, revenues and expenses are recorded separately. From Exhibit 2, calculate the revenues and expenses for the period January 2 through 8 by completing the following table:

Date	Revenues	Expenses
5	$	$
7		
8		
Total	$	$

Date	Revenues	Expenses
5	$ 300	$ 200
7	800	500
8	900	600
Total	$ 2,000	$1,300

8-87. If in Year 2 Monkton Company used tax depreciation, it would pay $_______________ . . . [more / the same / less] income tax than if it used accounting depreciation. If it used tax depreciation, it would pay . . . [more / the same / less] income tax in each of the early years and correspondingly . . . [more / the same / less] in the later years of the asset's life.

$770 (= $1,050 – $280) less

less

more

8-88. Accelerated depreciation results in a . . . [higher/lower] tax depreciation in the early years of an asset's life and hence in . . . [higher / lower] taxable income and . . . [higher / lower] income taxes during those early years.

higher

lower

lower

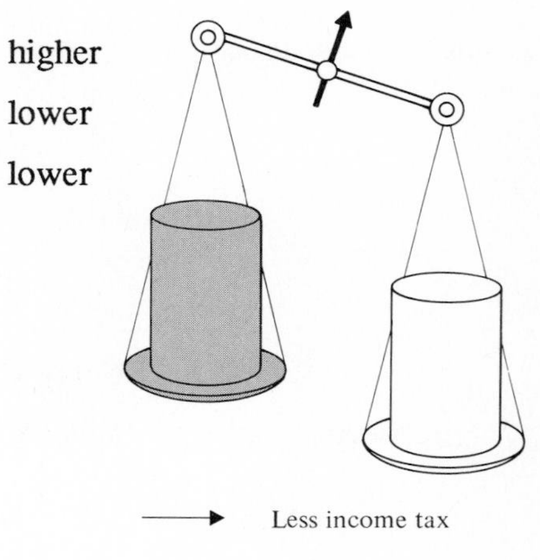

8-89. In the later years of the asset's life, accelerated depreciation will result in . . . [higher / lower] depreciation expense and . . . [higher / lower] taxable income and income taxes.

lower higher

8-90. The higher taxable income in later years will offset the lower taxable income in earlier years. However, during the earlier years the company will have the use of the money not paid out in taxes. For this reason, most companies use a _ _ _ _ _ _ _ _ _ _ d depreciation for calculating taxable income.

accelerated

8-91. In some circumstances, income tax regulations forbid a company from counting as tax deductions certain items that appear as expenses on its accounting income statement. For example, payments of fines or bribes are not tax deductible. In these circumstances, taxable income will be . . . [lower / higher] than accounting income.

higher

3-52. You can now prepare an income statement. Its heading shows the name of the accounting entity, the title of the statement, and the period covered. Complete the heading for Glendale Market's income statement for January 2–8:

GLENDALE MARKET

[ ] Statement

For the period [ ]

Income

January 2–8

3-53. The income statement reports revenues and expenses for the period and the difference between them, which is income. Label the amounts in the following income statement for Glendale Market.

GLENDALE MARKET
Income statement
for the period January 2–8

[ ]	$ 2,000
[ ]	1,300
[ ]	$ 700

Revenues

Expenses

Income

Revenues	$2,000
Expenses $1,300	
	Income $700

3-54. As the name suggests, Retained Earnings refers to the amount of income that has been r________ in the entity. On January 13, Smith withdrew $600 of assets for his personal use. This reduced R________ E________ by $________.

retained

Retained Earnings; $600

3-55. No other changes in Retained Earnings occured during the period January 2–13. Complete the following table:

Retained Earnings, January 2	$ 0
Income	+____
Withdrawal	−____
Retained Earnings, January 13	$____

700

600

100

8-85. To study the effect of tax depreciation, let's assume that in Year 2 (the first full year) Monkton Company had revenues of $4,000, that its only expense was depreciation expense, and that it paid income tax of 35% of its taxable income. Complete the calculation of its income tax for Year 2, using the tax depreciation you calculated in Frame 8-82:

		Answer
Revenues	$4,000	
Tax depreciation	______	$3,200
Taxable income	$______	$ 800
Income tax (35%)	$______	$ 280

8-86. Now calculate what its income tax would have been if it had used accounting (straight-line) depreciation in calculating its taxable income:

	Using tax depreciation	Using accounting depreciation	Answer
Revenues	$4,000	$4,000	
Tax depreciation	3,200	______	$1,000
Taxable income	800	______	$3,000
Income tax (35%)	$280	______	$1,050

The amount of Retained Earnings calculated above . . . [would / would not] equal the amount shown on the balance sheet of January 13.

would

3-56. Assume that in the remainder of January 7 Glendale Market had additional income of $800 and there were no additional withdrawals. Since Retained Earnings was $100 as of January 13, it would be $________ on January 31. Thus, the amount of Retained Earnings on a balance sheet is:

A. the amount earned in the current period.
B. the total amount retained since the entity began operations.

$900

B

3-57. The terms **profit, earnings,** and **income** all have the same meaning. They all are the differences between the r _ _ _ _ _ _ _ of an accounting period and the e _ _ _ _ _ _ _ of that period.

revenues
expenses

Note: Some people use the term **income** when they mean **revenue**; this can be confusing.

3-58. Another name for the income statement is **profit and loss statement.** This suggests that if revenues are less than expenses, the bottom line on the income statement is labeled l _ _ _, rather than income.

loss

3-59. In later parts, we shall describe various revenue and expense items, such as sales revenue, interest revenue, salary expense, and rent expense. These explain in more detail the reasons for the change in Retained Earnings during a period.

(No answer required.)

3-60. Remember that the Equities section of the balance sheet reports the amount of capital that the entity has obtained from two different sources:

1. The amount paid in by the owner(s), which is called P_____ - ____ C______________.

2. The amount of income that has been retained in the entity, which is called R __________ E ______________ .

Paid-in
Capital

Retained Earnings

8-83. Assume that a machine that qualifies for the above treatment has a service life of 10 years. The table below gives the accounting depreciation and the tax depreciation for the $10,000 machine. Calculate the differences between these accounts.

Year	Accounting Depreciation	Tax Depreciation	Tax higher by	Accounting higher by
1	$500	$2,000	$______	
2	1,000	3,200	______	
3	1,000	1,920	______	
4	1,000	1,150	______	
5	1,000	1,150	______	
6	1,000	580	$______	______
7–11	4,500	0		
Total	$10,000	$10,000	$	$______

	Tax higher by	Accounting higher by
	$1,500	
	2,200	
	920	
	150	
	150	
		$ 420
		$4,500
Total	$4,920	$4,920

8-84. As you can see from the table above, the total amount of tax depreciation is . . . [higher than / the same as / lower than] the total amount of accounting depreciation. However, in the early years of life, tax depreciation is . . . [higher than / the same as / lower than] accounting depreciation. This is why it is called an ______________ed appreciation.

the same as

higher than

accelerated

Income tax regulations state depreciation percentages for various types of assets. They all are based on the half-year convention and depreciate the asset faster than straight-line depreciation.

(No answer required.)

3-61. The two financial statements may be compared to two reports on a reservoir. One report may show how much water *flowed through* the reservoir during the period, and the other report may show how much water *was in* the reservoir as of the end of the period. Similarly, the ... [balance sheet / income statement] reports flows during a period of time, whereas the ... [balance sheet / income statement] reports status as of a point of time.

income statement
balance sheet

Thus, the income statement may be called a ... [flow / status] report, and the balance sheet may be called a ... [flow / status] report.

flow
status

KEY POINTS TO REMEMBER

- Every accounting transaction affects at least two items and preserves the basic equation: Assets = Liabilities + Equities. Accounting is a double-entry system.
- Some events are not transactions; they do not affect the accounting amounts. Examples in this part were: a change in the value of land, "goodwill" that was not purchased, and the changing of the entity from a proprietorship to a corporation.
- Other events affect assets and/or liabilities but have no effect on equities. Examples in this part were: borrowing money, purchasing inventory, purchasing insurance protection, acquiring an asset, giving a mortgage, buying land, selling land at its cost, and repaying a bank loan.
- Still other events affect equities as well as assets and/or liabilities. Revenues are increases in equities resulting from operations during a period. Expenses are decreases. Their effect is shown in the equity item called Retained Earnings. Equities also increase when owners pay in capital.
- A sale has two aspects: a revenue aspect and an expense aspect. Revenue results when the sale is made, whether or not cash is received at that time. The related expense is the cost of the merchandise that was sold. The income of a period is the difference between the revenues and expenses of that period.

8-79. Haydol Company purchased a machine for $3,000. It had an estimated service life of three years. If we use the straight-line method, the full year depreciation expense for this asset would be $______________ per year.

$1,000

8-80. Using the half-year convention, we would record depreciation expense as follows:

In Year 1	$______
In Year 2	______
In Year 3	______
In Year 4	______
Total	$______

In Year 1	$ 500
In Year 2	1,000
In Year 3	1,000
In Year 4	500
Total	$ 3,000

8-81. Monkton Company purchased a machine for $10,000 with an estimated service life of 10 years. Using the straight-line method and the half-year convention, we would record depreciation expense as follows:

In Year 1	$______
In each of Years 2 through 10, 9 years @ $______ per year	______
In Year 11	______
Total	$ 10,000

Year 1	$ 500
9 years @ $1,000 per year	9,000
Year 11	500
Total	$ 10,000

8-82. Based on accelerated depreciation and the half-year convention, income tax regulations specify the annual depreciation rates for various types of assets. For example, certain machines can be depreciated over a period of 6 years at rates given below. Calculate the tax depreciation for a machine costing $10,000.

Year	Allowed Percentage	Tax Depreciation Amount
1	20.0%	$______
2	32.0	______
3	19.2	______
4	11.5	______
5	11.5	______
6	5.8	______
Total	100%	$10,000

$2,000
3,200
1,920
1,150
1,150
580

(Note: These percentages applied in 1987. They may be changed by future tax laws.)

You have completed Part 3 of this program. If you think you understand the material in this part, you should now take Post Test 3, which is in the separate booklet. If you are uncertain about your understanding, you should review Part 3.

The post test will serve both to test your comprehension and to review the highlights of Part 3. After taking the post test, you may find that you are unsure about certain points. You should review these points before continuing with Part 4.

8-74. The Internal Revenue Service publishes regulations explaining how to calculate income that is subject to the income tax, that is, how to calculate the t _ _ _ _ _ _ income. We shall refer to these regulations as **tax accounting principles** to distinguish them from the **financial accounting principles** that govern the preparation of financial statements. Most tax accounting rules are consistent with financial accounting principles, but some are not. As a result, taxable income and financial accounting income . . . [may differ / are identical].

taxable

may differ

8-75. When a choice is possible, a business usually chooses the tax accounting method that results in the . . . [higher / lower] taxable income.

lower

8-76. In its accounting income statement, a business attempts to report its income as *fairly* as possible. In determining the taxes it owes, a business tries to show a taxable income that is as *low* as legally possible. These two objectives . . . [are / are not] the same.

are not

(Note: The remaining frames in this part get complicated. Try them, but if you have difficulty, be satisfied with the general idea, and learn the details in a more advanced course.)

ACCELERATED DEPRECIATION AND TAX DEPRECIATION

8-77. If you want an automobile to go faster, you press down on the accelerator. Income tax regulations permit the use of **accelerated depreciation,** which writes off the cost of an asset . . . [faster / slower] than straight-line depreciation.

faster

8-78. Before describing accelerated depreciation, we shall introduce the **half-year convention,** which is used in both tax accounting and financial accounting. Accountants often assume, in the interest of simplicity, that all depreciable assets purchased in a year were purchased in the middle of the year. As a result, in the year of purchase, depreciation expense will be ____________ (what fraction?) of a full year's depreciation.

1/2

Part 4

Accounting Records and Systems

Learning Objectives

In this part you will learn:

- The nature of the **account** and how entries are made to accounts.
- The meaning of debit and credit.
- Use of the ledger and the journal.
- The closing process.

THE ACCOUNT

4-1. In Part 3 you recorded the effect of each transaction by changing the appropriate items on a balance sheet. Erasing the old amounts and writing in the new amounts . . . [would / would not] be a practical method for handling the large number of transactions that occur in most entities.

would not

4-2. Instead of changing balance sheet amounts directly, we use in practice a device called an **account** to record each change. In its simplest form, an account looks like a large letter T, and it is therefore called a ____ -account.

T

8-69. Company *A* reports $1,000,000 of trademarks on its balance sheet, but Company *B* reports no such item. Which statement is more likely to be correct?

(A) Company *A* has more trademarks than Company *B*, *or*

(B) Company *A* has purchased trademarks, but Company *B* has not.

(B)

8-70. Three terms that refer to the writing off of an asset's cost are:

(A) ____________tion, which refers to ____________ (what type of?) assets,

(B) ____________tion, which refers to ____________ (what type of?) assets,

(C) ____________tion, which refers to ____________ (what type of?) assets.

(A) depreciation plant

(B) depletion wasting

(C) amortization intangible
(any order)

8-71. Although we have used the word **amortization** just for intangible assets, amortization is sometimes used as a general term for expensing the cost of all assets; that is, some people call **depreciation** and **depletion** special cases of amortization.

(No answer required.)

INCOME TAX REGULATIONS

8-72. Both corporations and individuals are subject to a tax on their income. The income tax is calculated as a percentage of taxable income. If a corporation has taxable income of $1 million, and if the income tax rate is 35%, the corporation would pay an income tax of $ ____________ .

$350,000 (=$1,000,000 x 0.35)

8-73. Any business quite properly tries to minimize its taxes. Therefore, it tries to . . . [maximize / minimize] the amount of taxable income that it reports to the Internal Revenue Service.

minimize

4-3. The title of the account is written on top of the T. Draw a T-account and title it "Cash."

(Note: As a matter of accounting custom, the name of an account is treated as a proper name, that is, the first letter is capitalized.)

Cash	

4-4. Following is how a T-account looks at the beginning of an accounting period.

Cash	
Beg. bal.. 10,000	

Evidently the amount of cash at the beginning of the accounting period was $____________.

$10,000

(Note that although the amounts are in dollars, the dollar sign is not used.)

4-5. Transactions that affect the Cash account during the accounting period can either **increase** cash or **decrease** cash. Thus, one side of the T-account is for _ _ _ _ _ _ _ _ s, and the other side is for _ _ _ _ _ _ _ _ s.

increases; decreases *(either order)*

4-6. Increases in cash add to the beginning balance. Because the beginning balance is recorded on the left side of the T-account, increases in cash are recorded on the . . . [left / right] side of the T-account. Decreases are recorded on the . . . [left / right] side.

left

right

8-63. The . . . [depletion / depreciation] of a wasting asset is similar to the . . . [depletion / depreciation] of a plant asset. However, in accounting for **depletion,** the asset account is reduced directly. Therefore an accumulated depletion account . . . [is / is not] ordinarily used.

depletion
depreciation

is not

8-64. Depletion is usually calculated by multiplying the quantity of the resource used in a period by a unit cost. If in 19x1 Cecil Company purchased a coal mine for $3,000,000 and estimated that the mine contained 1,000,000 tons of coal, it would use a unit cost of $________ per ton.

$3 (= $3,000,000 ÷ 1,000,000 tons)

8-65. In 19x2, Cecil Company mined 100,000 tons of coal. The cost of this coal was estimated to be $3 per ton. The depletion expense in 19x2 was $______________ .

$300,000 (= $3 x 100,000)

8-66. On December 31, 19x1, Cecil Company owned a coal mine, which was listed on its balance sheet at $3,000,000. In 19x2, $300,000 of depletion expense was recognized.

How will the coal asset appear on the balance sheet for December 31, 19x2?

Coal .... $ [ ]

$2,700,000

INTANGIBLE ASSETS

8-67. In accordance with the cost concept, intangibles such as goodwill, trademarks, and patents are not treated as assets unless . . . [their market value can be determined / they have been acquired at a measurable cost].

they have been acquired at a measurable cost.

8-68. When intangibles such as goodwill are recognized as assets, their cost is written off over their service life, but not longer than 40 years. The process is called **amortization**. Amortization therefore means ....
....

writing off the cost of intangible assets.

4-7. Here is the T-account for Cash.

Cash	
(increases)	(decreases)
Beg. bal.. 10,000	

Record the effect of the following transactions on Cash:

(a) The entity received $300 cash from a customer.

(b) The entity borrowed $5,000 from a bank.

(c) The entity paid $2,000 cash to a supplier.

(d) The entity sold merchandise for $800 cash.

Cash	
(increases)	(decreases)
Beg. bal. 10,000	2,000
300	
5,000	
800	

4-8. At the end of an accounting period, the increases are added to the beginning balance, and the total of the decreases is subtracted from it. The result is the **new balance**. Calculate the new balance for the Cash account shown below.

Cash	
(Increases)	(Decreases)
Beg. bal.10,000	2,000
300	
5,000	
800	
Total	Total

New balance

Cash	
(Increases)	(Decreases)
Beg. bal. 10,000	2,000
300	
5,000	
800	
Total 16,100	2,000 Total

New balance 14,100

4-9. The amount of Cash shown on the balance sheet at the end of the accounting period would be $_________. The amount shown as the beginning balance of Cash in the next accounting period would be $_________ .

$14,100

$14,100

8-57. Actually, an asset may be as valuable at the end of a year as at the beginning. Depreciation expense for a given year . . . [represents / does not necessarily represent] a decrease in the asset's real value or usefulness during the year.

does not necessarily represent

8-58. Also, don't forget that in accounting for plant asset, original cost is . . . [known / an estimate], service life is . . . [known / an estimate], and residual value is . . . [known / an estimate].

known; an estimate
an estimate

8-59. The book value of a plant asset represents . . . [what the asset can be sold for / that portion of the cost not yet expensed].

that portion of the cost not yet expensed

8-60. Therefore the statement "book value reports what the asset is worth" is . . . [correct / incorrect].

incorrect
(This is a very common error.)

DEPLETION

8-61. Natural resources such as coal, oil, other minerals, and timber are called **wasting assets**. Which of the following are wasting assets?

building
natural gas
freight car
iron ore
cash

natural gas

iron ore

8-62. When the supply of oil in a well or coal in a mine is reduced, the asset is said to be **depleted**. This word, when used as the noun dep _ _ _ ion, is the name for the process of writing off the cost of such w _ _ _ _ _ _ assets.

depletion
wasting

RULES FOR INCREASES AND DECREASES

4-10. In the T-account for Cash, increases were recorded on the . . . [left / right] side. This is the rule for all asset accounts; that is, increases in ________ accounts are recorded on the ________ side.

left

asset; left

4-11. Suppose Ellen Jones pays $300 cash to Brown Company to settle her account receivable. In the T-account below, the increase in Brown Company's cash that results is recorded on the . . . [left / right] side. Enter the amount.

left

Cash

(increases)	(decreases)
Beg. bal. 10,000	

Cash

(Increases)	(Decreases)
Beg. bal.. 10,000	
300	

4-12. Jones, a customer of Brown Company paid $300 cash to settle her account receivable. The Cash account increased by $300. Jones no longer owed $300, so the A _ _ _ _ _ _ _ R _ _ _ _ _ _ _ _ _ account decreased by $300. In the T-account below, enter the name of this second account that must be changed to complete the record of the transaction.

Accounts Receivable

Cash

(Increases)	(Decreases)
Beg. bal. 10,000	
300	

(Increases)	(Decreases)
Beg. bal. 2,000	

Accounts Receivable

4-13. Accounts Receivable is an asset account. The dual-aspect concept requires that if the asset account, Cash, increases by $300, the change in the other asset account, Accounts Receivable, must be a(n). . . [increase / decrease] of $300.

decrease

8-52. After the cost of an asset has been completely written off as depreciation expense, no more depreciation is recorded, even though the asset continues to be used. In the example given above, the book value at the end of 19x5 is zero. If the asset continued to be used in 19x6, depreciation expense in 19x6 would be $ ________________ .

zero

8-53. To calculate the book value of an asset you must subtract the ________________ ________________ from the original ________________ .

accumulated depreciation

cost

SALE OF A PLANT ASSET

8-54. The calculation of book value depends on estimates of service life and residual value. Because the actual residual value may differ from these estimates, the amount realized from the sale of a plant asset will probably be . . . [equal to / different from] its book value.

different from

8-55. The difference between book value and the amount actually realized from a sale of a plant asset is call a **gain** (or **loss**) **on the disposition of plant.** For example, if an asset whose book value is $10,000 is sold for $12,000, $________________ would be the . . . [gain / loss] on the disposition of plant and would be so reported on the income statement.

$2,000 (=$12,000 – $10,000); gain

SIGNIFICANCE OF DEPRECIATION

8-56. The purpose of depreciation is to . . . [show the decline in an asset's value / write off a fair share of the cost of the asset in each year in which it provides service].

write off a fair share of the cost of the asset in each year in which it provides service

4-14. Record the change in Accounts Receivable resulting from the $300 payment in the account below.

Accounts Receivable

(Increases)	(Decreases)
Beg. bal. 2,000	

Accounts Receivable

(Increases)	(Decreases)
Beg. bal. 2,000	300

4-15. The decrease in accounts receivable was recorded on the . . . [left / right] side of the account. This balanced the . . . [left / right] -side amount for the increase in cash.

right left

4-16. Another customer of Brown Company settled an $800 Account Receivable by paying $600 Cash and giving a note for $200. Record this transaction in the Brown Company's accounts, given below.

Cash

(Increases)	(Decreases)
Beg. bal. 10,000	
300	

Accounts Receivable

(Increases)	(Decreases)
Beg. bal. 3,000	300

Notes Receivable

(Increases)	(Decreases)
Beg. bal. 1,000	

Cash

(Increases)	(Decreases)
Beg. bal. 10,000	
300	
600	

Accounts Receivable

(Increases)	(Decreases)
Beg. bal. 3,000	300
	800

Notes Receivable

(Increases)	(Decreases)
Beg. bal. 1,000	
200	

4-17. As you can see, accounting requires that each transaction give rise to . . . [equal / unequal] totals of left-side and right-side amounts.

equal

4-18. An **increase** in any asset account is recorded on the left side. Therefore, since the totals of left-side and right-side amounts must equal each other, a **decrease** in any asset must always be recorded on the . . . [left / right] side.

right

8-50. The table below shows the original cost, annual depreciation expense, accumulated depreciation (at year end), and book value (at year end) for a plant asset with an original cost of $5,000, a service life of five years, and zero residual value.

Year	Original Cost	Depreciation Expense	Accumulated Depreciation	Book Value
19x1	$5,000	$1,000	$1,000	$4,000
19x2	5,000	1,000	2,000	3,000
19x3	5,000	1,000	3,000	2,000
19x4	5,000	1,000	4,000	1,000
19x5	5,000			

1,000 5,000 zero

Complete the table. What is the total amount charged as depreciation expense during the service life of the asset? $________ .

$5,000

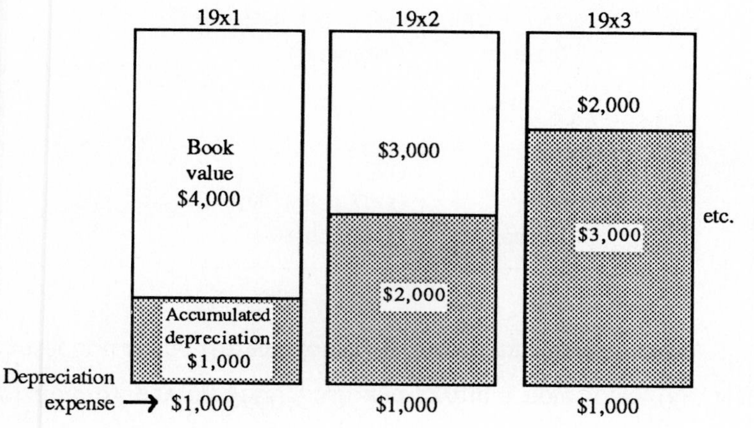

8-51. Refer to the table above and indicate how the asset would be shown on the company's balance sheet at the end of 19x3.

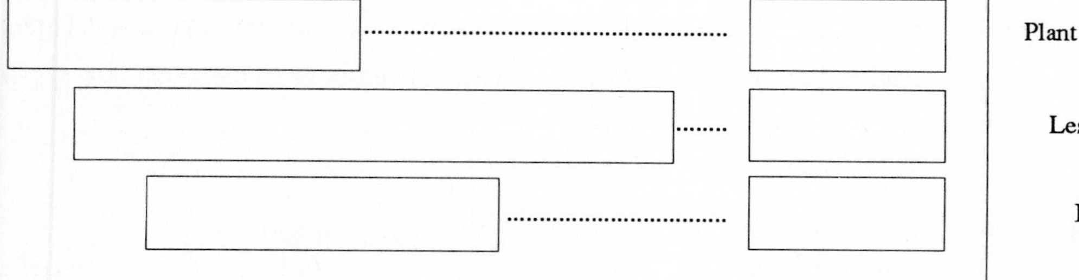

Plant .... $ 5,000

Less accumulated depreciation 3,000

Book value .... $ 2,000

4-19. Black Company borrowed $700 from Federal Bank, signing a note.

Black Company's Cash account. . . [increased / decreased] by $700, and its Notes Payable account, which is a liability account, . . . [increased / decreased] by the same amount.

increased
increased

4-20. Black Company borrowed $700 from Federal Bank, signing a note.

The increase in Black Company's cash is recorded on the . . . [left / right] side of its Cash account. Record the $700 increase in the Cash account below.

left

Cash	
(Increases)	(Decreases)

Notes Payable	

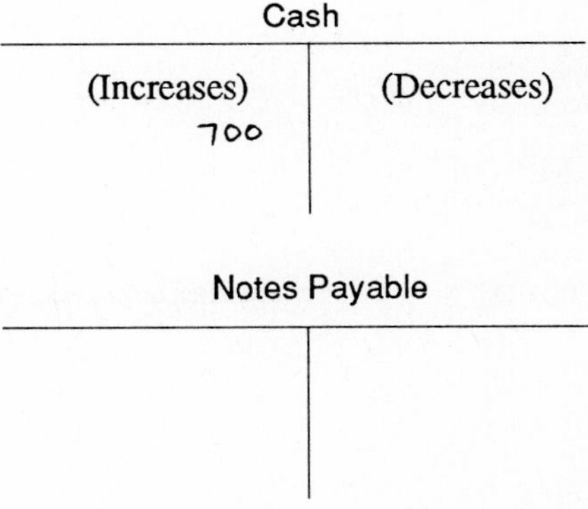

4-21. Black Company borrowed $700 from Federal Bank, signing a note.

In order to show equal totals of right and left side amounts, the corresponding change in the Notes Payable account should be recorded on the . . . [left / right]-hand side. Complete the record of this transaction in the accounts below.

right

Cash	
(Increases)	(Decreases)
700	

Notes Payable	

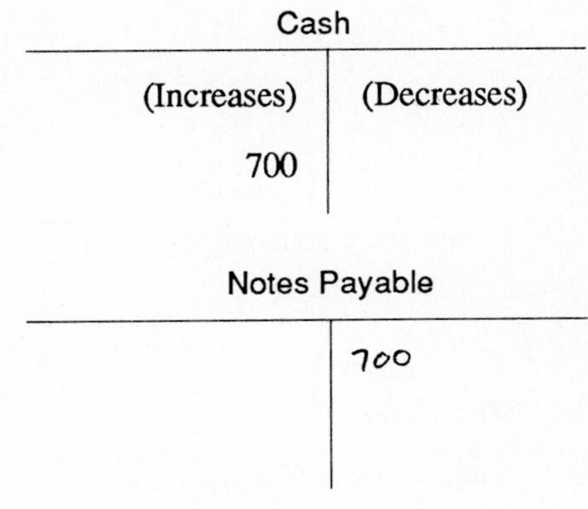

8-47. Suppose that the ledger showed the following account balances on January 1, 19x5, and that annual depreciation expense was $1,000. Enter the amounts for depreciation in 19x5.

Plant	
Balance 10,000	

Depreciation Expense	

Accumulated Depreciation	
	4,000 Balance

Plant	
Balance 10,000	

Accumulated Depreciation	
	4,000 Balance
	1,000

Depreciation Expense	
1,000	

8-48. The balance sheet for December 31, 19x5, would include the following items.

Plant .... $______

Less______ ______ ...... ______

Book value .... $______

Plant $10,000

Less accumulated depreciation 5,000

Book value .... $ 5,000

The income statement for 19x5 would include an item:

Depreciation expense .... $ ______

Depreciation expense $1,000

8-49. Each year, the write-off of $1,000 of the cost of the asset would be recorded with the following journal entry.

Dr. ______ ______ .... ______

Cr. ______ ______ ...... ______

Dr. Depreciation expense 1,000

Cr. Accumulated depreciation 1,000

4-22. Since left-side and right-side amounts must have equal totals, and since increases in assets are always recorded on the left side, increases in liability accounts, such as Notes Payable, are always recorded on the . . . [left / right] side.

right

4-23. Similarly, since **decreases** in assets are always recorded on the *right* side, **decreases** in liabilities are always recorded on the . . . [left side / right side].

left side

Show which side of the Notes Payable account is used to record increases and which side is used to record decreases by filling in the boxes below.

Cash

(Increases)	(Decreases)
700	

Notes Payable

[ ]	[ ]
	700

Cash

(Increases)	(Decreases)
700	

Notes Payable

(Decreases)	(Increases)
	700

4-24. The rules for Equity accounts are the same as those for Liability accounts, that is:

Equity accounts increase on the . . .[left / right] side.

Equity accounts decrease on the . . .[left / right] side.

right

left

4-25. One way to remember the above rules is to think of the two sides of the balance sheet.

Asset accounts are on the *left* side of the balance sheet, and they increase on the . . .[left / right] side.

left

Liability and equity accounts are on the *right* side of the balance sheet, and they increase on the [left / right] side.

right

8-43. Suppose $1,000 of depreciation expense is recognized for a given year. What would be the appropriate journal entry?

Dr. ______________ ______________ .... ________

Cr. ______________ ______________ ...... ________

Dr. Depreciation expense 1,000

Cr. Accumulated depreciation 1,000

8-44. Here is a journal entry:

Dr. Depreciation expense	1,000	
Cr. Accumulated depreciation		1,000

On a separate piece of paper, set up and title the appropriate T-accounts and post the entries to these accounts.

Depreciation Expense	
1,000	

Accumulated Depreciation	
	1,000

8-45. On the balance sheet, the balance in the Accumulated Depreciation account is shown as a deduction from the original cost of the asset, and the remaining amount is called **Book Value.** For example, the listing:

Plant	$10,000
Less accumulated depreciation	4,000
Book value	$6,000

shows that the plant originally cost $______________, that $______________ of its original cost has so far been recognized as depreciation expense, and that $______________ of book value remains to be depreciated in future years.

$10,000

$ 4,000

$ 6,000

8-46. If the depreciation expense on this machine was $1,000 per year, we know from the above that depreciation expense has been taken for ________ (how many?) years, and that it will be taken for ________ (how many?) more years in the future, assuming zero residual value.

four; six

DEBIT AND CREDIT

4-26. In the language of accounting, the left side of an account is called the **debit** side, and the right side is called the **credit** side. Thus, instead of saying that increases in cash are recorded on the left side of the Cash account and decreases are recorded on the right side, accountants say that increases are recorded on the ____________ side and decreases are recorded on the ____________ side.

debit
credit

4-27. Debit and **Credit** are also verbs. To record an increase in cash, you ________ the Cash account. To record a decrease in cash, you ________ the Cash account. Instead of saying, "Record an amount on the left side of the Cash account," the accountant simply says, "________ Cash."

debit; credit

Debit

4-28. Increases in all asset accounts, such as Cash, are recorded on the. . . [debit / credit] side. To increase an asset account, you. . . [debit / credit] the account.

debit; debit

4-29. The rules we just developed in terms of "left side" and "right side" can now be stated in terms of debit and credit.

Increases in assets are	[debits / credits]	debits
Decreases in assets are	[debits / credits]	credits
Increases in liabilities are	[debits / credits]	credits
Decreases in liabilities are	[debits / credits]	debits
Increases in equities are	[debits / credits]	credits
Decreases in equities are	[debits / credits]	debits

4-30. In everyday language the word **credit** sometimes means "good" and **debit** sometimes means "bad." In the language of accounting, debit means only. . . [left / right], and credit means only. . . [left / right].

left; right

8-37. For example, if an entity had a fuel oil asset of $2,000 at the beginning of March and used $500 of fuel oil during March, the entity would recognize $________ of fuel oil expense for March, and it would balance this by a decrease of $________ in the fuel oil asset. On the balance sheet of March 31, the fuel oil asset would be reported at $________.

$500

$500

$1,500 (= $2,000 – $500)

8-38. Similarly, if a company purchased a three-year insurance policy in advance for $9,000 on December 31, 19x1, the following journal entry would be made to record Insurance Expense in 19x2.

Dr. ________ ________ .... ________

Cr. ________ ________ .... ________

Dr. Insurance expense 3,000

Cr. Prepaid expense 3,000
(*or* Prepaid insurance)

8-39. In accounting for depreciation, the procedure is similar. First, we recognize the appropriate amount of expense for the period. In this case the title of the expense account is D________ Expense.

Depreciation

8-40. Next, we must recognize an equal . . . [decrease / increase] in the amount of the asset.

decrease

8-41. However accountants prefer to show the original cost of plant assets on the balance sheet at all times. Therefore, decreases in the amount of a plant asset . . . [are / are not] shown by a direct reduction in the asset amount.

are not

8-42. Instead, decreases in the asset amount of a plant asset because of depreciation expense are accumulated in a separate account called **Accumulated Depreciation.**

A decrease in an asset is alway a . . . [Dr. / Cr.]. Accumulated Depreciation is a decrease in an asset, and therefore has a . . . [Dr. / Cr.] balance.

Cr.

Cr.

4-31. The word **debit** is abbreviated as "Dr.," and the word **credit** is abbreviated as "Cr." Label the two sides of the Cash account below with these abbreviations.

Cash

[ ]	[ ]
Beg. bal. 1,000	

Cash

(Dr.)	(Cr.)
Beg. bal. 1,000	

(In practice, these labels are not shown in the accounts, but we shall use them in the next few frames, to help you fix them in your mind.)

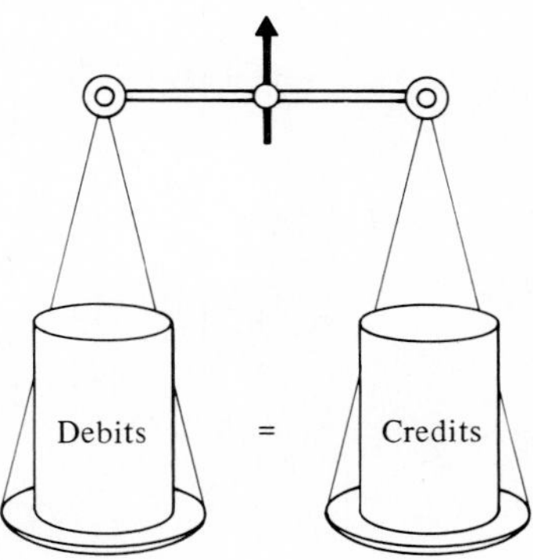

4-32. Exhibit 3 (in your booklet) shows the accounts for Green Company, arranged as they would appear on a balance sheet. The sum of the debit balances is $______________ , and the sum of the credit balances is $______________ .

$18,000

$18,000

4-33. These totals are equal in accordance with the d_ _ _-a_ _ _ _ _ concept.

dual-aspect

4-34. Record the following transactions in the accounts of Exhibit 3. Record increases in assets on the debit side and make sure that in each transaction the debit and credit amounts are equal.

- Inventory costing $600 was purchased for cash.
- Inventory costing $400 was purchased on credit.
- Green Company paid $300 to a creditor.
- Green Company received $500 in cash from a credit customer.

ACCOUNTS FOR GREEN COMPANY

Assets

Cash

(Dr.)	(Cr.)
Beg. bal. 1,000	600
500	300

Accounts Receivable

(Dr.)	(Cr.)
Beg. bal. 3,000	500

Inventory

(Dr.)	(Cr.)
Beg. bal. 4,000	
600	
400	

Other Assets

(Dr.)	(Cr.)
Beg. bal. 10,000	

Liabilities and Equities

Accounts Payable

(Dr.)	(Cr.)
300	2,000 Beg. bal.
	400

Paid-in Capital

(Dr.)	(Cr.)
	7,000 Beg. bal.

Retained Earnings

(Dr.)	(Cr.)
	9,000 Beg. bal.

8-33. Complete the following table.

If the estimated life of an asset is:	The straight-line depreciation rate is:	
2 years	____ %	50%
3 years	____ %	33 1/3%
4 years	____ %	25%
5 years	20%	

8-34. In the straight-line method, the amount of **depreciation expense** for a given year is determined by multiplying the depreciable cost by the depreciation rate. Thus, if the depreciable cost is $9,000 and the depreciation rate is 20%, the amount of depreciation expense each year will be $________.

$1,800 (= $9,000 x 0.20)

8-35. Here is a list of factors that are relevant to the depreciation of an asset:

(1) original cost
(2) residual value
(3) service life

Depreciable cost
??? Service life
Cost (known)
Residual value ???

Which factor(s) enter(s) into a determination of the depreciation rate? . ... (3)

the depreciable cost? .... (1) and (2)

the amount of depreciation expense in a given year? .... (1), (2), and (3)

Which factors are estimates? .... (2) and (3)

ACCOUNTING FOR DEPRECIATION

8-36. In Part 6 we described how certain types of assets were converted into expenses with the passage of time. When this occurs, there is a . . . [Dr. / Cr.] entry to the asset account, which shows the . . . [decrease/increase] in the amount of the asset, and there is an equal . . . [Dr. / Cr.] to the expense account.

Cr.
decrease
Dr.

4-35. Now calculate the new balances for each account and enter them in the accounts of Exhibit 3.

The new balances are:

Cash	600 Dr.
Accounts Receivable	2,500 Dr.
Inventory	5,000 Dr.
Other Assets	10,000 Dr.
Accounts Payable	2,100 Cr.
Paid-in Capital.	7,000 Cr.
Retained Earnings	9,000 Cr.

4-36. The total of the new balances of the asset accounts is $________. The total of the new balances of the liability and equity accounts is $________. Also, the total of the debit balances equals the total of the ________ balances.

$18,100

$18,100

credit

4-37. Because the total of the debit entries for any transaction will always equal the total of the credit entries, it is . . . [difficult / easy] to check the accuracy with which bookkeeping is done. (We owe this ingenious arrangement to Venetian merchants, who invented it more than 500 years ago.)

easy

INCOME STATEMENT ACCOUNTS

4-38. The accounts in Exhibit 3 were for items that appear on the balance sheet. Accounts are also kept for items that appear on the other financial statement, the i _ _ _ _ _ statement. As we saw in Part 3, this statement reports the revenues and the expenses of an accounting period and the difference between them, which is i _ _ _ _ _.

income

income

4-39. Revenues are. . . [increases / decreases] in equity during a period, and expenses are. . . [increases / decreases] in equity.

increases

decreases

4-40. For equity accounts, increases are recorded as . . . [debits / credits]. Since revenues are increases in equity, revenues are recorded as . . . [debits / credits].

credits

credits

8-29. When the residual value is subtracted from the cost of a fixed asset, the result is called the **depreciable cost**. Thus, if an automobile purchased for $10,000 is expected to have a six-year life, and to have a residual value of $1,000 at the end of that life, $10,000 is the ________ and $9,000 is the ________ ________.

cost (*or* gross cost)
depreciable cost

STRAIGHT-LINE DEPRECIATION

8-30. The depreciation of a plant asset with a cost of $10,000, no residual value, and a five-year life, may be graphed as follows:

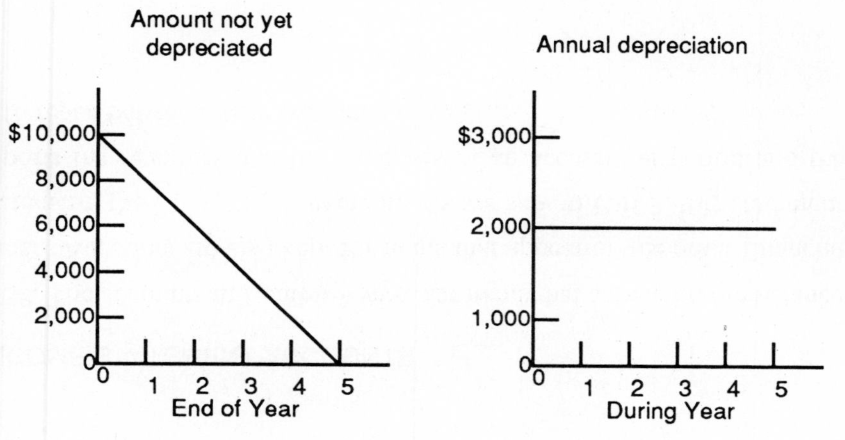

The line showing depreciation expense as a function of time is . . . [straight / curved].

straight

8-31. Because of this, charging off an equal fraction of the asset cost each year is called the s _ _ _ _ _ _ _ -line method of depreciation. Most companies use this method.

straight

8-32. The percentage of cost charged off each year is called the depreciation rate. In the straight-line method, we obtain the rate by finding:

$$\frac{1}{\text{number of years of service life}}$$

For example, if an asset is to be depreciated over five years, the d ________ r ________ is ________ %.

depreciation rate; 20% (1/5)

4-41. Similarly, decreases in equity are recorded as . . . [debits / credits]. Since expenses are decreases in equity, expenses are recorded as. . . [debits / credits].

debits
debits

4-42. The complete set of rules for making entries to accounts is as follows:

Increases in assets are .... [debits / credits].
Decreases in assets are ....[debits / credits].
Increases in liabilities and equities are ....[debits / credits].
Decreases in liabilities and equities are ....[debits / credits].
Increases in revenues are ....[debits / credits].
Increases in expenses are ....[debits / credits].

debits
credits
credits
debits
credits
debits

(Note: Make sure you learn these rules. They govern all accounting transactions.)

THE LEDGER AND THE JOURNAL

4-43. A group of accounts, such as those for Green Company in Exhibit 3, is called a **ledger.** There is no standard form, so long as there is space to record the d _ _ _ _ s and c _ _ _ _ _ s to each account. Exhibit 5 is the ____________ of Glendale Market, the same company we examined in Part 3.

debits; credits
ledger

4-44. In practice, transactions are not recorded directly in the ledger. First, they are written in a record such as Exhibit 4. The title of Exhibit 4 shows that this record is called a ____________________ . The record made for each transaction is called a ____________________ entry.

journal
journal

4-45. In the journal, entries are recorded as they happen; that is, the transactions for January 3 are recorded . . . [before / after] the transactions for January 2.

after

8-24. To summarize:

(1) Depreciation is the process of converting the cost of an asset into expense over its service life.

(2) This process recognizes that an asset gradually loses its usefulness.

(3) An asset can lose its usefulness for either of two reasons:

(a) ....

(b) ....

(4) The asset's service life is the . . . [longer / shorter] of these two causes.

it wears out

it becomes obsolete

shorter

8-25. In the summary above, no mention was made of market value. Depreciation . . . [is / is not] related to changes in the market value of an asset. This is consistent with the ______________ concept.

is not

cost

8-26. In some cases, an entity expects to be able to sell the plant asset at the end of its service life. The amount that it expects to sell it for is called its **residual value.** For example, if an entity buys a truck for $20,000 and expects to sell it for $4,000 five years later, the estimated residual value is $________________.

$4,000

8-27. In most cases, an entity expects that a plant asset will be worthless at the end of its service life. If so, the asset has zero r ______________ v______________ .

residual

value

Total cost $22,000

Depreciable cost $20,000

Residual value $2,000

8-28. Suppose a restaurant oven that cost $22,000 is expected to have a residual value of $2,000 at the end of its 10-year life. In this case, the total amount of depreciation that should be recorded during the service life of the asset is only $________________. The depreciation expense for each of the ten years would be $________________.

$20,000

$2,000 (= 1/10 x $20,000)

4-46. As Exhibit 4 shows, the account to be . . . [debited / credited] is listed first, and the . . . [Dr. / Cr.] amount is entered in the first of the two money columns. The account to be . . . [debited / credited] is listed below, and is indented. The . . . [Dr. / Cr.] amount is entered in the second money column.

debited

Dr.

credited

Cr.

4-47. On January 8 merchandise costing $600 was sold for $900, and the customer agreed to pay $900 within 30 days. Using the two journal entries for January 7 as a guide, record the two parts of this transaction in the journal. (If you are not sure about how to record this transaction, go to Frame 4-48.)

8	Accounts Receivable	900	
	Revenues		900
8	Expenses	600	
	Inventory		600

(If you did this correctly, skip to Frame 4-50.)

4-48. On January 8 merchandise costing $600 was sold for $900, and the customer agreed to pay $900 within 30 days.

The first part of this transaction is that the business earned **revenues** of $900, and an asset, Accounts Receivable, increased by $900. Record this part of the transaction by completing the blanks below.

Dr. [ ] 900

Cr. [ ] 900

Dr. Account Receivable 900

Cr. Revenues 900

(Hint: if in doubt as to whether a particular account is to be debited or credited, you usually can find out by referring to the other account in the entry. For example, the entry to Accounts Receivable is an increase in an asset, which is a debit, so the entry to Revenues must be a credit.)

4-49. On January 8, merchandise costing $600 was sold for $900, and the customer agreed to pay $900 within 30 days.

The other part of this transaction is that the business had an **expense** of $600 because its **inventory** was decreased by $600. Record this part of the transaction by completing the blanks below.

Dr. [ ] 600

Cr. [ ] 600

Dr. Expenses 600

Cr. Inventory 600

8-18. Since some portion of a plant asset is used up during each year of its service life, a portion of the cost of the asset is treated as a(n) . . . [revenue / expense] in each year.

expense

8-19. For example, suppose a computer is purchased at a cost of $50,000 and has an estimated service life of five years. It would be reasonable to charge __________ (what fraction?) or $ __________ as expense in each of the five years.

1/5; $10,000 (= 1/5 x $50,000)

8-20. The process of recognizing a portion of the cost of a plant asset as an expense during each year of its estimated service life is called **depreciation**. The $10,000 recorded as an expense during each one of the five years of service life of the computer that cost $50,000 is called the __________________ expense for that year.

depreciation

8-21. A plant asset can become useless for either of two reasons: (1) it may *wear out* physically; or (2) it may become obsolete. The latter reason is called **obsolescence**. Loss of usefulness because of the development of improved equipment, changes in style, or other causes not related to the physical condition of the asset are examples of __________________.

obsolescence

8-22. The ***service life*** of an asset considers both physical wear and obsolescence. The service life is the shorter of the two periods. Thus an asset with an estimated physical life of ten years that is estimated to become obsolete in five years has an estimated service life of . . . [five / ten] years.

five

8-23. Since depreciation considers obsolescence, it is . . . [correct / not correct] to regard depreciation and obsolescence as two different things.

not correct

4-50. Journal entries are transferred to the l _ _ _ _ _ (as in Exhibit 5). This process is called **posting**.

ledger

4-51. The entries through January 7 have already been posted to the ledger, as indicated by the check mark opposite each one. Post the journal entries for January 8 to the proper ledger accounts in Exhibit 5, and make check marks to show that you have posted them.

Accounts Receivable

Debit	Credit
900	

Revenues

Debit	Credit
	300
	800
	900

Inventory

Debit	Credit
2,000	200
2,000	500
	600

Expenses

Debit	Credit
200	
500	
600	

4-52. To summarize, any transaction requires at least (how many?)________ changes in the accounts. These changes are recorded first in the . . . [ledger / journal]. They are then posted to the . . . [ledger / journal].

two

journal

ledger

4-53. We have used a handwritten journal and ledger to illustrate the bookkeeping process. Most entities today do this work on computers. What goes on inside the computer is essentially the same as what has been described above.

(No answer required)

THE CLOSING PROCESS

4-54. The Revenues account in Exhibit 5 shows. . . [increases / decreases] in Retained Earnings during the period, and the Expenses account shows . . . [increases / decreases] in Retained Earnings. The difference between revenues and expenses is the i _ _ _ _ _ of the period.

increases

decreases

income

8-12. Even though the entity does not own the item, a capital lease is treated like other plant assets. A capital lease is an exception to the general rule that assets are property or property rights that are _ _ _ _ _ by the entity.

owned

DEPRECIATION

8-13. Except in rare cases, land retains its usefulness indefinitely. Land therefore continues to be reported on the balance sheet at its acquisition cost, in accordance with the ______________ concept.

cost

If Hanover Hospital purchased a plot of land in 1970 at a cost of $100,000, it would have been reported at $________________ on the December 31, 1970 balance sheet. If Hanover Hospital still owned the land in 1987, and its market value then was $200,000, it would be reported on the December 31, 1987, balance sheet at . . . [$100,000 / $200,000].

$100,000

$100,000

8-14. Unlike land, plant assets eventually become useless. They have a(n) . . . [limited / unlimited] life.

limited

8-15. Plant assets will become completely useless at some future time. At that time, the item is no longer an asset. Usually this process occurs gradually; that is, a portion of the asset is used up in each year of its life, until finally it is . . . [partially / completely] used up.

completely

8-16. The period of time over which a plant asset is estimated to be of **service** to the company is called its s _ _ _ _ _ _ life.

service

8-17. At the time a machine or other item of plant is acquired, we . . . [know / do not know] how long it actually will be of service. Therefore, we . . . [can know with certainty / must estimate] its service life.

do not know

must estimate

4-55. The income for the period is an increase in the equity account, R _ _ _ _ _ _ _E _ _ _ _ _ _ _ _. Income is added to this account by a series of journal entries called **closing entries.**

Retained Earnings

4-56. First, an account called **Income Summary** is established. The balances in Revenues and Expenses are transferred to this ________________ ____________________ (give its title) account.

Income Summary

4-57. In order to do this, we first must find the balance in the account that is to be closed. What is the balance in the Revenues account in Exhibit 5? $____________________.

$2,000 (=$300 + $800 + $900)

4-58. An entry is made that reduces the balance in the account to be closed to zero and records the same amount on the opposite side of Income Summary. Since the Revenues account has a . . . [Dr. / Cr.] balance, the entry that reduces revenues to zero must be on the opposite side; that is, it must be a. . . [Dr. / Cr.].

Cr.

Dr.

4-59. In Exhibit 4, write the journal entry that closes the $2,000 balance in the Revenues account to Income Summary. (Date it January 8, the end of the accounting period).

		Dr.	Cr.
8	Revenues	2,000	
	Income Summary		2,000

4-60. Using similar reasoning, write the journal entry that closes the $1,300 balance in the Expenses account to Income Summary.

		Dr.	Cr.
8	Income Summary	1,300	
	Expenses		1,300

8-7. Transportation and installation costs are usually included as part of equipment cost.

Plymouth Bank purchased a computer for $40,000. The entity also paid $200 in freight charges and $1,000 in installation charges. This equipment should be recorded in the accounts at its cost, $ ___________.

$41,200 (= $40,000 + $200 + $1,000)

8-8. If an entity constructs a machine or a building with its own personnel, all costs incurred in construction are included in the asset amount.

Thayer Company built a new building for its own use. It spent $200,000 in materials, $300,000 in salaries to persons engaged in the building's construction, and $100,000 in overhead costs related to the building. This building should be recorded in the accounts at its cost, $ ______________.

$600,000 (= $200,000 + $300,000 + $100,000)

CAPITAL LEASES

8-9. Most assets are *owned* by the entity. When an entity leases a building, a machine, or other tangible item, the item is owned by someone else (the **lessor**); the entity . . . [does / does not] own it. Therefore, most leased items . . . [are / are not] assets of the entity that leases them (the **lessee**).

does not

are not

8-10. However, if an entity leases an item for a long period of time, it has as much control over the use of that item as if it owned it. A lease for a long time—almost the whole life of the asset—is called a **capital lease**. Because the entity controls the item for almost its whole life, a c _ _ _ _ _ _ l _ _ _ _ is recorded as an asset.

capital lease

8-11. The amount recorded for a capital lease is the amount the entity would have paid if it had purchased the item rather than leased it. If an entity leased a machine for 10 years, agreeing to pay $1,000 per year, and if the purchase price of this machine was $7,000, this c _ _ _ _ _ _ l _ _ _ _ would be recorded as an asset at an amount of . . . [$7,000 / $10,000], as in this entry:

capital lease

$7,000

Capital lease	__________	
Lease obligation		__________

$7,000

$7,000

4-61. Next, post these two entries to the ledger in Exhibit 5.

The accounts affected are:

Revenues

2,000	300
	800
	900

Expenses

200	1,300
500	
600	

Income Summary

1,300	2,000

4-62. The balance in the Income Summary account is now $ ________. It represents the i _ _ _ _ _ for the period. Since income is an increase in retained earnings, the Income Summary account is closed to that account. In Exhibit 4, write the journal entry that closes Income Summary and increases Retained Earnings. Post the entry to the ledger, Exhibit 5.

$700

income

		Dr.	Cr.
8	Income Summary	700	
	Retained Earnings		700

4-63. To get ready for preparing the financial statements, the balance in each asset, liability, and equity account is calculated. (Revenue and expense accounts have zero balances because of the closing process.) For the Cash account in Exhibit 5, the calculation is as follows:

Cash

	Dr.	Cr.
	10,000	2,000
	5,000	
	300	
	800	
	16,100	2,000
Balance	14,100	

(Note: Each side is totaled. A single line is drawn above the total. A double line is drawn beneath the total. The difference between the two totals is entered beneath the double line.)

Calculate the balance for each account in Exhibit 5.

(Details not shown here. The amounts can be checked against the amounts in Frame 4-65.)

8-2. Tangible assets are assets than can be seen or touched. Intangible assets are assets that have no physical substance (other than pieces of paper) but give the entity valuable rights. Which of the following are tangible assets?

Current Assets	Noncurrent assets
1. Account receivable	5. Land
2. Notes receivable	6. Goodwill
3. Inventory	7. Buildings
4. Prepaid rent	8. Investment in another entity

(3), (5), and (7)

(Note: Although a note receivable is evidenced by a paper that can be seen, the asset is the sum of money that is promised. This is an intangible asset.)

8-3. On the balance sheet, tangible noncurrent assets are often labeled **fixed assets,** or **property, plant, and equipment**. Equipment is a . . . [current / noncurrent] . . . and [tangible / intangible] asset.

noncurrent; tangible

8-4. For brevity, we shall use the word **plant** for all tangible noncurrent assets except land. Thus buildings, equipment, and furniture are items of ________________ . These assets are expected to be useful for longer than ______ ___________ .

plant

one year

ACCOUNTING FOR ACQUISITIONS

8-5. When an item of property, plant, or equipment is acquired, it is recorded in the accounts at its ____________ (what value?) in accordance with the fundamental accounting concept known as the ___________ concept.

cost

cost

8-6. The cost of an asset includes all costs incurred to make the asset ready for its intended use.

Bird Corporation paid $50,000 for a plot of land. It also paid $1,500 as a brokers' fee, $600 for legal fees, and $5,000 to tear down the existing structures in order to make the land ready for its intended use. The land should be recorded in the accounts at an amount of $ ________________ .

$57,100 (=$50,000 + $1,500 + $600 + $5,000)

(Note: Some accountants charge the $5,000 as a cost of the new building.)

4-64. Journal entries change the balance in the account. The *calculation* of the balance does not change the balance. Therefore the calculation of a balance. . . [does / does not] require a journal entry.

does not

4-65. The balance sheet is prepared from the balances in the asset and equity accounts. Complete the balance sheet for Glendale Market as of January 8, in Exhibit 6.

GLENDALE MARKET

Balance Sheet as of January 8

Assets		Liabilities and Equity	
Cash	$14,100	Accounts payable	$ 2,000
Accounts receivable	900	Note payable	5,000
Inventory	2,700	Paid-in capital	10,000
		Retained earnings	700
Total Assets	$17,700	Total Equities	$17,700

4-66. The income statement is prepared from information in the Income Summary account. Complete the income statement in Exhibit 6.

GLENDALE MARKET
Income Statement
for the period January 2-8

Revenues	$ 2,000
Expenses	1,300
Income	$ 700

4-67. After the closing process, the revenues, expenses, and income summary accounts have. . . [debit / credit / zero] balances. These accounts are therefore **temporary** accounts. They are started over at the beginning of each period. By contrast, the asset accounts have. . . [debit / credit / zero] balances, and the liability and equity accounts have. . . [debit / credit / zero] balances, and these balances are carried forward to the next period. Income statement accounts are. . . [temporary / permanent] accounts, and balance sheet accounts are. . . [temporary / permanent] accounts.

zero

debit

credit

temporary

permanent

Part 8

Noncurrent Assets and Depreciation

Learning Objectives

In this part you will learn:

- How plant assets are recorded in the accounts.
- The meaning and significance of depreciation.
- Straight-line and accelerated methods of depreciation.
- How depreciation is recorded.
- The meaning of depletion and how it is recorded.
- How intangible assets are recorded.
- Differences between income-tax principles and accounting principles.

8-1. Earlier, you learned that current assets are cash or items likely to be converted to cash within one ______________ (what time period?).	year
Evidently **noncurrent assets** are expected to be of use to the entity for longer than _________ _______________.	one year

4-68. Most entities report individual items of revenues and expenses (such as salary expense, maintenance expense, insurance expense) on their income statement. In order to do this, they set up an account for each item. Thus, if the income statement reported 2 revenue items and 10 expense items, there would be at least ________ (how many?) revenue and expense accounts. We shall describe these accounts in later parts. The entries to them are made in exactly the same way as in the simple example given here.

12

4-69. Management needs more detailed information than is contained in the financial statements. For example, instead of one account, Accounts Receivable, it needs an account for each customer so that the amount owed by each customer is known. Therefore the ledger usually contains... [the same number of / many more] accounts than there are items on the financial statements.

many more

4-70. There is no point in memorizing the bookkeeping process described in this part. Its purpose is to show where the numbers in the financial statements come from. This helps you understand what the numbers mean.

(No answer required)

KEY POINTS TO REMEMBER

- If an entity has no record of the cost of the specific items that were sold during a period, it deduces cost of sales by (1) adding purchases to the beginning inventory, which gives the goods available for sale and (2) subtracting the cost of the ending inventory.
- In doing this, it must make an assumption as to which items were sold.
- The First-In First-Out (FIFO) method assumes that the oldest items are the first to be sold.
- The Last-In First-Out (LIFO) method assumes that the most recently purchased items are the first to be sold. In periods of inflation, it results in the highest cost of sales and hence the lowest taxable income.
- The average-cost method costs both cost of sales and the ending inventory at the average cost of the goods available for sale.
- If the market value of items in inventory decreases below their cost, the inventory is written down to cost.
- The cost of goods produced in a manufacturing company is the sum of their direct materials cost, direct labor cost, and production overhead cost.
- Period costs are those charged as expenses in the period in which the costs were incurred. Product costs become Cost of Sales in the period in which the products are sold, which may be later than the period in which the products were manufactured.
- Overhead is charged to products by means of an overhead rate, such as a rate per direct labor hour.
- The inventory turnover ratio shows how many times the inventory turned over during a year.

You have now completed Part 7 of this program. If you think you have understood the material in this part, you should now take Post Test 7 which is in the separate booklet. If you are uncertain about your understanding, you should review Part 7.

The post test will serve both to test your comprehension and to review the highlights of Part 7. After taking the post test, you may find that you are unsure about certain points. You should review these points before continuing with Part 8.

KEY POINTS TO REMEMBER

- Debit refers to the left side of an account and credit to the right side.
- Increases in asset and expense accounts are debits. Increases in liability, equity and revenue accounts are credits. Decreases are the opposite.
- For any transaction, debits must equal credits. For the whole set of accounts, debit balances must equal credit balances.
- Transactions are first recorded in a journal. Amounts are then posted to the accounts in a ledger.
- Revenue and expense accounts are temporary accounts. At the end of each accounting period, they are closed to Retained Earnings. The change in Retained Earnings during a period is income. Explanation of income is given on an income statement.
- Asset, liability, and equity accounts are permanent accounts. Their balances are carried forward to the next accounting period.

You have completed Part 4 of this program. If you think you understand the material in this part, you should now take Post Test 4, which is in the separate booklet. If you are uncertain about your understanding, you should review Part 4.

The post test will serve both to test your comprehension and to review the highlights of Part 4. After taking the post test, you may find that you are unsure about certain points. You should review these points before continuing with Part 5.

7-72. A useful ratio for analyzing inventory is the **inventory turnover ratio,** which shows how many *times* the inventory turned over during a year. It is found by dividing Cost of Sales for a period by I _ _ _ _ _ _ _ _ at the end of the period.

Inventory

7-73. Cost of Sales for 19x1 was $1,000,000. Inventory on December 31, 19x1, was $200,000. Calculate the inventory turnover ratio to determine how many times the inventory turned over.

$$\frac{\boxed{}}{\boxed{}} = \frac{\$\boxed{}}{\$\boxed{}} = \boxed{} \text{ times}$$

$$\frac{\text{Cost of Sales}}{\text{Inventory}} = \frac{\$1{,}000{,}000}{\$200{,}000} = 5 \text{ times}$$

7-74. Slow-moving inventory ties up capital and increases the danger that the goods will become obsolete. Thus, an inventory turnover of 5 times is generally . . . [better / worse] than an inventory turnover of 4 times. However, if inventory is too small, orders from customers may not be filled promptly, which can result in lost sales revenue.

better

7-75. Look back at the calculation of the inventory turnover ratio. The turnover ratio can be increased either by selling . . . [more / less] goods with the same level of inventory or by having . . . [more / less] inventory for the same amount of sales volume.

more

less

Part 5

Revenues and Monetary Assets

Learning Objectives

In this part you will learn:

- Three more of the nine basic accounting concepts:
    - Conservatism concept.
    - Materiality concept.
    - Realization concept.
- What accrual accounting is.
- How revenue items are measured.
- How monetary assets are measured.
- The days' receivable ratio.

5-1. In Part 4 we introduced the idea of income, which is the difference between r _ _ _ _ _ _ _ and e _ _ _ _ _ _ _ .

revenues; expenses

5-2. Income increases Retained Earnings. Retained Earnings is an item of . . . [liabilities / equities] on the balance sheet. Any increase in Retained Earnings is also an increase in . . . [liabilities / equities].

equities

equities

7-67. Lee Shoe Company incurred $40,000 of production overhead costs during January. If 5,000 hours of direct labor were used during January, then $ ________ of overhead cost might be charged for each hour of direct labor. This amount per hour is the o _ _ _ _ _ _ _ r _ _ _ .

$8 (= $40,000 ÷ 5,000)
overhead rate

7-68. If a certain pair of shoes requires 1/2 hour of direct labor, and if the overhead rate is $8 per direct labor hour, the amount of overhead cost charged to those shoes would be $ ________ .

$4 (= 0.5 x $8)

7-69. Suppose the direct materials used in a certain pair of shoes cost $10. One-half hour of direct labor at $12 per hour is also used. The overhead rate is $8 per direct labor hour. The cost of the shoes is recorded at $ ________ .

$20 [= $10 + (0.5 x $12) + (0.5 x $8)]

7-70. There are many other types of overhead rates: a rate per machine hour, a rate per labor dollar, and a rate per material dollar. Whatever the rate, its purpose is to assign a fair share of overhead cost to each product.

(No answer required.)

INVENTORY TURNOVER

7-71. In earlier parts we described ratios and percentages that are useful in analyzing financial statements. For example, the gross margin percentage is a ratio of which items on the Income Statement?

$$\frac{\boxed{}\ \$\ 600{,}000}{\boxed{}\ \$1{,}500{,}000} = 40\%\ \text{gross margin}$$

$$\frac{\text{Gross Margin}}{\text{Sales (or Sales Revenue)}}$$

5-3. Income results from the profitable operation of an entity. The amount of income is one of the most important items of information that accounting reports. In this part we shall describe how the revenue portion of income is measured.

(No answer required)

ACCOUNTING PERIOD

5-4. An income statement reports the amount of income . . . [at a moment in time / over a period of time]. The period of time covered by one income statement is called the **accounting period.**

over a period of time

5-5. For most entities, the official accounting period is one year. However, income statements, called **interim statements,** usually are prepared for shorter periods. In Part 4 you prepared an income statement for Glendale Market for the period January 2 through January 8. This was an . . . [annual / interim] statement, and the accounting period was one . . . [week / month / year.]

interim; week

5-6. For most entities, the accounting period is the **calendar year,** that is, the year that ends on the last day of the calendar, which is ______________ (what date?).

December 31

5-7. Some entities end their year when activities are at a relatively low level. For example, a school might end its year on June 30, when students have left for the summer. The accounting period for such entities is the . . . [calendar year / natural business year.]

natural business year

5-8. The income statement that describes changes in equity for the period January 1, 19x2, through December 31, 19x2, is an income statement for the a _ _ _ _ _ _ _ _ _ p _ _ _ _ _ 19x2.

accounting period

7-63. Since Lee Shoe Company recognized $60,000 as a period cost for January, this $60,000 will be charged as an expense . . . [in January / whenever the products manufactured in January are sold]. (The word "charged" means "debited.")

in January

7-64. Suppose the shoes manufactured in January are sold in February. The $40,000 of product overhead costs will be included in ________________ (what account?) at the end of January and will be part of Cost of Sales in ________________ (what month?).

Inventory

February

		January	February
January overhead $100,000	Product cost	Inventory cost $40,000	Expense $40,000
	Period cost	Expense $60,000	

7-65. . . . [Period / Product] costs affect income in the period in which the costs are incurred . . . [Period / Product] costs affect income in the period in which the products are sold, which is often a later period.

Period

Product

OVERHEAD RATES

7-66. Another problem regarding overhead is how to divide the total product overhead cost among the various products produced. For example, it is hard to say how much of the cost of heating a shoe factory should be charged to each pair of shoes made in the factory. Any of several methods may be used to charge overhead costs to various products. Usually these methods make use of an overhead rate.

(No answer required.)

5-9. Entities don't fire their employees and cease operations at the end of an accounting period. They continue from one accounting period to the next. The fact that accounting divides the stream of events into a _ _ _ _ _ _ _ _ _ periods makes the problem of measuring revenues and expenses in a single accounting period . . . [an easy / the most difficult] problem in accounting.

accounting

the most difficult

ACCRUAL ACCOUNTING

5-10. On January 3, Glendale Market borrowed $5,000 from the bank. As a result of this transaction, its cash . . . [increased / decreased / did not change], a liability . . . [increased / decreased / did not change], but its equity . . . [increased / decreased / did not change]. Increases in equities that result from operating activities are revenues. Therefore, the receipt of cash on January 3 . . . [was / was not] associated with revenues.

increased
increased
did not change

was not

5-11. On January 4, Glendale Market purchased $2,000 of inventory, paying cash. This was an increase in one asset and a decrease in another asset. Since equity was unchanged, the payment of cash on January 4 . . . [was / was not] associated with an expense.

was not

5-12. On January 8, Glendale Market sold merchandise for $900, and the customer agreed to pay $900 within 30 days. This transaction resulted in . . . [an increase / decrease / no change] in cash. Revenue was $___________. This revenue . . . [was / was not] associated with an increase in cash on January 8.

no change
$900; was not

5-13. Evidently revenues and expenses . . . [are / are not] necessarily accompanied, at the same time, by increases or decreases in cash. Moreover, increases or decreases in cash . . . [are / are not] necessarily associated with increases or decreases in revenues or expenses.

are not

are not

7-58. It is relatively easy to keep track of the first two elements of the product cost mentioned earlier: the ______________ ______________ and the ______________ ______________. However, the measurement of overhead costs is more difficult.

direct labor

direct materials
(either order)

7-59. Overhead costs that are classified as product costs are added to direct labor costs and direct material costs in order to find the amount at which the products are costed in the Inventory account. If, during 19x1, Jones Manufacturing Company spent $10,000 on production overhead, $100,000 on direct labor and $20,000 on direct materials, and if no products were sold, its Inventory item on the balance sheet will . . . [decrease / increase] by $______________. If these products (and no others) were sold in 19x2, Cost of Sales in 19x2 would be $______________.

Product costs

19x1		→	19x2
Material	$ 20,000		
Labor	100,000	→	Cost of sales
Overhead	10,000		$130,000
Total	$130,000		

	19x1	19x2
Inventory, Dec. 31	$130,000	
Cost of Sales	0	$130,000

increase

$130,000 (= $10,000 + $100,000 + $20,000)

$130,000

7-60. Product costs do not affect income until the product is sold. At that time, product costs become Cost of Sales. Thus, if $10,000 of overhead is counted as a product cost in 19x1, and if the goods with which these product costs were associated are sold in 19x2, the $10,000 of overhead costs will appear as a part of Cost of Sales in . . . [19x1 / 19x2].

19x2

7-61. By contrast, costs that are classified as **period** costs are treated as part of the operating expenses of the period in which they are incurred. For example, if Jones Manufacturing Company's 19x1 period costs were $50,000, and if the shoes produced in 19x1 were not sold until 19x2, the $50,000 of period costs would nevertheless be an expense in . . . [19x1 / 19x2].

19x1

7-62. Suppose that in January the total overhead costs in Lee Shoe Company were $100,000, and that 40% of this overhead was associated with the production activities of the business and 60% with the sales and general activities.

In this example, the amount of overhead that is a product cost is $______________, and the amount that is a period cost is $______________.

$40,000 (= 0.4 x $100,000)

$60,000 (= 0.6 x $100,000)

5-14. Increases or decreases in cash are changes in an . . . [equity / asset] account. Revenues or expenses are changes in an . . . [equity / asset] account.

asset
equity

5-15. Income is measured as the difference between . . . [cash increases and cash decreases / revenues and expenses].

revenues and expenses

5-16. Income measures the increase in e _ _ _ _ _ during an accounting period that was associated with the entity's operations.

equity

5-17. Many individuals and some small businesses keep track only of cash receipts and cash payments. This type of accounting is called c _ _ _ accounting. If you keep a record of your deposits, the checks you write, and the balance in your bank account, you are doing _ _ _ _ accounting. Cash accounting . . . [does / does not] measure changes in equity.

cash
cash
does not

5-18. Most entities, however, account for revenues and expenses, as well as for cash receipts and cash payments. This type of accounting is called **accrual accounting**. Evidently, accrual accounting is . . . [simpler / more complicated] than cash accounting, but accrual accounting . . . [does / does not] measure changes in equity. The most difficult problems in accounting are problems of . . . [cash / accrual] accounting.

more complicated
does
accrual

5-19. In order to measure the income of a period, we must measure r _ _ _ _ _ _ s and e _ _ _ _ _ _ s of that period, and this requires the use of _ _ _ _ _ _ _ accounting.

revenues; expenses
accrual

5-20. In this part, we describe the measurement of revenues. The measurement of expenses is described in later parts. First, we shall introduce three more accounting concepts: conservatism, materiality, and realization.

(No answer required)

7-54. Production overhead consists of all other production costs, that is, costs that are not d______________ m ______________ or d______________ l______________ .

direct materials
direct labor

7-55. The three elements of production cost—**direct labor, direct materials,** and **overhead**—are added together to determine the total cost of the finished product. Until the product is sold, this amount is held in inventory. When the product is sold, this amount becomes Cost of Sales. Thus, if a product requires $5 of direct labor, $7 of direct materials, and $3 of overhead, the product will be costed at $ ______________ as long as it is in the Inventory account. When it is sold, C _ _ _ of S _ _ _ _ will be $______________ .

$15 (= $5 + $7 + $3)
Cost of Sales
$15

7-56. The process of assigning these production costs to products is called **cost accounting**. The assignment of costs to various services in banks, schools, hotels, and all types of service organizations also involves c _ _ _ a _ _ _ _ _ _ _ _ _ _ . We shall discuss some of its major aspects.

cost
accounting

PRODUCT COSTS AND PERIOD COSTS

7-57. Costs are divided into two categories, that are treated differently for purposes of accounting:

(1) **product costs**—those that are associated with the production of products, and

(2) **period costs**—those that are associated with the sales and general activities of the accounting period.

For example, the cost of heating the offices of the sales department would be considered a . . . [product / period] cost. The cost of heating the production plant itself would be a . . . [product / period] cost.

period
product

CONSERVATISM CONCEPT

5-21. Suppose that in January Lynn Jones agrees to buy an automobile from Ace Auto Company; the automobile is to be delivered to Jones in March. Since Ace Auto Company is in the business of selling automobiles, it . . . [would / would not] be happy that Jones has agreed to buy one.

would

5-22. Jones agrees in January to buy an automobile for delivery in March. Although Jones is . . . [likely / unlikely] to take delivery in March, it is possible that she will change her mind. The sale of this automobile therefore is . . . [absolutely certain / uncertain.]

likely

uncertain

Recognize revenue when delivered

5-23. Jones agrees in January to buy an automobile for delivery in March.

Because in January the sale of this automobile is uncertain, accounting . . . [does / does not] recognize the revenue in January. If Jones does accept delivery in March, accounting recognizes r _ _ _ _ _ _ in March. This is a . . . [conservative / liberal] way to account for the transaction.

does not

revenue

conservative

5-24. Revenue is an increase in e _ _ _ _ _ . The conservatism concept requires that increases in equity not be recognized until they are *reasonably* c _ _ _ _ _ _.

equity

certain

5-25. Increases in equity are recognized only when they are **reasonably certain**. To be conservative, decreases in equity should be recognized as soon as they have occurred. Suppose an automobile is stolen from Ace Auto Company in January, and the company waits until March to decide that the automobile is gone for good. Conservatism requires that the decrease in equity be recognized when it is **reasonably possible**; that is, in . . . [January /March].

January

INVENTORY IN A MANUFACTURING COMPANY

7-49. Retail stores, wholesalers, and distributors are . . . [merchandising / manufacturing] companies. A company that makes shoes is a . . . [merchandising / manufacturing] company.

merchandising

manufacturing

7-50. A . . . [merchandising / manufacturing] business sells finished items acquired from other businesses. A . . . [merchandising / manufacturing] business converts raw materials into finished, salable products and then sells these products.

merchandising

manufacturing

7-51. A merchandising company buys its goods in salable form and receives an invoice showing the cost for each item. The costs on these invoices are the amounts used to record the additions to inventory. A manufacturing company adds value to the raw material it buys; it must include these **conversion costs** in its inventory and in its cost of sales.

Evidently measuring inventory and cost of sales is complicated in a . . . [merchandising / manufacturing] company.

manufacturing

7-52. In a **manufacturing** business, the cost of a finished product consists of three things:

(1) cost of materials used directly on that product;
(2) cost of labor used directly on that product;
(3) a fair share of overhead, or general, costs associated with the production process.

Circle one word in each of (1), (2), and (3) above that best summarizes the whole phrase.

materials

labor

overhead

7-53. Some materials, such as oil for lubricating machinery, are not used directly on a product. The materials that are used *directly* on the product are called d _ _ _ _ _ materials. Similarly, the labor used directly to make the product is called ________________ labor.

direct

direct

5-26. The conservatism concept therefore has two parts:

(1) Recognize **increases** in equity only when they are reasonably . . . [certain / possible].

certain

(2) Recognize **decreases** in equity as soon as they are reasonably . . . [certain / possible].

possible

These are general ideas only. Specifics will be given in later parts of this program.

(No answer required)

MATERIALITY CONCEPT

5-27. A brand new pencil is a(n) . . . [asset / liability / equity] of the entity that owns it.

asset

5-28. Every time an employee writes with a pencil, part of the asset's value . . . [increases / decreases], and the entity's equity also . . . [increases / decreases].

decreases
decreases

5-29. Would it be possible, theoretically, to find out each day the number of partly used pencils that are owned by the entity and to make a journal entry showing the amount of assets that have been used up and the corresponding "pencil expense" of that day? . . . [Yes / No]. Would it be practical? . . . [Yes / No].

Yes
No

5-30. The accountant considers that the asset value of pencils was entirely used up at the time they were purchased. To do otherwise would be a waste of time. This solution is simple and . . . [impractical / practical], but . . . [more / less] exact than the theoretically correct treatment.

practical
less

7-44. Any of the methods described above is permitted in calculating taxable income. However, a company cannot switch back and forth between methods from one year to the next.

(No answer required.)

INVENTORY VALUATION: ADJUSTMENT TO MARKET

7-45. We have assumed so far that inventory is recorded at its cost. Suppose, however, that the market value of the inventory falls below its original cost. The conservatism concept requires that we should record the inventory at the . . . [higher / lower] amount.

lower

7-46. For this reason, if the market value of an item of inventory at the end of an accounting period is lower than its original cost, the item is "written down" to its market value. For example, an item whose original cost was $100 and whose current market value is $80 should be written down by $__________. (This is an exception to the general rule that assets are reported at cost.)

$20 (= $100 – $80)

7-47. In "writing down" inventory, the Inventory account is . . . [debited / credited], and Cost of Sales is . . . [debited / credited].

credited; debited

7-48. If inventory is written down by $20, what would the appropriate journal entry be?

Dr. __________ ____ ________ 20

Cr. ________________ 20

Dr. Cost of Sales 20

Cr. Inventory 20

5-31. The treatment of pencils is an example of the **materiality** concept. The materiality concept is that the accountant may disregard im _ _ _ _ _ _ _ _ transactions. When accountants consider the asset value of pencils to be entirely used up at the time of purchase, they are applying the _ _ _ _ _ _ _ _ _ _ _ _ concept.

immaterial

materiality

5-32. Material transactions are those that make a difference in understanding an entity's financial affairs. Deciding which transaction are material is a matter of judgment. There are no mechanical rules.

(No answer required)

5-33. The other side of the coin is that the financial statements must disclose all material facts. For example, if a large fraction of a company's inventory is found to be worthless, the m____________________ concept requires that this fact be disclosed.

materiality

5-34. The materiality concept has two aspects:(1) . . . [disregard / disclose] trivial (i.e., unimportant) matters, and (2) . . . [disregard / disclose] all important matters.

disregard

disclose

5-35. To review, the conservatism concept is: recognize increases in equity only when they are r _ _ _ _ _ _ _ _ _ c _ _ _ _ _ _, but recognize decreases as soon as they are r _ _ _ _ _ _ _ _ _ p _ _ _ _ _ _ _. The materiality concept is: . . . [disregard / disclose] trivial matters, but . . . [disregard / disclose] all important matters.

reasonably certain

reasonably possible

disregard

disclose

REALIZATION CONCEPT

5-36. Consider an entity that manufactures goods and then sells them. In accounting, the revenue from these goods is recognized at the time they are delivered to the customer, *not* at the time they are manufactured.

19x1	19x2	19x3
Goods manufactured	Goods delivered	Cash received
	Revenue recognized	

Suppose that in 19x2 an entity delivers to a customer an item that it manufactured in 19x1. The revenue is recognized in . . . [19x1 / 19x2].

19x2

7-37. Using the average cost of $1.09 per unit, complete the average cost section of Exhibit 9.

$$\frac{\$1,090}{1,000} = \$1.09 \text{ cost per unit}$$

Ending inventory: 600 units @ $1.09 = $654
Cost of sales: 400 units @ $1.09 = $436

COMPARISON OF INVENTORY METHODS

7-38. Most businesses try to sell their oldest goods first, so the goods that were first out are likely to be the goods . . . [first in / last in]. The . . . [FIFO / LIFO] method reflects this practice.

first in; FIFO

7-39. From Exhibit 9, we see that cost of sales under FIFO was $____________ and under LIFO it was $____________. Cost of sales was . . . [lower / higher] under LIFO.

$400; $470
higher

7-40. In most companies, in periods of inflation (when prices are rising) this same relationship holds; that is, cost of sales is . . . [lower / higher] under LIFO than under FIFO.

higher

7-41. In calculating income taxes, cost of sales is one of the items subtracted from revenue in order to find taxable income.

Assume the revenue of Lewis Fuel Company was $1,000. Disregarding other expenses, if cost of sales was $470, taxable income would be $______. If cost of sales was $400, taxable income would be $______.

$530
$600

7-42. As can be seen from the above, the higher the cost of sales, the . . . [lower / higher] the taxable income. The lower the taxable income, the . . . [lower / higher] the income tax based on that income will be.

lower
lower

7-43. Companies usually prefer to pay as low an income tax as they legally can. Therefore, they prefer the method that results in the . . . [lower / higher] cost of sales. If prices are rising, this is usually the . . . [FIFO / LIFO] method.

higher
LIFO

5-37. If a company sells services rather than goods, revenue is recognized at the time the services are . . . [contracted for / delivered].

delivered

5-38. Goods (such as shoes) are *tangible* products. Services (such as repairing TV sets) are *intangible* products. Both goods and services are products. Thus, the general rule is that revenue from a product is recognized when the product is . . . [manufactured / contracted for / delivered].

delivered

5-39. At the time of delivery, revenue is said to be realized. The realization concept is that revenue is recognized in the period in which it is r _ _ _ _ _ ed.

realized

5-40. In January, Smith Company contracts to paint Herbert's house. The house is painted in February, and Herbert pays Smith Company in March. Smith Company would recognize revenue in ______________ (what month?).

January	February	March
Services ordered	Services delivered	Cash received
	Revenue recognized	

February

5-41. Gordon Company manufactures some imitation carrots in May. In June it receives an order from Peter Rabbit, Esq., for one carrot. Gordon Company delivers the carrot in July. Peter Rabbit pays the bill in August and eats the carrot in September. Gordon Company would recognize revenue in ______________ .

July

5-42. Revenue is realized when a *sale* is completed by the delivery of a product. Because of this, the word "sales" is often used along with revenue, as in the phrase "s _ _ _ _ r _ _ _ _ _ _ ."

sales revenue

5-43. A salesperson may say that he or she has "made a sale" when the order was written, even though the product is to be delivered at some future time. In accounting, writing a sales order . . . [is / is not] a sale because the revenue has not yet been _ _ _ _ _ _ ed.

is not

realized

LAST-IN, FIRST-OUT (LIFO) METHOD

7-33. The FIFO method assumes that the oldest units, that is, those F________ I____, were the first to be sold, i.e., that they were the F________ O_____. The **LIFO** method assumes the opposite, namely, that the . . . [oldest / newest] units, which were the Last In, were the first to be sold, i.e., that they were the First Out, hence the name **Last-In First-Out**.

First In
First Out
newest

7-34. Since the LIFO method assumes that the units sold were the last ones purchased, the ending inventory is assumed to consist of the units in beginning inventory, plus the earliest units purchased. In Exhibit 9, the ending inventory was 600 units, and in the LIFO method these 600 units are assumed to be the ________ (how many?) units in beginning inventory plus ________ (how many?) of the 300 units purchased on April _____.

400
200; April 10

7-35. In the LIFO section in Exhibit 9, enter the amount available for sale, $1,090, calculate the ending inventory, and subtract to find the cost of sales.

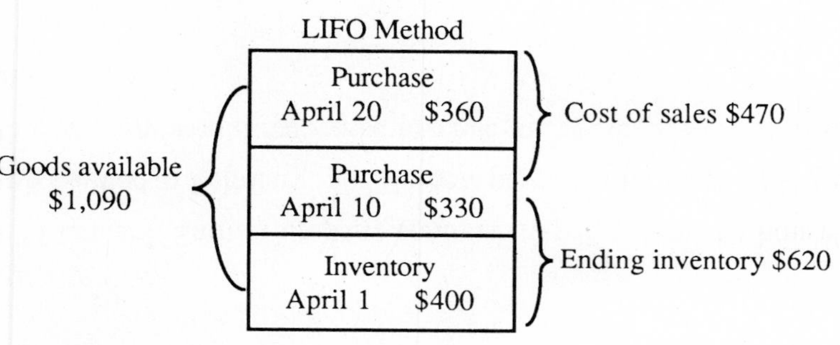

	Goods available		$1,090
	Ending inventory		
	400 units @ $100	=$400	
	200 units @ $1.10	= 220	
Total	600 units		620
	Cost of sales		$ 470

AVERAGE COST METHOD

7-36. The third method is the **average-cost** method. It calculates the cost of both the ending inventory and the cost of sales at the average cost per unit of the goods available. In Exhibit 9, the number of units available in April was __________, and the total cost of these goods was $ __________, so the average cost per unit was $ __________.

1,000
$1,090
$1.09 (= $1,090 ÷ 1,000)

5-44. Revenue may be recognized (1) before, (2) during, or (3) after the period in which the cash from the sale is received. First, let's consider a case in which revenue is recognized in the same period as when the cash is received.

In January, Mugar TV Company repaired Freund's television set, and Freund paid $50 cash.

In keeping with the dual-aspect concept, this transaction had two effects on the accounts of Mugar TV Company. It increased Cash, and it increased Sales Revenue. Complete the journal entry for this transaction by entering the proper account titles.

Dr. [__________] 50

Cr. S[__________] R[__________] 50

Dr. Cash 50

Cr. Sales Revenue 50

5-45. In January, Loren Company sold and delivered a motorcycle to Jerry Paynter, who paid $1,800 cash.

In this example, revenue is recognized in the . . . [month before / same month as / month after] the related cash receipt.

same month as

5-46. In January, Loren Company sold a motorcycle on credit to Jean Matthews for $3,800. Matthews agreed to pay for the motorcycle in 30 days.

In this case revenue is recognized in the . . . [month before / same month as / month after] the related cash receipt.

month before

5-47. When revenue is recognized before the related cash receipt, as in the preceding transaction, the revenue is accompanied by the right to collect the cash, which is an Accounts Receivable. Thus, the entry for the sale of the motorcycle on credit would be:

Dr. [__________] 3,800

Cr. [__________] 3,800

Dr. Accounts Receivable 3,800

Cr. Sales Revenue 3,800

FIRST-IN, FIRST-OUT (FIFO) METHOD

7-28. In this situation, many companies make the **First-In First-Out (FIFO)** assumption. They assume that the goods that came into the inventory . . . [first / last] are the . . . [first / last] to move out.

first; first

7-29. If you applied the FIFO method to the data of Exhibit 9, you would assume that the . . . [newer / older] fuel oil was sold during the month and that the . . . [newer / older] fuel oil remains in the ending inventory.

older

newer

7-30. The FIFO method assumes that the older units were sold during the period; therefore the ending inventory of 600 units of fuel oil is the most recently purchased fuel oil—that is, the 300 units that were purchased on April ________ at $________ per unit, and the 300 units that were purchased on April ________ at $________ per unit.

20; $1.20

10; $1.10

7-31. In the "FIFO Method" section of Exhibit 9, enter these amounts and calculate the ending inventory.

Ending Inventory

	300 units @ $1.20 =	$360
	300 units @ $1.10 =	330
Total	600 units	$690

7-32. Earlier, you found the amount of goods available for sale to be $1,090. Enter this amount in your calculation, and subtract the ending inventory of $690 from it. The difference is the FIFO c________ of s________, which is $________.

cost of sales

$400

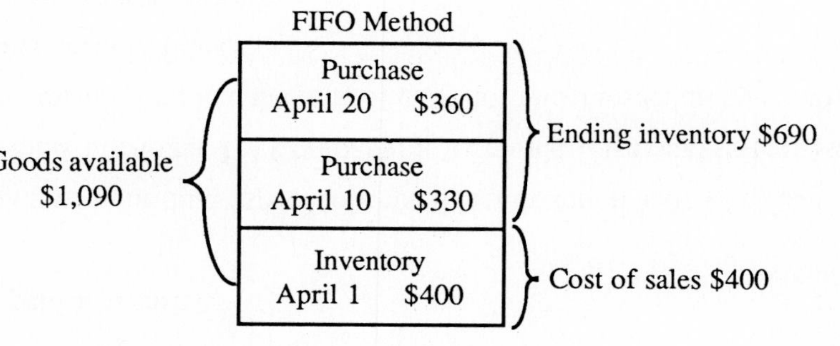

5-48. When a customer pays an entity for a credit purchase, the entity records an increase in Cash and a corresponding decrease in Accounts Receivable. Thus, when Loren Company receives a check for $3,800 from Matthews, Loren Company makes the following entry:

Dr. [ ] 3,800

Cr. [ ] [ ] 3,800

Dr. Cash 3,800

Cr. Accounts Receivable .. 3,800

5-49. So far we have treated the cases in which

(1) revenue is recognized *in the same period* as the associated cash receipt; and

(2) revenue is recognized *before* the associated receipt of cash.

There remains the case in which

(3) revenue is recognized ____________ the associated receipt of cash.

after

5-50. When a customer pays an entity in advance of delivery of the product, the entity has an obligation to deliver the product. This obligation, like any obligation, is a(n) . . . [asset / liability / equity]. It is listed on the . . . [left / right] side of the balance sheet with the title **Advances from Customers**.

liability

right

5-51. Thus, when an entity receives cash in advance of delivery, it records a debit to Cash and a corresponding credit to the liability, Advances from Customers.

In March, Maypo Company received $3,000 cash in advance from a firm to prepare an advertising brochure. Write the entry that Maypo Company should make in March to record this transaction.

Dr. [ ] 3,000

Cr. [ ] [ ] [ ] 3,000

Dr. Cash 3,000

Cr. Advances from Customers .. 3,000

INVENTORY VALUATION: THE PROBLEM

7-23. Complete the following table, filling in all empty boxes.

	Quantity	Unit Cost	Total Cost
Beginning inventory, April 1	400	$1.00	$
Purchases, April 6	300	1.00	
Purchases, April 20	300	1.00	
Total goods available		1.00	
Ending inventory, April 30	600	1.00	
Cost of sales, April			

Quantity	Unit Cost	Total Cost
400	$1.00	$ 400
300	1.00	300
300	1.00	300
1,000	1.00	1,000
600	1.00	600
400	1.00	400

7-24. Lewis Fuel Company deals in fuel oil. Its inventory and purchases during April are shown in Exhibit 9 in the separate booklet. Fill in the two empty boxes in the column titled "Units."

Total goods available 1,000

Cost of sales 400

7-25. The "Unit Cost" column of Exhibit 9 shows that fuel oil entered the inventory at . . . [identical / different] unit costs during April.

different

7-26. In Exhibit 9 fill in the first four boxes in the column headed "Total Cost."

Units	Unit Cost	Total Cost
400	$1.00	$ 400
300	1.10	330
300	1.20	360
1,000		1,090

7-27. The problem now is: What unit cost should we assign to the ending inventory? There are three choices: (1) we could assume that the older fuel oil was sold, leaving the newer fuel oil in inventory; (2) we could assume that the newer fuel oil was sold, leaving the older fuel in inventory; or (3) we could assume that a mixture of old and new oil was sold. Since the fuel oil has been mixed together in the storage tank, we . . .[have / do not have] a record of the cost of the particular fuel oil actually sold during the month. Therefore the solution . . .[is / is not] clearcut.

do not have

is not

5-52. In March, Maypo Company received $3,000 in advance from a firm to prepare an advertising brochure. It delivered the brochure in June. It therefore no longer had the liability, Advances from Customers. Write the entry that should be made in June.

Dr. [ ] [ ] [ ] 3,000

Cr. [S] [R] 3,000

March	April	May	June
Cash received	Product made		Product delivered
			Revenue recognized

Dr. Advances from Customer .. 3,000

Cr. Sales Revenue 3,000

5-53. A magazine publisher received a check for $50 in 19x1 for a magazine subscription. The magazines will be delivered in 19x2. Write the entry that the publisher should make in 19x1.

Dr. [ ] 50

Cr. [ ] [ ] [ ] 50

Dr. Cash 50

Cr. Advances from Customers . 50

(Note: The terms "Deferred Revenue" and "Precollected Revenue" are sometimes used instead of "Advances from Customers.")

5-54. A publisher received $50 for a magazine subscription in 19x1. In 19x2, when the magazines are delivered, the publisher will recognize the $50 revenue and will record a corresponding decrease in the liability, Advances from Customers.

Write the names of the accounts and the amounts for the entry that should be made in 19x2.

Dr. [ ] [ ] [ ] .... [ ]

Cr. [ ] [ ] .. [ ]

Dr. Advances from Customers 50

Cr. Sales Revenue 50

5-55. The customer's advance may cover revenue that will be earned over several future accounting periods. Suppose in 19x1 a publisher received $80 for a magazine subscription, with the magazines to be delivered in 19x2 and 19x3. The entry for 19x1 should be:

Dr. [ ] .... [ ]

Cr. [ ] [ ] [ ] .... [ ]

Dr. Cash 80

Cr. Advances from Customers 80

The amount of the liability at the end of 19x1 would be . . . [$80 / $40 / $20 / $0].

$80

7-20. A hardware store . . . [does / does not] keep track of individual items in inventory. It finds its cost of sales by the process of d ________________, which requires taking a . . . [perpetual / physical] inventory. An automobile dealership finds its cost of sales directly from its . . . [perpetual / physical] inventory records.

does not

deduction

physical

perpetual

(Note: The automobile dealer takes a physical inventory at least annually, as a check on its perpetual inventory records.)

7-21. It finds cost of sales by subtracting the ending inventory from the total goods available, as in the following table:

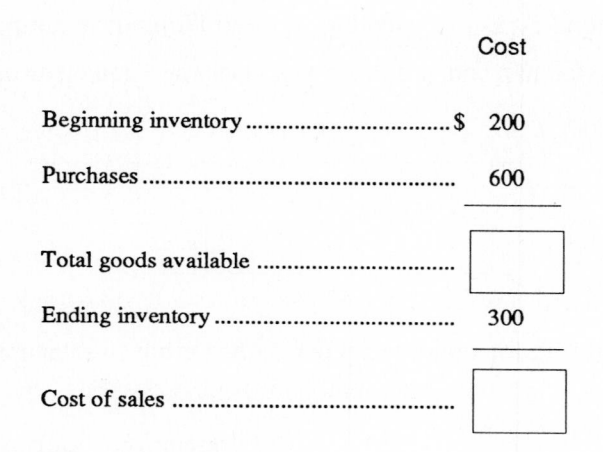

	Cost
Beginning inventory	$ 200
Purchases	600
Total goods available	[ ]
Ending inventory	300
Cost of sales	[ ]

	Cost
Beginning inventory	$ 200
Purchases	600
Total goods available	800
Ending inventory	300
Cost of sales	500

7-22. The same situation is shown in the following diagram. Fill in the boxes.

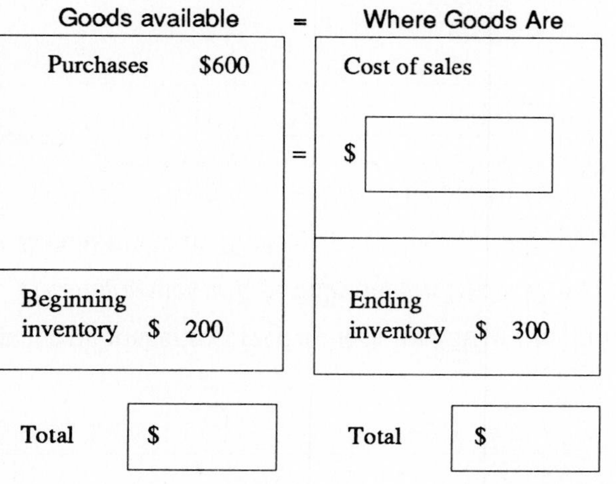

$500

$800; $800

5-56. In 19x1 a publisher received $80 for a magazine subscription, with the magazines to be delivered in 19x2 and 19x3. The entry for 19x2 should be:

Dr. [ ] [ ] [ ] .... [ ]

Cr. [ ] [ ] ..... [ ]

Dr. Advances from Customers 40

Cr. Sales Revenue 40

At the end of 19x2 . . . [$80 / $40 / $20 / $0] would be reported as a liability on the balance sheet.

$40

5-57. In 19x1 a publisher received $80 for a magazine subscription, with the magazines to be delivered in 19x2 and 19x3. The entry for 19x3 would be:

Dr. [ ] [ ] [ ] 40

Cr. [ ] [ ] 40

Dr. Advances from Customers 40

Cr. Sales Revenue 40

At the end of 19x3, . . . [$80 / $40 / $20 / $0] would be reported as a liability on the balance sheet.

$0

SERVICE REVENUE

5-58. Revenue is recognized in the period in which services are delivered. If a landlord receives cash from a tenant in January and in return permits the tenant to use an apartment in February, March, and April, the landlord recognizes revenue in . . . [January / February / March / April].

February, March, April

5-59. In January, a tenant paid the landlord $2,400 cash covering rent for February, March, and April. This type of revenue is called **rental revenue**. How much revenue would the landlord recognize each month, and how much liability would be reported at the end of each month?

	Rental Revenue for the month	Liability at the end of month
January	$	$
February	$	$
March	$	$
April	$	$

	Rental Revenue for the month	Liability at the end of month
January	$ 0	$2,400
February	$800	$1,600
March	$800	$ 800
April	$800	$ 0

7-14. On January 1, 19x1, Cantal Hardware had an inventory that cost $200,000. During 19x1 it purchased $600,000 of additional merchandise. The cost of goods **available for sale** in 19x1 was $ ______________.

$800,000 (= $200,000 + $600,000)

7-15. Accountants assume that goods available for sale during a period either were in inventory at the end of the period or they were sold. Thus, if goods costing $800,000 were available for sale during 19x1 and goods costing $300,000 were in inventory on December 31, 19x1, cost of sales in 19x1 is assumed to be $ ______________.

$500,000 (= $800,000 – $300,000)

7-16. At the end of each accounting period, all goods currently on hand are counted. This process is called **taking a physical inventory**. Since its purpose is to find the cost of the goods that were sold, each item is reported at its . . . [cost / selling price].

cost

7-17. In order to determine the ending inventory of one period and the beginning inventory of the next period, how many physical inventories must be taken? ______________

Just one (because the ending inventory on December 31, 19x1 is the same as the beginning inventory on January 1, 19x2).

7-18. "Cost of sales" and "Cost of goods sold" mean the same thing. We shall use the shorter term, **cost of sales**. In the deduction method for determining cost of sales, the rationale is as follows: Goods are assumed to have been sold if they . . . [are / are not] in inventory at the . . . [beginning / end] of the period.

are not
end

7-19. Sometimes goods in inventory are stolen, damaged, or spoiled. The assumption that goods not in the closing inventory have been sold . . . [is / is not] necessarily valid. However, steps are taken to discover and record this **shrinkage**.

is not

5-60. When a bank lends money, it delivers a service; that is, the bank provides the borrower with the use of the money for a specified period of time. The bank earns revenue for the service it delivers during this period.This type of revenue is called **interest revenue**. In accordance with the realization concept, interest revenue is recognized in the period(s) . . . [in which the interest is received / in which the borrower has the use of the money].

in which the borrower has the use of the money

(Note: the term "interest income" is sometimes used, but the amount actually is revenue, not income. Income is always a difference between revenue and expense.)

5-61. Interest revenue is similar to rental revenue. Banks deliver a service when they "rent" money; landlords deliver a service when they rent apartments. In both cases, revenue is realized in the period(s) in which the service is d _ _ _ _ _ _ _ _ .

delivered

5-62. To summarize, accountants recognize revenue *before* the related cash receipt by crediting Revenues and debiting a(n) . . . [asset / liability / equity] account entitled A _ _ _ _ _ _ _ R _ _ _ _ _ _ _ _ _ .

asset
Accounts Receivable

5-63. Accountants recognize revenue *after* the related cash receipt by debiting Cash and crediting a(n) . . . [asset / liability / equity] account when the cash is received. Revenue is recognized when the product is d _ _ _ _ _ _ _ _ in accordance with the r _ _ _ _ _ _ _ _ _ _ concept.

liability

delivered; realization

(Note: There are exceptions to the concept that revenues are recognized when products are delivered. They involve certain types of installment sales, certain long-term contracts, and a few other special situations. They are outside the scope of this introductory treatment.)

AMOUNT OF REVENUE

5-64. The realization concept describes *when* revenue is recognized. The conservatism concept governs *how much* revenue is recognized.

(No answer required)

7-8. Refrigerators that cost $1,800 were sold in May for $2,500. Complete the following partial income statement, assuming these were the only items sold.

Income Statement
May

Sales revenue	$
Cost of sales	$
G______ M _________	

Income Statement
May

Sales revenue	$2,500
Cost of sales	1,800
Gross Margin	700

FINDING COST OF SALES BY DEDUCTION

7-9. If an entity has a p_______________ inventory, as illustrated above, finding cost of sales in a month is easy. We shall next show how to deduce cost of sales in a business that does not have this record. This method is the process of **deduction**.

perpetual

7-10. Many hardware stores carry so many relatively low-value items that keeping a perpetual inventory record for each separate item is not practical. When the salesperson rings up a sale on the cash register, a record is made of the . . . [cost of sales / sales revenue] but not the . . . [cost of sales / sales revenue].

sales revenue; cost of sales

7-11. If a hardware store does not keep a record of the cost of each item in inventory, it . . . [can arrive at cost of sales by direct tally / must deduce cost of sales by an indirect method].

must deduce cost of sales by an indirect method

7-12. Items in a hardware store's **beginning inventory** on January 1, 19x1 . . . [were / were not] available for sale during 19x1. Additional items **purchased** and placed on the shelves during 19x1 . . . [were / were not] available for sale during 19x1.

were
were

7-13. The goods available for sale in a period are the sum of the b_______________ inventory plus p_______________ during the period.

beginning; purchases

5-65. Loren Company sold a motorcycle to James Austin for $3,000 on credit, but Austin never paid the $3,000. Since Loren Company's assets decreased by one motorcycle but there was no actual increase in another asset, Loren Company's equity actually . . . [increased / stayed the same / decreased] as a result of this transaction. Loren Company . . . [did / did not] realize revenue from this transaction.

decreased did not

5-66. Obviously, if Loren Company knew that Austin would not pay for the motorcycle, Loren would not have delivered it. Although Loren would not knowingly sell a motorcycle to someone who is not going to pay, experience indicates that some customers do not pay; in this case there is a **bad debt**. Loren . . . [must / need not] take this possibility into account in measuring its income. It does this by estimating the amount of revenue that it is **reasonably certain** to receive from all its sales during the accounting period.

must

5-67. In 19x1 Loren Company sold $500,000 of motorcycles to customers, all on credit. It estimated that 2% of these credit sales would never be collected; that is, they would become **bad debts**. Its estimate of bad debts for 19x1 was $________________, and its revenues in 19x1 were therefore only $________________.

$10,000 (=.02 x $500,000)
$490,000 (= $500,000 – $10,000)

5-68. Loren Company recorded each sale as revenue at the time the motorcycles were delivered. In order to measure its revenues properly, it must . . . [increase / decrease] the amount of recorded revenue by $________________.

decrease
$10,000

(Note: Some companies increase expense rather than decreasing revenue. The effect on income is the same.)

5-69. After this decrease, the amount recognized as revenue is $________________. This is the amount that is reasonably . . . [possible / certain] to be realized. This is in accordance with the . . . [conservatism / materiality] concept.

$490,000
certain; conservatism

This is called a **perpetual inventory** record. "Receipts" are . . . [increases / decreases] in inventory, and "Shipments to Customers" are . . . [increases / decreases] in inventory.

increases

decreases

7-6. Information in the perpetual inventory records corresponds to that in the Inventory account. Considering only Refrigerator #602, we see that the beginning balance in the Inventory account on May 1 was $__________. There were receipts during May of $__________, which added to Inventory; these were . . . [Dr. / Cr.] to the Inventory account. Shipments during May decreased inventory by $__________ which was a . . . [Dr. / Cr.]. This decrease in inventory represented Cost of Sales in May, which was $__________.

$800; $2,000

Dr.

$1,800

Cr.

$1,800

7-7. Using the *totals* in the perpetual inventory record, enter the inventory transactions for May in the T-accounts given below. (The inventory purchases were on credit.)

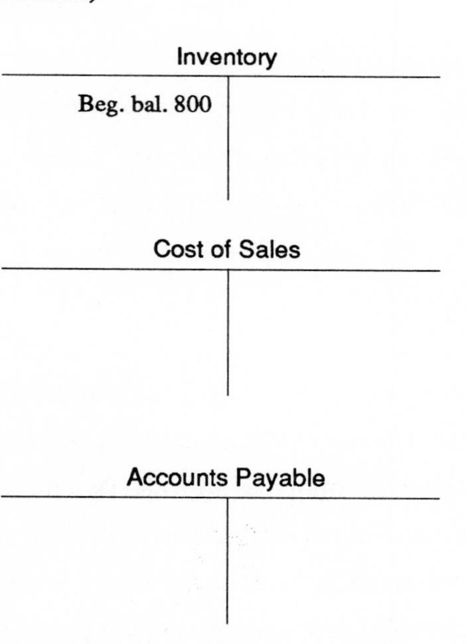

Refer back to Frame 7-6 if you are uncertain. Remember that debits must equal credits.

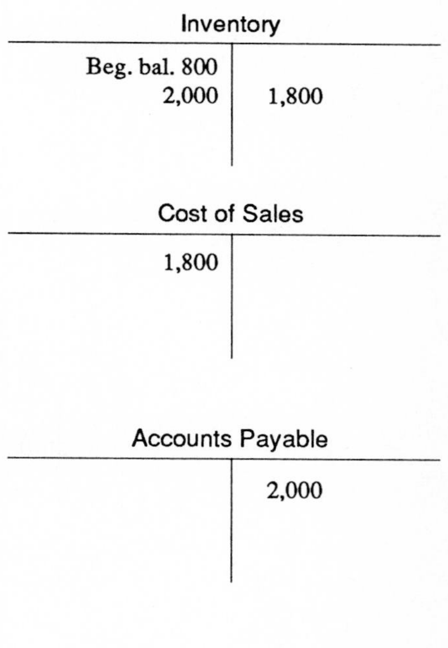

5-70. Since the Accounts Receivable account includes amounts from customers who probably will never pay their bills, it overstates the real asset value. Thus, if the Loren Company decreases its Sales Revenue account by $10,000, it must also . . . [increase / decrease] its Accounts Receivable account by $10,000.

decrease

5-71. However, accountants usually can't decrease the Accounts Receivable account directly because they don't know *which* customers will not pay their bills. Therefore, accountants usually set up a separate account, called **Allowance for Doubtful Accounts**, and record the decrease in this account. Accounts Receivable, like all asset accounts, has a . . . [debit / credit] balance. Allowance for Doubtful Accounts, which is subtracted from Accounts Receivable, therefore must have the opposite balance, that is, a . . . [debit / credit] balance.

debit

credit

5-72. The entry to record Loren Company's estimate that Sales Revenue should be decreased by $10,000 and an Allowance for Doubtful Accounts of $10,000 should be established is:

Dr. [ ] [ ] 10,000

Cr. [ ] [ ]

[ ] [ ] 10,000

Dr. Sales Revenue 10,000

Cr. Allowance for Doubtful Accounts 10,000

5-73. On December 31, 19x1, Loren Company had $125,000 of Accounts Receivable before subtracting the Allowance for Doubtful Accounts. Fill in the amounts that would be reported on Loren Company's December 31, 19x1, balance sheet.

		Answer
Accounts receivable, gross	$	$125,000
Less Allowance for doubtful accounts	–	10,000
Accounts receivable, net	$	$115,000

7-2. In some entities, matching cost of sales and sales revenue is easy. For example, an automobile dealer keeps a record of the cost of each automobile in its inventory. If the dealer sold two automobiles during a given month, one for $8,000 that had cost $6,000, and the other for $10,000 that had cost $7,500, sales revenue for the period would be recorded as $ __________ and cost of sales as $ __________ .

$18,000 (= $8,000 + $10,000)
$13,500 (= $6,000 + $7,500)

7-3. A dealer sold an automobile costing $6,000 for $8,000 cash. What would be the journal entry that records the effect of this transaction solely on the Sales Revenue and Cash accounts?

Dr. __________ .... __________

Cr. __________ .... __________

Dr. Cash 8,000
Cr. Sales Revenue 8,000

7-4. A dealer sold an automobile costing $6,000 for $8,000 cash. What would the journal entry be for recording the effect of this transaction solely upon the Inventory and Cost of Sales accounts?

Dr. __________ .... __________

Cr. __________ .... __________

Dr. Cost of Sales 6,000
Cr. Inventory 6,000

7-5. A dealer that sells refrigerators might keep a record of its inventory of each type of refrigerator, something like the following:

Item: Refrigerator #602, Cost $200 each

Date	Receipts		Shipments to Customers		On Hand	
	Quantity	Cost	Quantity	Cost	Quantity	Cost
May 1					4	800
6			1	200	3	600
10	10	2,000			13	2,600
13			6	1,200	7	1,400
31			2	400	5	1,000
Totals	10	2,000	9	1,800	5	1,000

5-74. Sometime in 19x2, Loren Company decides it is never going to collect the $3,000 owed by Austin. It therefore *writes off* the bad debt. It does this by decreasing Accounts Receivable and also decreasing Allowance for Doubtful Accounts. Write the entry for this transaction.

Dr. [__________] [______]
[______] [__________] 3,000

Cr. [______] [__________] .. 3,000

Dr. Allowance for
Doubtful Accounts 3,000

Cr. Accounts Receivable 3,000

5-75. Loren Company's revenue in 19x1 was reduced by the estimated bad debts on sales made in 19x1, but its revenue in 19x2 . . . [was / was not] affected by this write-off of a bad debt.

was not
(Since revenue was decreased in 19x1, it should not be decreased again for the same motorcycle.)

MONETARY ASSETS

5-76. Monetary assets are cash and promises by an outside party to pay the entity a specified amount of money. Which of the following assets are monetary assets?

(a) Inventory
(b) Accounts receivable
(c) Notes receivable
(d) Buildings
(e) Equipment
(f) Bonds owned by the entity

(b), (c) and (f)

5-77. As with accounts receivable, other monetary assets are usually reported on the balance sheet at the amounts that are r _ _ _ _ _ _ _ _ _ c _ _ _ _ _ _ to be received. By contrast, nonmonetary assets, such as buildings and equipment, are reported at their c _ _ _.

reasonably
certain
cost

DAYS' RECEIVABLES

5-78. In Part 2 we described the current ratio, which is:

current a _ _ _ _ s
―――――――――
current l _ _ _ _ _ _ _ _ _ s

current assets
―――――――――
current liabilities

Part 7

Inventories and Cost of Sales

Learning Objectives

In this part you will learn:

- How the cost of sales is calculated.
- Methods of arriving at inventory amounts.
- When inventory amounts on the balance sheet are reduced.
- How inventory is measured in a manufacturing company.
- The distinction between product costs and period costs.
- How overhead rates are calculated.

FINDING COST OF SALES

7-1. As we saw in the income statement in Part 6, the first item subtracted from sales revenue is called **Cost of sales**. It is the cost of the same products whose revenues are included in the sales amount. This is an example of the m _ _ _ _ _ _ _ concept. (Some businesses call this item **Cost of goods sold**.) In most businesses the cost of sales is the . . . [smallest / largest] item of expense, amounting to as much as 85–90% of sales revenues in a profitable supermarket.

matching

largest

5-79. Another useful ratio is Days' Receivables. This is the number of days of sales that are in Accounts Receivable at the end of the accounting period. Sales per day are total credit sales for the year divided by 365. The formula is:

Days' Receivables = [A ______] [R ______] / Credit sales ÷ 365

Accounts Receivable / Credit Sales ÷ 365

5-80. Calculate the Days' Receivables ratio for Worley Company from the following data:

Accounts receivable, December 31, 19x1 .... $50,000
Credit sales for the Year 19x1 .... $365,000

Days' Receivables = [$ ______] / [$ ______] ÷ 365 = [______] days

$50,000 / $365,000 ÷ 365 = 50 days

5-81. The Days' Receivable ratio indicates whether customers are paying their bills when they are due. If Worley Company expects customers to pay within 30 days from the date of the sale, the ratio of 50 days indicates that customers . . . [are / are not] paying on time.

are not

(Note: This is only a rough indication because it assumes sales are made evenly throughout the year.)

KEY POINTS TO REMEMBER

- Expenditures are made when goods or services are acquired. If these goods or services are used up during the current period, they are expenses of the period. If not used up, they are assets at the end of that period. These assets will become expenses in future periods as they are used up.
- Some expenditures result in liabilities that will be paid in future periods. An example is accrued salaries.
- Expenses are expired costs. Assets are unexpired costs.
- Matching concept: Costs associated with the revenues of a period are expenses of the period.
- Expenses of a period are (1) cost of the products (i.e., goods and services) that were delivered to customers during the period; (2) other expenditures that benefit operations of the period; and (3) losses, that is, assets whose benefits expired during the period, or liabilities that were created during the period.
- The income statement summarizes revenues and expenses of the period. Its "bottom line," or net income, shows the increase in equity resulting from activities during the period.
- Dividends are a distribution of earnings to shareholders. Dividends are *not* expenses.
- Retained Earnings at the beginning of the period + Net Income − Dividends = Retained Earnings at the end of the period.
- Percentages are calculated for various income statement items, especially gross margin and net income, taking sales revenue as 100 percent.

You have completed Part 6 of this program. If you think you understand the material in this part, you should now take Post Test 6, which is in the separate booklet. If you are uncertain about your understanding, you should review Part 6.

The post test will serve both to test your comprehension and to review the highlights of Part 6. After taking the post test, you may find that you are unsure about certain points. You should review these points before continuing with Part 7.

KEY POINTS TO REMEMBER

- The official accounting period is one year, but financial statements can be prepared for shorter interim periods.
- Accrual accounting measures revenues and expenses during an accounting period and the difference between them, which is income. Accrual accounting is more complicated, but more useful, than accounting only for cash receipts and payments.
- The conservatism concept: Recognize increases in equity only when they are reasonably certain; recognize decreases as soon as they are reasonably possible.
- The materiality concept: Disregard trivial matters, but disclose all important matters.
- The realization concept: Revenue is usually recognized when goods and services are delivered.
- If revenue is recognized before the cash receipt, an asset, Accounts Receivable, is debited. If cash is received before revenue is recognized, a liability, Advances from Customers, is credited. The liability is debited in the period(s) in which revenue is recognized.
- The gross amounts of sales revenue and associated accounts receivable in a period are reduced by estimated bad debt losses. When bad debts are later discovered, Accounts Receivable is reduced, but revenue in the later period is unaffected.
- Monetary assets are reported at the amounts reasonably certain to be realized, but nonmonetary assets are reported at cost.
- The days' receivables ratio is

$$\frac{\text{Account Receivable}}{\text{Credit sales} \div 365}$$

It indicates whether customers are paying their bills on time.

You have completed Part 5 of this program. If you think you understand the material in this part, you should now take Post Test 5, which is in the separate booklet. If you are uncertain about your understanding, you should review Part 5.

The post test will serve both to test your comprehension and to review the highlights of Part 5. After taking the post test, you may find that you are unsure about certain points. You should review these points before continuing with Part 6.

6-95. Cost concept: Accounting focuses on the __________ of assets, rather than on their ....

cost

market value

6-96. Conservatism concept: Revenues are recognized when they are __________ __________. Expenses are recognized when they are __________ __________.

reasonably certain

reasonably possible

6-97. Materiality concept: Disregard ....
Disclose ....

insignificant matters

all important matters

6-98. Realization concept: Revenues are recognized when goods or services are __________.

delivered

6-99. Matching concept: The expenses of a period are ....

costs associated with the revenues or activities of the period.

Part 6

Expense Measurement; The Income Statement

Learning Objectives

In this part you will learn:

- The difference between "expense" and "expenditure."
- How the expenses of a period are measured.
- The last of the nine basic accounting concepts:
  - The matching concept.
- The meaning of items reported on an income statement.
- Methods of analyzing an income statement.

6-1. In Part 5 you learned that the revenues recognized in an accounting period were not necessarily associated with the cash receipts in that period. If $1,000 of product were delivered to a customer in August, and the customer paid cash for these goods in September, revenue would be recognized in . . . [August / September].

August

6-2. Revenues are . . . [increases / decreases] in equity during an accounting period. Expenses are . . . [increases / decreases] in equity during an accounting period. Just as revenues in a period are not necessarily the same as cash receipts in a period, the expenses of a period . . . [are / are not] necessarily the same as the cash payments in that period.

increases
decreases

are not

6-88. An even more important percentage is the **net income percentage.** Calculate it for Garsden Company.

$$\frac{\text{Net income}}{\text{Sales revenue}} = \frac{\$\,\_\_\_\_}{\$\,\_\_\_\_} = \_\_\_\%^*$$

$$\frac{\$\ 6{,}122}{\$75{,}478} = 8\%$$

6-89. The net income of many American corporations is roughly 5% to 10% of sales revenue, but there is a wide variation from company to company.

(No answer required.)

REVIEW OF BASIC CONCEPTS

6-90. The nine basic concepts emphasized in this program are listed in the following frames, together with some guides that will refresh your memory as to their meaning. Complete the meaning of each concept. (These concepts are not stated as such in accounting literature, but most accountants would agree that they are the basic underpinnings of accounting.)

(No answer required)

6-91. Dual-aspect concept: ________ = ________ + ________

assets = liabilities + equities

6-92. Money-measurement concept: Accounting reports only facts that can be expressed ....

in monetary amounts

(Note: If you have the general idea, fine. Your words need not be exactly like those given here.)

6-93. Entity concept: Accounts are kept for ____________ as distinguished from ....

entities

the persons associated with those entities

6-94. Going-concern concept: Accounting assumes that an entity will...

....

and that it is not ....

continue to operate indefinitely

about to be sold

EXPENSE AND EXPENDITURE

6-3. When an entity acquires goods or services, it makes an **expenditure**. If Mogul Shop purchased goods for its inventory at a cost of $1,000, paying cash, it had an e__________ of $1,000 in August. It would record this transaction with the following journal entry:

Dr. I __________	1,000	
Cr. C __________		1,000

expenditure

Inventory	1,000	
Cash		1,000

6-4. If in August Mogul Shop purchased $2,000 of goods for inventory, agreeing to pay in 30 days, it had an e__________ of $2,000 in August. Accounts Payable, which is a liability account, was increased. It would record this transaction with the following journal entry:

Dr. I __________	2,000	
Cr. A ________ P________		2,000

expenditure

Inventory

Accounts Payable

6-5. Thus, an expenditure for the purchase of goods or services results either in a decrease in the asset C___ or an increase in a l________, such as Accounts Payable.

Cash; liability

[Note: Occasionally an expenditure results in a decrease in an asset other than cash. When an old automobile is traded in for a new automobile, part of the expenditure is the decrease in the asset, Automobiles.]

6-6. Mogul Shop had e__________s of $3,000 in August for the purchase of goods for inventory. If $500 of these goods were sold in August, there was an **expense** in August of $500. The remaining $2,500 of goods are still in inventory at the end of August; they therefore are an **asset**. Thus, the expenditures of a period are either __________ of the period or __________s at the end of the period.

expenditures

expenses

assets

6-7. Mogul Shop sold the remaining $2,500 of goods in September. In September it had an . . . [expenditure / expense] of $2,500, but it did not have any . . . [expenditure / expense] for these goods in September.

expense

expenditure

6-82. During 19x2 profitable operations resulted in net income of $__________, which increased Retained Earnings by this amount. (Net income is the "bottom line" on the income statement.)

$6,122,000

6-83. **Retained Earnings** was decreased by $4,390,000, representing a distribution to the shareholders in the form of __________.

dividends

6-84. As a result, the total Retained Earnings on December 31, 19x2, was $__________.

$15,372,000

6-85. Remember that dividends are . . . [an expense / a distribution of earnings to owners]. Dividends are *not*. . . . [an expense / a distribution of earnings to owners].

a distribution of earnings to owners
an expense

INCOME STATEMENT PERCENTAGES

6-86. In an analysis of a business's performance, **percentages** of certain income statement items are usually calculated. **Sales revenue** is taken as 100 percent. One percentage is the **gross margin percentage**, which is found by dividing g _ _ _ _ m _ _ _ _ _ by s _ _ _ _ r _ _ _ _ _ _.

gross margin; sales revenue

6-87. Calculate the gross margin percentage for Garsden Company in 19x2.

$$\frac{\text{Gross margin}}{\text{Sales revenue}} = \frac{\$\_\_\_\_}{\$\_\_\_\_} = \_\_\_\%*$$

$$\frac{\$23,251}{\$75,478} = 31\%$$

*Show only the nearest percent.

6-8. In August, Mogul Shop paid an employee $800 cash for services rendered in August. It had both an ____________________ and an ____________________ of $800 for labor services in August.

expense

expenditure
(either order)

6-9. When an asset is used up or consumed in the operations of the business, an expense is incurred. Thus, an asset gives rise to an . . . [expenditure / expense] when it is acquired, and to an . . . [expenditure / expense] when it is consumed.

expenditure

expense

6-10. When an asset is purchased, there is an ____________________ . When an asset is consumed, there is an ____________________ .

expenditure

expense

6-11. For example, suppose that Irwin Company purchased a supply of fuel oil in 19x1, paying $10,000 cash. No fuel oil was consumed in 19x1. In 19x2, $8,000 of fuel oil was consumed, and in 19x3, $2,000 was consumed. There was an expenditure in ____________ (when?), and there was an expense in ____________________ (when?).

19x1

19x2 and 19x3

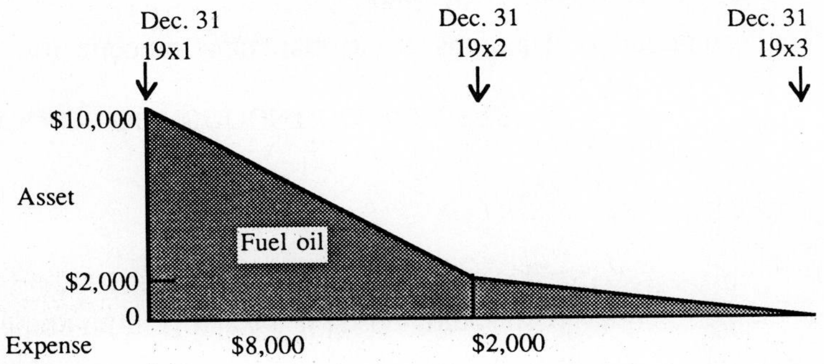

6-12. Between the time of their purchase and the time of their consumption, the resources of a business are assets. Thus, when fuel oil is purchased, there is an expenditure. The fuel oil is an ______________ until consumed. When consumed, it becomes an ____________________ .

asset

expense

6-75. To arrive at net income, **dividends** . . . [are / are not] subtracted from revenues. Therefore dividends . . . [are / are not] an expense. Dividends are a distribution of earnings to shareholders.

are not
are not

6-76. Revenues are defined as . . . [increases / decreases] in the __________ __________ item on the balance sheet. Expenses are . . . [increases / decreases] in that item. Net income is the difference between __________ and __________.

increases
retained earnings
decreases
revenues; expenses

6-77. Because income is always supposed to be the *difference* between sales revenue and expenses, a term such as "sales income" . . . [is / is not] a misleading term. However, it is sometimes used.

is

A PACKAGE OF ACCOUNTING REPORTS

6-78. An income statement is a summary of certain changes in R_ _ _ _ _ _ _ E_ _ _ _ _ _ _ that have taken place during a(n) __________ __________.

Retained Earnings
accounting period

6-79. In other words, a(n) __________ __________ (what accounting report?) reports certain changes in Retained Earnings that have taken place between two __________ __________ (what accounting reports?).

income statement
balance sheets

6-80. Thus, a useful accounting "report package" consists of a(n) __________ __________ *at the beginning of* the accounting period, a(n) __________ __________ *for* the period, and a(n) __________ __________ *at the end of* the period.

balance sheet
income statement
balance sheet

6-81. Exhibit 8 shows a financial report package consisting of an income statement and two balance sheets. Exhibit 8 shows that the Retained Earnings on December 31, 19x1, was $__________.

$13,640,000

6-13. Irwin Company purchased a two-year supply of fuel oil in 19x1 paying $10,000. None of it was consumed in 19x1, $8,000 was consumed during 19x2, and $2,000 in 19x3. The balance sheet item for the asset Fuel Oil Inventory will show the following amounts:

As of December 31, 19x1	$	$10,000
As of December 31, 19x2	$	$ 2,000
As of December 31, 19x3	$	$ 0

6-14. Irwin Company purchased a two-year supply of fuel oil in 19x1, paying $10,000. None was consumed in 19x1, $8,000 was consumed in 19x2, and $2,000 in 19x3. The item Fuel Oil Expense on the income statements will be as follows:

For the year 19x1	$	$ 0
For the year 19x2	$	$ 8,000
For the year 19x3	$	$ 2,000

6-15. Over the life of a business, most expenditures . . . [will / will not] become expenses, but in a single accounting period, expenses . . . [are / are not] necessarily the same as expenditures.

will

are not

UNEXPIRED AND EXPIRED COSTS

6-16. All expenditures result in costs. When inventory or other assets are acquired, they are recorded at their acquisition c _ _ _. Expenses are the c _ _ _ of the resources used up in an accounting period.

cost

cost

6-17. Expenditures result in costs. Costs that are used up or consumed in a period are e _ _ _ _ _ _ s. Costs that are represented by resources on hand at the end of the period are a _ _ _ _ s.

expenses

assets

6-18. Costs that have been consumed are gone; they have **expired**. Costs of resources still on hand are **unexpired**. You will find it useful to think of expenses as . . . [expired / unexpired] costs and assets as . . . [expired / unexpired] costs.

expired; unexpired

6-68. The item on the second line is labeled ________ ___ ________. It reports the cost of the goods or services whose revenue is reported on the first line. This is an example of the ____________________ concept.	Cost of Sales matching
6-69. The difference between sales and cost of sales is called __________ ______________ on Exhibit 8. Write an equation (i.e., in the form $A = B - C$) using the terms **cost of sales, sales revenue,** and **gross margin.**	gross margin
______________ = ______________ - ______________	gross margin = sales revenue – cost of sales
6-70. Exhibit 8 shows that ______________ ______________ are subtracted from gross margin, leaving ______________ __________ ____________.	operating expenses income before taxes
6-71. In accordance with the m _ _ _ _ _ _ _ concept, these expenses include costs related to the current p _ _ _ _ _ and costs that do not benefit future periods.	matching period
6-72. The next item on Exhibit 8, ______________ ______ ______________ ________, is shown separately because it is an especially important expense.	provision for income taxes
6-73. The final item on an income statement is called ____________ ________________ (or **net loss,** if expenses were larger than revenues).	net income
6-74. If the entity had a large, unusual, and nonrecurring loss or gain, this amount would be shown separately just above net income and labeled **extraordinary loss or gain.**	
Loss from destruction caused by an earthquake is an example of an ______________________ loss, and a profit from the sale of part of the business is an example of an ______________________ gain.	extraordinary extraordinary

6-19. Irwin Company purchased $10,000 of fuel oil in 19x1, consumed $8,000 of it in 19x2, and consumed $2,000 in 19x3. At the end of 19x1, the total expenditure of $10,000 was an an . . . , [asset / expense] because none of the cost had expired. In 19x2, $8,000 of the cost expired, and $8,000 was therefore an . . . [asset / expense] in 19x2. At the end of 19x2, $2,000 was an unexpired cost and therefore an . . . [asset / expense]. The remaining $2,000 expired in 19x3, so it was an . . . [asset / expense] in 19x3.

asset

expense

asset

expense

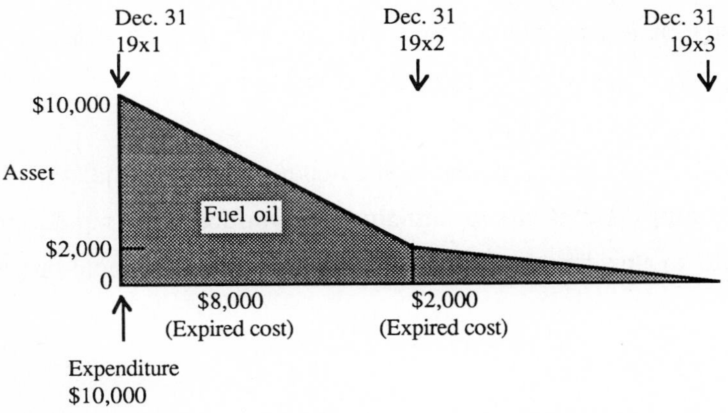

MATCHING CONCEPT

6-20. The principal task of the accountant is to measure the income of an accounting period. Income is the difference between r _ _ _ _ _ _ s and e _ _ _ _ _ _ s of the period.

revenues

expenses

6-21. As you learned in Part 5, the concept governing the recognition of revenues of a period is the r _ _ _ _ _ _ _ _ _ _ concept, which is that revenue is recognized in the period in which goods or services are d _ _ _ _ _ _ ed.

realization

delivered

6-22. The concept governing the recognition of expenses of a period is the **matching** concept. It is that **costs associated with the revenues of a period are expenses of that period.**

(No answer required.)

6-23. To illustrate, consider an automobile that Bryan Company, an automobile dealer, bought for $6,000 in March and sold (i.e. delivered) for $8,000 in May. At the end of March, the automobile was in the Bryan Company inventory, so its cost was . . . [expired / unexpired]. At the end of April, its cost was still . . . [expired / unexpired].

unexpired

unexpired

6-64. According to Exhibit 7, cash transactions in June were:

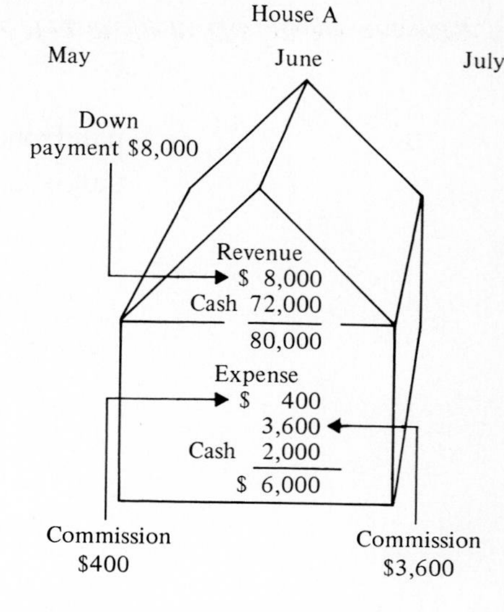

	Event	Cash Increases	Cash Decreases
2	Down payment on House *B*	$12,000	
5	Final payment on House *A*	72,000	
30	Commission on House *B*		$600
	General expenses for June		2,000

In June, Cash increased by a net amount of $________. This increase . . . [was approximately the same as / had no relation to] the $4,000 income for June.

$81,400 (= $84,000 – $2,600)
had no relation to

THE INCOME STATEMENT

6-65. The equities section of a balance sheet shows the two sources of equity capital: (1) the capital supplied by equity investors (i.e., proprietors, partners, shareholders), which is called Paid-in C_ _ _ _ _ _; and (2) that portion of the earnings resulting from profitable operations that have been retained in the entity, which is called R_ _ _ _ _ _ _ E_ _ _ _ _ _ _ .

Capital

Retained Earnings

6-66. The amount added to Retained Earnings as a result of profitable operations during a period is the **income** of the period. An i_ _ _ _ _ statement explains how this income was earned.

income
(The income statement is also called a Profit and Loss, or P&L statement.)

6-67. There is no standard format for an income statement. The lower portion of Exhibit 8 shows one common format. The first item on this income statement is ________ __________, which is the amount of products (i.e. goods and services) __________ during the period.

Sales Revenue
delivered

6-24. Bryan Company bought an automobile for $6,000 in March and sold it for $8,000 in May.

In May, Bryan Company recognizes $8,000 of ____________________ from the sale of this automobile. It must m _ _ _ _ the $6,000 of cost with this revenue. Thus, its expense in May is $6,000. The $8,000 of revenue and the $6,000 of expense relate to the same automobile. The expense **matches** the revenue.

revenue
match

OTHER ASSETS THAT WILL BECOME EXPENSES

6-25. When products are delivered, their costs are matched with revenues in the period in which the sale takes place. These costs become expenses of that period. This is one application of the m _ _ _ _ _ _ _ concept. Other costs associated with activities of the period are also expenses.

matching

6-26. If expenditures were made in an earlier period, the unexpired costs are a _ _ _ _ s until the period in which the expense is recognized. We shall consider serveral examples. The first is an intangible asset.

assets

6-27. A **tangible asset** has physical substance; an **intangible asset** does not have physical substance. Buildings, equipment, and inventories of goods are . . . [tangible / intangible] assets. The protection provided by an insurance policy is a(n) . . . [tangible / intangible] asset.

tangible
intangible

6-28. The general name for intangible assets that will become expenses in a future period is **prepaid expenses**. The asset account may identify the particular type of prepaid expense. Thus, the name of the asset account that shows the cost incurred for insurance protection in future periods is P________________ Insurance.

Prepaid

6-60. The **matching** concept requires that the costs associated with the revenues of a period be recognized as expenses of that period. Therefore, the two commissions associated with House *A*, totaling $__________ , should be recognized as expenses in __________ (what month?), even though they were not paid in that month.

$4,000
June

6-61. In accordance with the realization concept, the $12,000 down payment received on House B in June . . . [was / was not] revenue in June. It will be revenue in __________ (what month?). Because Homes, Inc., has an obligation to deliver the house, the $12,000 is a(n) . . .[asset / liability] on the balance sheet at the end of June.

was not
July
liability

6-62. The matching concept says that general costs of operations during any period are expenses of that period. Thus the $2,000 general costs of operations in June are expenses in __________ (what month?)

June

6-63. Refer to Frames 6-57 through 6-62 and complete the income statement for Homes, Inc., for the month of June, applying the realization concept and the matching concept.

HOMES, INC.

Income Statement for June

			Answer
Sales Revenue		$	$80,000 (= $8,000 + $72,000)
Expenses:			
Cost of House	$		$70,000
Commission Expense			4,000 (= $400 + $3,600)
General Expense			2,000
Total Expense			76,000
Income		$	$ 4,000

6-29. Bryan Company purchased a two-year insurance policy on December 31, 19x1, for $2,000.

The effect of this expenditure is a decrease in Cash and an increase in the asset Prepaid Insurance. Record the journal entry for this transaction.

Dr. ______________ ______________ 2,000

Cr. ______________ 2,000

Dr. Prepaid Insurance 2,000

Cr. Cash 2,000

6-30. Bryan Company purchased a two-year insurance policy on December 31, 19x1, for $2,000.

During 19x2 Bryan Company used up half of this insurance protection, thereby incurring $1,000 of insurance expense. The effect on the accounts in 19x2 is a decrease in the asset Prepaid Insurance and a corresponding amount of Insurance Expense. Make the journal entry for 19x2.

Dr. ______________ ______________ ...... ________

Cr. ______________ ______________ ...... ________

Dr. Insurance Expense 1,000

Cr. Prepaid Insurance ... 1,000

On December 31, 19x2, the balance in the asset account Prepaid Insurance would be $______________.

$1,000

6-31. Bryan Company purchased a two-year policy on December 31, 19x1, for $2,000.

During 19x3 Bryan Company received the remaining $1,000 of insurance protection. Make the journal entry for 19x3.

Dr. ______________ ______________ ...... ________

Cr. ______________ ______________ ...... ________

Dr. Insurance Expense 1,000

Cr. Prepaid Insurance ... 1,000

On December 31, 19x3, the amount of insurance protection has completely expired. The balance in the Prepaid Insurance account on that date therefore is $ ______________ .

zero

6-56. Delivery of the deed to a house is delivery of the ownership of the house. Exhibit 7 states that for House *A* this happened in ________ (what month?); therefore, revenue from the sale of House *A* is recognized in ____________ (what month?).

June

June

6-57. The amount of revenue for House *A* is measured by two transactions. List these below and find the revenue for House *A*.

Date	Transaction*	Amount
May 2		$
June 5		
	Revenue from House *A*	$

*Write a brief description of the transaction.

Date	Transaction	Amount
May 2	Down payment	$ 8,000
June 5	Final payment	72,000
	Revenue from House *A*	$80,000

6-58. Now consider the costs that are associated with this total revenue of $80,000 in June. One of these costs was the cost of House A, which was $________________.

$70,000

6-59. Two of the cash payments related to the sale of House *A*. What were these cash decreases?

Date	Transaction	Amount
		$
	Total	$

Date	Transaction	Amount
May 15	Commission	$ 400
July 2	Commission	$ 3,600
	Total	$ 4,000

6-32. Similarly, if Carter Company made an advance payment of $1,800 to its landlord on January 31 for two months' rent, its asset account P _ _ _ _ _ _ Rent would have a balance of $________ on January 31, a balance of $__________ on February 28, and a balance of $__________ on March 31. Its rent expense would be $________ in February and $__________ in March.

Prepaid; $1,800
$900; $0
$900
$900

6-33. Buildings and equipment also benefit future periods. They are assets like Prepaid Insurance and Prepaid Rent, except that they usually have a longer life and therefore benefit . . . [more / fewer] future periods. The amount reported as an asset on the balance sheet is the . . . [expired / unexpired] cost as of the balance sheet date.

more
unexpired

6-34. Also, as with insurance and rent, the amount of building and equipment cost that is reported as an expense in each period is the amount of . . . [expired / unexpired] cost in that period.

expired

6-35. The expired cost for buildings and equipment is called **Depreciation Expense**. If Bryan Company bought a machine for $5,000 and expected it to provide service for five years, the amount of expired cost in each year would be 1/5 of $5,000. In each of the five years D _ _ _ _ _ _ _ _ _ _ _ E _ _ _ _ _ _ would be reported as $__________. Procedures for estimating depreciation expense and accounting for depreciation are described in Part 8.

Depreciation
Expense; $1,000

EXPENSES THAT CREATE LIABILITIES

6-36. So far we have described expenditures that first were assets and then became expenses as the costs expired. We now describe expenses for which the related expenditures are liabilities.

(No answer required.)

SUMMARY OF MATCHING CONCEPT

6-50. Three types of costs are expenses of the current period. First, there are the costs of the goods and services that are delivered in the current period and whose r _ _ _ _ _ _ _ are recognized in that period.

revenues

6-51. Second, there are costs that are associated with activities of the period. The expenditures for these costs were made either in the current period or in an earlier period. If made in an earlier period, these amounts are a__________ on the balance sheet as of the beginning of the current period.

assets

6-52. Third, there are losses that are recognized in the current period. These may recognize a reasonably possible decrease in a(n) . . . [asset / liability] because of fire, theft or other reasons. Or, they may recognize a reasonably possible increase in a(n) . . . [asset / liability] arising from events occurring in the period, such as a law suit.

asset

liability

6-53. The cash payments associated with these expenses may have been made in a prior period or in the current period; or they may be made in a future period, when the . . . [assets / liabilities] are paid.

liabilities

6-54. The balance sheet at the **beginning** of a period reports assets obtained as a result of e _ _ _ _ _ _ _ _ _ _ _ s made in earlier periods. Part of these assets will expire and therefore are e _ _ _ _ _ _ s of the current period. The remainder will be carried forward to future periods and will be reported as a _ _ _ _ _ on the balance sheet at the end of the current period.

expenditures

expenses

assets

AN EXAMPLE OF MATCHING

6-55. Homes, Inc. is a company that buys and sells houses. Exhibit 7 in your booklet describes some of its transactions during May, June, and July. These events relate to the sale of two houses, House *A* and House *B*.

We shall measure the income for Homes, Inc. for the month of June.

(No answer required.)

6-37. Amounts earned by the employees of Eastman Company for services performed in 19x1 are e ______ s of 19x1. If Eastman paid its employees one week after the week they worked, the amounts earned in the last week of 19x1 would be a cash disbursement in 19x__(what year?).

expenses

19x2

6-38. Employees of Eastman Company earned $10,000 in the last week of 19x1, for which they were paid in 19x2.

	19x1	Dec. 31	19x2
	Employees earn $10,000		Employees paid $10,000
Expenditure	Yes		No
Expense	Yes		No
Cash paid	No		Yes
		Liability $10,000	

On December 31, 19x1, Eastman Company owed its employees $10,000, and it would report a l _______ y of $10,000 on its December 31, 19x1, balance sheet.

liability

6-39. Liabilities for expenses incurred but not yet paid for are called **accrued liabilities.** Account titles may describe the nature of the liability, in this case A ______ Salaries.

Accrued

6-40. In the last week of 19x1, Eastman Company had a salary expense of $10,000, which was not paid to its employees. Write the journal entry for this transaction.

Dr. __________ __________ .... ______

Cr. __________ __________ .... ______

Dr. Salary Expense 10,000

Cr. Accrued Salaries 10,000

6-45. Prepaid expenses are turned into expenses by a debit to the . . . [asset / expense] account and a credit to the . . . [asset / expense] account. Accrued Liabilities are discharged by a debit to . . . [Cash / Accrued Liabilities] and a credit to . . . [Cash / Accrued Liabilities].

expense; asset
Accrued Liabilities
Cash

6-46. Of course, many items of expense are paid for in cash during the accounting period. Salaries of $90,000 earned in 19x1 and paid for in cash in 19x1 would be recorded in the following entry.

Dr. ______________ ______________ .... ________

Cr. ______________.. ________

Dr. Salary Expense 90,000
Cr. Cash 90,000

LOSSES

6-47. Assets provide benefits to future periods. Suppose Bryan Company owned an uninsured machine that was destroyed by fire in 19x1. The machine . . . [will / will not] benefit future periods. The asset amount carried for the machine expired in 19x1, and this amount is therefore recorded as an ______________ in 19x1.

will not

expense

6-48. Thus, even though an asset does not provide benefits during a period, it is an expense of that period if its cost has expired for any reason. Such expenses are called **losses.** A loss is recorded as an expense . . . [in the period in which the loss occurs / over the periods that the asset was supposed to benefit].

in the period in which the loss occurs

6-49. A loss is recorded as an expense if it is **reasonably possible** that the loss occurred, even though it is not certain. Thus, if a customer sues Bryan Company in 19x1, and if it seems reasonably possible that Bryan Company will lose the law suit, the estimated loss is recorded as an expense . . . [in 19x1 / when the law suit is settled]. This is in accordance with the concept that requires expenses to be recognized when they are reasonably possible, which is the c _ _ _ _ _ _ _ _ _ _ m concept.

in 19x1

conservatism

6-41. Employees are not paid the total amount that they earn. Part of their salary is withheld by the employer, who pays it to the federal government for income taxes. Amounts are also deducted for social security taxes and for other reasons. We shall disregard these complications and assume that total earnings are paid in cash to the employees. In January 19x2, Eastman Company employees are paid the $10,000 owed them for work done in 19x1. This payment removes the liability Accrued Salaries. The journal entry for this transaction would be:

Dr. ______ ______ ...... ______

Cr. ______ .... ______

Dr. Accrued Salaries 10,000

Cr. Cash 10,000

6-42. If Eastman Company paid its December rent of $5,000 in January, it would record the Rent Expense of December 19x1 and the related liability, Accrued Rent, by the following journal entry:

Dr. ______ ______ ...... ______

Cr. ______ ______ .. ______

Dr. Rent Expense 5,000

Cr. Accrued Rent... 5,000

6-43. In January 19x2, Eastman Company paid $5,000 to its landlord for the December 19x1 rent. The journal entry in January would be:

Dr. ______ ______ ...... ______

Cr. ______ .... ______

Dr. Accrued Rent 5,000

Cr. Cash 5,000

6-44. Earlier we saw that if rent is paid *prior to* the period in which the expense was incurred, the amount is first debited to Prepaid Rent, which is a(n) . . . [asset / liability] account. As the previous frame indicates, if rent is paid *after* the period in which the expense was incurred, the entry is made to Accrued Rent, which is a(n) . . . [asset / liability] account.

asset

liability

(Please turn the book around and continue with Frame 6–45.)

EXHIBITS
POST TESTS
ANSWERS TO POST TESTS
GLOSSARY/INDEX

FOR USE WITH

ROBERT N. ANTHONY

4th Edition

ESSENTIALS OF ACCOUNTING

Reprinted with corrections May, 1990.

ISBN 0-201-05906-1
10 11 12 13 14 15 AL 95949392

Exhibits

(Do not consult any Exhibit until you are instructed to do so.)

EXHIBIT 1

GARSDEN COMPANY

Balance Sheet
as of December 31, 1986
(000 omitted)

ASSETS		LIABILITIES AND EQUITIES	
CURRENT ASSETS:		CURRENT LIABILITIES:	
Cash	$ 1,449	Accounts payable	$ 5,602
Marketable Securities (market $248)	246	Bank loan payable	1,000
Accounts receivable, net	9,944	Accrued liabilities	876
Inventories	10,623	Estimated tax liability	1,541
Prepaid expenses	389	Current portion of long-term debt	500
Total current assets	22,651	Total current liabilities	9,519
NONCURRENT ASSETS:		NONCURRENT LIABILITIES:	
Property, plant, equipment, cost	$26,946	Long-term debt, less current portion	2,000
Accumulated depreciation	13,534	Deferred income taxes	824
Property, plant, equipment–net	13,412		
Investments	1,110		
Patents and trademarks	403	Total liabilities	12,343
Goodwill	663		
		EQUITIES	
		Common stock	1,000
		Other paid-in capital	11,256
		Total paid-in capital	12,256
		Retained earnings	13,640
		Total equities	25,896
TOTAL ASSETS	$38,239	TOTAL LIABILITIES AND EQUITIES	$38,239

EXHIBIT 2

GLENDALE MARKET

Transaction	Assets		Liabilities and Equities	
January 2. Glendale market received $10,000 from John Smith and banked the money.	Cash	$10,000	Paid-in capital	$10,000
		$10,000		$10,000
January 3. Glendale Market borrowed $5,000 from a bank, giving a note therefor.	Cash	$15,000	Note payable	$ 5,000
			Paid-in capital	10,000
		$15,000		$15,000
January 4. Glendale Market purchased inventory costing $2,000, paying cash for it.	Cash	$13,000	Note payable	$ 5,000
	Inventory	2,000	Paid-in capital	10,000
		$15,000		$15,000
January 5. Glendale Market sold merchandise for $300 cash that cost $200.	Cash	$13,300	Note payable	$ 5,000
	Inventory	1,800	Paid-in capital	10,000
			Retained earnings	100
		$15,100		$15,100
January 6. Glendale Market purchased and received merchandise for $2,000, agreeing to pay within 30 days.	Cash	$13,300	Account payable	$ 2,000
	Inventory	3,800	Note payable	5,000
			Paid-in capital	10,000
			Retained earnings	100
		$17,100		$17,100
January 7. Merchandise costing $500 was sold for $800, which was received in cash.	Cash	$14,100	Account payable	$ 2,000
	Inventory	3,300	Note payable	5,000
			Paid-in capital	10,000
			Retained earnings	400
		$17,400		$17,400
January 8. Merchandise costing $600 was sold for $900, the customer agreeing to pay $900 within 30 days.	Cash	$14,100	Account payable	$ 2,000
	Account receivable	900	Note payable	5,000
	Inventory	2,700	Paid-in capital	10,000
			Retained earnings	700
		$17,700		$17,700

EXHIBIT 3

ACCOUNTS FOR GREEN COMPANY

Assets

Cash

(Dr.)	(Cr.)
Beg. bal. 1,000	

Accounts Receivable

(Dr.)	(Cr.)
Beg. bal. 3,000	

Inventory

(Dr.)	(Cr.)
Beg. bal. 4,000	

Other Assets

(Dr.)	(Cr.)
Beg. bal. 10,000	

Liabilities and Equities

Accounts Payable

(Dr.)	(Cr.)
	2,000 Beg. bal.

Paid-in Capital

(Dr.)	(Cr.)
	7,000 Beg. bal.

Retained Earnings

(Dr.)	(Cr.)
	9,000 Beg. bal.

EXHIBIT 4

JOURNAL

19		Accounts		Dr.	Cr.
Jan.	2	Cash	√	10,000	
		Paid-in Capital	√		10,000
	3	Cash	√	5,000	
		Notes Payable	√		5,000
	4	Inventory	√	2,000	
		Cash	√		2,000
	5	Cash	√	300	
		Revenues	√		300
	5	Expenses	√	200	
		Inventory	√		200
	6	Inventory	√	2,000	
		Account Payable	√		2,000
	7	Cash	√	800	
		Revenues	√		800
	7	Expenses	√	500	
		Inventory	√		500

EXHIBIT 4 (continued)

JOURNAL

19		Transactions		Dr.	Cr.
Jan.					

EXHIBIT 5

GLENDALE MARKET LEDGER

Cash

Debit	Credit
10,000	2,000
5,000	
300	
800	

Accounts Payable

Debit	Credit
	2,000

Revenues

Debit	Credit
	300
	800

Accounts Receivable

Debit	Credit

Notes Payable

Debit	Credit
	5,000

Expenses

Debit	Credit
200	
500	

Inventory

Debit	Credit
2,000	200
2,000	500

Paid-in Capital

Debit	Credit
	10,000

Income Summary

Debit	Credit

Retained Earnings

Debit	Credit

EXHIBIT 6 FINANCIAL STATEMENTS

GLENDALE MARKET

Balance Sheet as of January 8

Assets		Liabilities and Equities	
Cash	$14,100	Accounts Payable	$
Account receivable		Notes payable	
Inventory		Paid-in capital	
		Retained earnings	
Total assets	$	Total equities	$

Income Statement
for the period January 2–8

Revenues	$
Expenses	
Income	$

EXHIBIT 7

TRANSACTIONS OF HOMES, INC.

Date	Event	Effects on Cash
May 2	Able agrees to buy House *A* from Homes, Inc., and makes an $8,000 down payment.	increase $8,000
May 15	Homes, Inc., pays $400 commission to the salesperson who sold House *A* (5% of cash received).	decrease $400
May	Homes, Inc., general expenses for May were $2,200 (assume for simplicity these were paid in cash in May).	decrease $2,200
June 2	Baker agrees to Buy House *B*, and makes a $12,000 downpayment.	increase $12,000
June 5	Able completes the purchase of House *A*, paying $72,000 cash. Homes, Inc., delivers the deed to Able thereby delivering ownership of the house. (House *A* cost Homes, Inc., $70,000.)	increase $72,000
June 30	Homes, Inc., pays $600 commission to the salesperson who sold House *B*.	decrease $600
June	Homes, Inc., general expenses for June were $2,000	decrease $2,000
July 2	Homes Inc., pays $3,600 additional commission to the salesperson who sold House *A*.	decrease $3,600
July 3	Baker completes the purchase of House *B*, paying $108,000 cash. Homes, Inc., delivers the deed to Baker, thereby delivering ownership of the house. (House *B* cost Homes, Inc., $100,000.)	increase $108,000
July 30	Homes, Inc., pays $5,400 commission to the salesperson who sold House *B*.	decrease $5,400
July	Homes, Inc., general expenses for July were $2,400.	decrease $2,400

EXHIBIT 8

A "PACKAGE" OF ACCOUNTING REPORTS
(000 omitted)

GARSDEN COMPANY

Condensed Balance Sheet
As of December 31, 19x1

Assets

Current assets	$22,651
Buildings and equipment	13,412
Othert assets	2,176
Total Assets	$38,239

Liabilities and Equities

Liabilities	$12,343
Equities:	
Paid-in capital	12,256
Retained earnings	13,640
Total Liabilities and Equities	$38,239

Condensed Balance Sheet
As of December 31, 19x2

Assets

Current assets	$24,062
Buildings and equipment	14,981
Other assets	3,207
Total Assets	$42,250

Liabilities and Equities

Liabilities	$14,622
Equities:	
Paid-in Capital	12,256
Retained Earnings	15,372
Total Liabilities and Equities	$42,250

Income Statement
For the Year 19x2

Sales Revenue	$75,478
Less cost of sales	52,227
Gross margin	23,251
Less operating expenses	10,785
Income before taxes	12,466
Provision for income taxes	6,344
Net income	$6,122

Statement of Retained Earnings

Retained earnings, 12/31/x1	$13,640
Add Net income, 19x2	6,122
	19,762
Less dividends	4,390
Retained earnings, 12/31/x2	$15,372

EXHIBIT 9

Lewis Fuel Company

	Units	Unit Cost	Total Cost
Beginning inventory, April 1	400	1.00	
Purchase, April 10	300	1.10	
Purchase, April 20	300	1.20	
Total goods available			
Ending inventory, April 30	600		
Cost of sales, April			

FIFO Method

Goods available .... $____________

Ending inventory:

______ units @ $______ = $____________

______ units @ $______ = ____________

Total 600 units .... ____________

Cost of sales ____________

LIFO Method

Goods available .... $____________

Ending inventory:

______ units @ $______ = $____________

______ units @ $______ = ____________

Total 600 units .... ____________

Cost of sales ____________

Average-Cost Method

Average cost of [$] / [ ] = ________ cost per unit

Goods available $1,090

Ending inventory 600 units @ $ ________ = ________

Cost of sales 400 units @ $ ________ = ________

EXHIBIT 10

GARSDEN COMPANY

Cash Flow Statement
For the Year 19x2 (000 omitted)

Cash flows from operating activities		
Net income		$ 6,122
Noncash items affecting net income:		
Depreciation	$ 864	
Deferred income taxes	226	
Change in receivables, inventory, payables	1,174	
Subtotal		1,264
Cash flow, operating activities		8,386
Cash flows from financing activities		
Payment of long-term debt	(500)	
Bank loan	1,000	
Dividends paid	(4,390)	
Other	(223)	
Cash flow, financing activities		(4,113)
Cash flows from investing activities		
Acquisition of plant and equipment	(2,433)	
Investments	(731)	
Other	(300)	
Cash flow, investing activities		(3,464)
Net increase in cash		809

( ) indicates decrease in cash

EXHIBIT 11

Accountants' Report

The Shareholders and the Board of Directors of Garsden Company:

We have examined the balance sheets of Garsden Company as of December 31, 1987 and 1986, and the related income statements and cash flow statements for the three-year period ended December 31, 1987. Our examinations were made in accordance with generally accepted auditing standards, and such other auditing procedures as we considered necessary in the circumstances.

In our opinion, the aforementioned financial statements present fairly the financial position of Garsden Company at December 31, 1987 and 1986 and the results of their operations and changes in cash for each of the years in the three year period ended December 31, 1987, in conformity with generally accepted accounting principles applied on a consistent basis.

Deane and Burnham

Boston, Massachusetts
March 1, 1988

EXHIBIT 12

ARLEN COMPANY

Balance Sheet as of December 31, 19x2
(000 omitted)

Assets			Liabilities and Equities	
Current assets			**Current liabilities**	
Cash		$ 20	Accounts payable	$ 30
Accounts recevable		40	Accrued wages and taxes	10
Inventory		60	Estimated income taxes payable	20
Prepaid expenses		20		
Total current assets		140	Total current liabilities	60
Property and plant			**Noncurrent liabilities**	
Land		30	Mortgage bonds	40
Plant	120		Total liabilities	100
Less accumulated depreciation	70			
Net plant		50		
Total property and plant		80	**Shareholder equities**	
			Paid-in capital*	60
			Retained earnings	70
Other assets			Total shareholder equities	130
Goodwill and patents		10	Total liabilities and equities	230
Total assers		230		

* 4,800 shares of common stock outstanding

ARLEN COMPANY

Income Statement 19x2
(000 omitted)

	Dollars	Percentage
Sales revenue	$ 300	100.0
Less cost of sales	180	60.0
Gross margin	120	40.0
Operating expenses	78	26.0
Earnings before interest and taxes	42	14.0
Interest expense	5	1.7
Income before taxes	37	12.3
Provision for income taxes	13	4.3
Net income	24	8.0

EXHIBIT 13

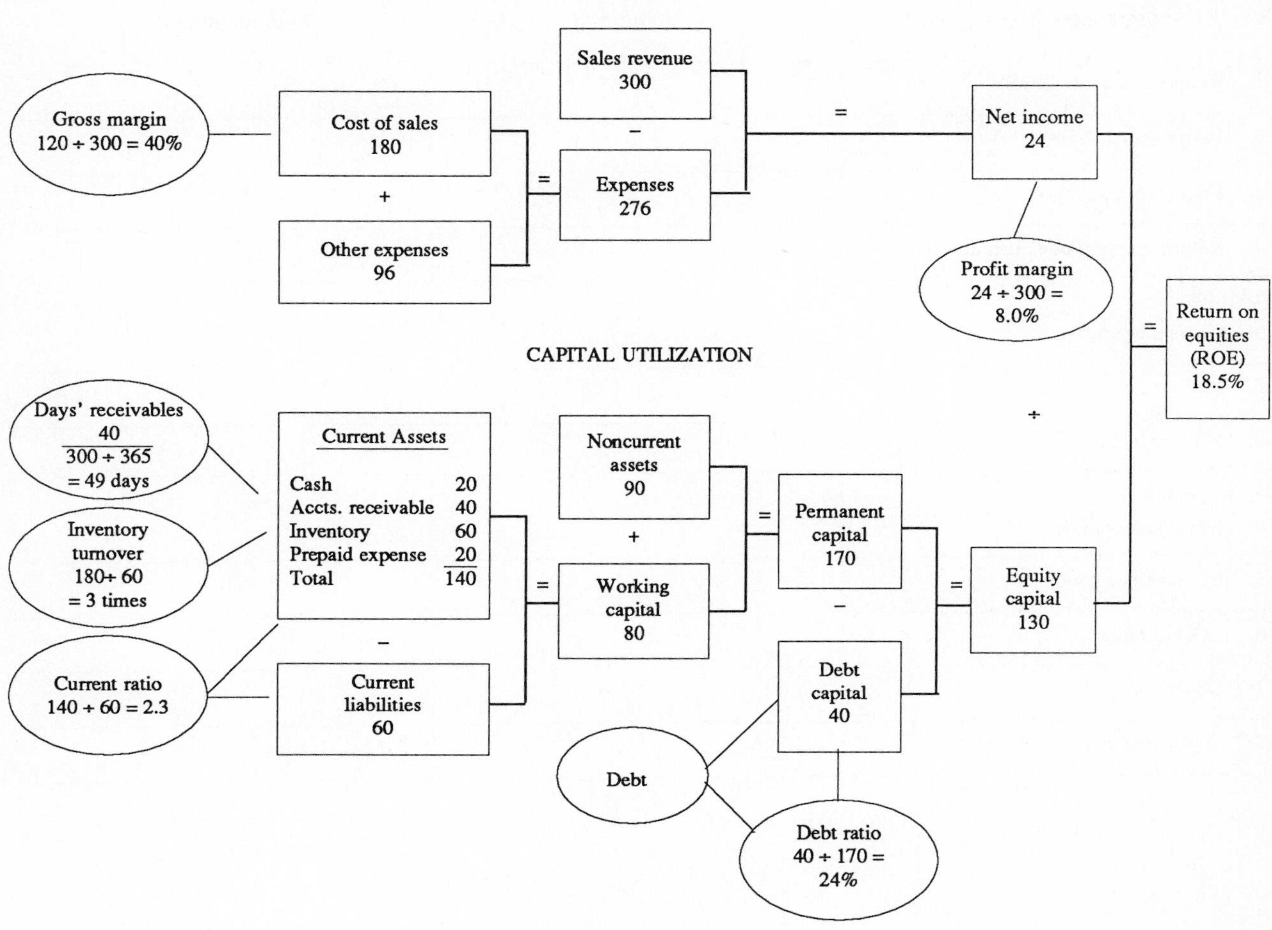

ARLEN COMPANY
Factors Affecting
Return on Equity
PROFITABILITY
Gross margin
120 ÷ 300 = 40%
Cost of sales
180
+
Other expenses
96
=
Sales revenue
300
–
Expenses
276
=
Net income
24
Profit margin
24 ÷ 300 =
8.0%
=
Return on
equities
(ROE)
18.5%
÷
CAPITAL UTILIZATION
Days' receivables
40
300 ÷ 365
= 49 days
Inventory
turnover
180÷ 60
= 3 times
Current ratio
140 ÷ 60 = 2.3
Current Assets
Cash 20
Accts. receivable 40
Inventory 60
Prepaid expense 20
Total 140
–
Current
liabilities
60
=
Noncurrent
assets
90
+
Working
capital
80
=
Permanent
capital
170
–
Debt
capital
40
=
Equity
capital
130
Debt
Debt ratio
40 ÷ 170 =
24%

EXHIBIT 13 (continued)

Some Common Ratios

Overall Performance	Numerator	Denominator
1. Return on equity (ROE)		
2. Earnings per share		
3. Price-earnings ratio		
4. Return on permanent capital		
Profitability 5. Gross margin %		
6. Profit margin %		
7. EBIT margin %		
Capital utilization 8. Days' receivables		
9. Inventory turnover		
10. Current ratio		
11. Debt ratio		
12. Capital turnover		

Post Tests

POST TEST 1

1. Give the accounting name for the following terms:

(a) Things of value owned by the entity ____________ .

(b) Money ____________ .

(c) Claims of creditors ____________ .

(d) Claims of investors ____________ .

2. List the two types of sources of funds, with the type having the stronger claim on the assets coming first:

Stronger claim ____________

Lesser claim ____________

3. A balance sheet reports the status of an entity . . . [at a point in time / over a period of time].

4. Give the fundamental accounting equation:

________ = ____________ + ____________

5. The above equation is consistent with what concept? ....

6. Why are amounts in accounting stated in monetary terms? ....

....

....

7. A balance sheet does not report all the facts about a business. What concept limits the amount of information that can be reported? ....

....

8. Brown Company has $10,000 cash. Fred Foy, its sole owner, withdraws $100 for his own use. Fred Foy is . . . [better off / worse off / no better or worse off] than he was before. Brown Company now has . . . [the same amount of / less] cash. The fact that this event affects Fred Foy differently than it affects Brown Company is an illustration of the ____________ concept.

9. The entity concept states that ....

....

....

10. On December 31, 19x1, Lewis Corporation has $12,000 in cash on hand and in the bank. It owns other things of value, totaling $25,000. Its only debt is a bank loan of $10,000. Prepare a balance sheet for Lewis Corporation as of December 31, 19x1, using the form below:

____

____

____________		____________	
____________	$ ______	____________	$ ______
____________	______	____________	______
Total	$ ______	Total	$ ______

Answers for Post Test 1 are on page 31.

POST TEST 2

1. What is the going-concern concept? ....

....

....

....

2. What is the cost concept? ....

....

....

....

3. Two reasons why assets are usually reported at their cost, rather than at their current market value, are:

(a) ....

....

(b) ....

....

4. An item can be reported as an asset only if it passes three of the following tests. Circle "yes" for these and "no" for the others.

(a) Item is valuable	yes	no
(b) Item is located in a building owned by the entity.	yes	no
(c) Item is used by the entity.	yes	no
(d) The entity has ordered the item	yes	no
(e) Item was acquired at a measurable cost.	yes	no
(f) Item is owned or controlled by the entity.	yes	no

5. The following items are *not* assets. Using the letters in Question 4, give the test each does not pass.

(a) Office space rented by the entity ______

(b) Inventory that no one will buy ______

(c) The entity's valuable reputation for providing excellent service to customers ______

6. "Goodwill'" refers to what things? ....

....

....

....

....

7. An asset is classified as "current" if it is cash or expected to be converted into cash in the near future, usually within .... [what time period?].

8. A liability is classified as "current" if it becomes due in the near future, usually within .... [what time period?].

9. Marketable securities are . . . [current / non-current] assets. Investments are. . . [current / non-current] assets.

10. Give an example of inventory ....

....

....

....

11. Give an example of a prepaid expense ....

....

....

....

....

12. Give an example of property and plant ....

....

....

....

....

13. On December 31, 19x1, Ace Company owed Chemical Bank $10,000, of which $5,000 is due July 1, 19x2, and $5,000 is due July 1, 19x3. How should this liability be reported?

(a) $10,000 as a current liability

(b) $5,000 as a current liability and $5,000 as a noncurrent liability

(c) $10,000 as a noncurrent liability

14. On December 31, 19x1, Ace Company had an asset, prepaid insurance, that provided insurance protection for the two years 19x2 and 19x3. How should this asset be reported?

(a) $2,000 as a current asset

(b) $1,000 as a current asset and $1,000 as a noncurrent asset

(c) $2,000 as a noncurrent asset

15. Parker Company operates a furniture store. On December 31, 19x1, it had 30 desks that it was holding for sale. These would be reported as ________________. The desk that is used by the president of Parker Company would be reported as ________________________________.

16. Fox Company sold $1,000 of goods on credit to Golden Company. This would be recorded as an account . . . [receivable / payable] of Fox Company and as an account . . . [receivable / payable] of Golden Company.

17. Indicate whether the following statements about the balance sheet of a corporation are true or false.

(a) Assets list all the valuable things owned by the entity................. T F

(b) The amount reported for the paid-in-capital item is approximately the market value of the stock ... T F

(c) The amount reported for total equities is approximately the market value of the corporation's stock .... T F

(d) Total equities (also called "net worth") show approximately what the entity is worth .... T F

(e) Retained earnings is the amount of cash retained in the entity .... T F

(f) Land is reported at approximately what it is worth .... T F

18. Give the numerator and the denominator of the current ratio:

Numerator ________________________

Denominator

Answers for Post Test 2 are on page 31–32.

POST TEST 3

1. On January 2, John Brown started the Brown Company. In January, Brown Company did the following things.

(a) It received $5,000 cash from John Brown as its capital.

(b) It borrowed $10,000 from a bank, giving a note therefor.

(c) It purchased $4,000 of inventory for cash.

(d) It sold $2,000 of its inventory for $6,000 to a customer, who paid $3,500 cash and agreed to pay $2,500 within 30 days.

(e) It purchased an auto for $7,000. It paid $2,000 down and gave a note to the automobile dealer for the remaining $5,000.

(f) Brown withdrew $1,000 cash for his personal use.

(g) Brown was offered $10,000 for his equity in the business, but he refused the offer.

Prepare a balance sheet for Brown Company as of the close of business January 31, and prepare an income statement for January.

2. Brown Company's income was $4,000, but its Retained Earnings was only $3,000. Explain the difference.

3. John Brown claims that the inventory as of January 31 is worth $6,000, as shown by the fact that inventory costing $2,000 was actually sold for $6,000. Would you change the balance sheet? ______ Why or why not? ....

....

....

....

....

....

....

Answers for Post Test 3 are on page 32.

POST TEST 4

1. The following transactions occurred in Kay Company in March. Prepare journal entries for each of them in the journal given on the next page:

March 5 Purchased $6,000 of inventory, paying cash.

March 10 Made a $15,000 sale to a customer who paid $6,000 cash and agreed to pay the other $9,000 in 30 days. The merchandise sold had cost $8,000.

2. Post these entries to the ledger accounts on the next page.

3. Prepare closing entries for March in the journal and post these entries.

4. Prepare a balance sheet as of March 31 and an income statement for March.

5. Complete the following Table, by placing an X in the proper column.

	Debits	Credits
Increases in asset accounts are	______	______
Decreases in asset accounts are	______	______
Increases in liability accounts are	______	______
Decreases in liability accounts are	______	______
Increases in equity accounts are	______	______
Decreases in equity accounts are	______	______
Increases in revenue accounts are	______	______
Increases in expense accounts are	______	______

6. A critic said that the company had $25,000 cash at the beginning of March and $25,000 at the end of March, and since its cash balance was unchanged, it couldn't be said to have any income in March. Explain why this criticism is incorrect.

JOURNAL

19x1		Transactions	L.F.	Dr.	Cr.

Cash

Bal. 25,000

Accounts Receivable

Bal. 11,000

Inventory

Bal. 40,000

Property and Plant

Bal. 30,000

Accounts Payable

16,000 Bal.

Paid-in Capital

60,000 Bal.

Retained Earnings

30,000 Bal.

Revenues

Expenses

Income Summary

Answers for Post Test 4 are on page 33.

POST TEST 5

1. What are the two parts to the conservatism concept?

(a) ....

....

(b) ....

....

2. What are the two parts to the materiality concept?

(a) ....

....

(b) ....

....

3. What is the length of the usual accounting period? .... Financial statements prepared for shorter periods are called ________________ statements.

4. Cash accounting reports only items that increase or decrease cash. Accrual accounting reports items that change .... (what balance sheet category?), even though these changes may not affect cash.

5. Increases in equity associated with the entity's operations during a period are ________________, and decreases are ________________. The difference between them is labeled ________________.

6. The realization concept states that revenues are recognized when goods or services are ....

....

7. Hartwell Company manufactures a table in August and places it in its retail store in September. Ralph Smith, a customer, agrees to buy the table in October, it is delivered to him in November, and he pays the bill in December. In what month is the revenue recognized? ....

8. The receipt of cash is a debit to Cash. What is the offsetting credit for the following types of sales transaction?

	Account credited
(a) Cash received prior to delivery	____________
(b) Cash received in same period as delivery	____________
(c) Cash received after the period of delivery	____________

9. Similarly, revenue is a credit entry. What is the offsetting debit when revenue is recognized in each of these periods?

	Account debited
(a) Revenue recognized prior to receipt of cash	____________
(b) Revenue recognized in same period as receipt of cash	____________
(c) Revenue recognized in period following receipt of cash	____________

10. In February, Hartwell Company agrees to sell a table to a customer for \$600, and the customer makes a down payment of \$100 at that time. The cost of the table is \$400. The table is delivered to the customer in March, and the customer pays the remaining \$500 in April. Using the journal on the next page, give the entries (if any) that would be made in February, March, and April for both the revenue and expense aspects of this transaction. Be sure to label each entry with the proper month.

JOURNAL

19x1		Transactions	L.F.	Dr.	Cr.

11. At the end of 19x1, Maypo Company had accounts receivable of $200,000, and it estimated that $2,000 of this amount was a bad debt. Its revenue in 19x1, with no allowance for the bad debts, was $600,000.

(a) What account should be debited for the $2,000 bad debt? ....

....

(b) What account should be credited? ....

....

(c) What amount would be reported as *net* accounts receivable on the balance sheet?

____

(d) What amount would be reported as revenue on the 19x1 income statement? __________

12. In 19x2, the $2,000 of bad debt was written off.

(a) What account should be debited for this write off? ....

(b) What account should be credited? ....

....

13. Give the numerator and the denominator of the days' receivable ratio:

Numerator ____________________

Denominator

Answers for Post Test 5 are on page 34.

POST TEST 6

1. An expenditure occurs in the period in which goods or services are . . . [acquired / consumed]. An expense occurs in the period in which goods or services are . . . [acquired / consumed].

2. For each of the following events, state the month in which the expenditure and the expense should be recorded.

	Month of Expenditure	Month of Expense
(a) Inventory is ordered in February, received in March, paid for in April, delivered to a customer in May; customer pays in June.	________	________
(b) Wages are earned in February and paid to employees in March.	________	________
(c) Fuel oil was received in February, paid for in March, and consumed in April.	________	________
(d) Rent was paid in February for the use of the premises in March.	________	________

3. A certain asset was acquired in May. There was therefore an ________________ in May. At the end of May, the item was either on hand, or it was not. If it was on hand, it was an ____________; if not on hand, it was an ________________ in May.

4. Productive assets are . . . [expired / unexpired] costs. Expenses are . . . [expired / unexpired] costs.

5. State the matching concept: ....

....

....

....

6. Expenses of a period consist of:

(a) ....

....

....

(b) ....

....

....

(c) ....

7. If Brown Company pays rent prior to the period that the rent covers, the amount is initially reported as a credit to cash and a debit to ________________ Rent, which is a(n) . . . [asset / liability] account. If Brown Company pays rent after the period covered, the amount is initially recorded as a debit to Rent Expense and a credit to ________________ Rent, which is a(n) . . . [asset / liability] account.

8. A brand new machine owned by Fay Company was destroyed by fire in 19x1. It was uninsured. It had been purchased for $10,000 with the expectation that it would be useful for five years. The expense (i.e., loss) recorded in 19x1 should be . . . [$2,000 / $10,000].

9. What is gross margin? ....

....

10. Give the numerator and the denominator of the gross margin percentage:

$$\frac{\text{Numerator}}{\text{Denominator}}$$

11. The term *net income* means ....

....

....

12. Dividends are not an expense. They are .....

....

13. Give an equation that uses the terms (a) net income, (b) dividends, (c) retained earnings at the beginning of the period, and (d) retained earnings at the end of the period.

____

Answers for Post Test 6 are on page 34–35.

POST TEST 7

1. A dealer sells a television set for $800 cash. It had cost $600. Write journal entries for the *four* accounts affected by this transaction.

Dr. ________________________ ________

Cr. ________________________ ________

Dr. ________________________ ________

Cr. ________________________ ________

2. What is meant by the perpetual inventory method? ....

....

....

....

....

3. Write an equation that shows how the cost of sales is determined by deduction ....

....

....

....

4. In the equation above, how were the following amounts found:

(a) Ending inventory ....

....

(b) Beginning inventory ....

....

5. From the information given below, calculate cost of sales for July and inventory at the end of July by the (a) FIFO, (b) LIFO, and (c) average cost methods.

	Quantity of Units	Unit Cost	Total Cost
Inventory, July 1	400	$1.00	
Purchase, July 15	200	1.20	
Total goods available			
Inventory, July 31	300		

Method Used	Cost of Sales	Inventory July 31
(a) FIFO	$	$
(b) LIFO		
(c) Average Cost		

6. In periods of inflation, many companies use the LIFO method in calculating their taxable income. Why? ....

....

....

....

7. A company discovers that the market value of its inventory is $1,000 lower than its cost. What journal entry should it make?

Dr. ______________________ ________

Cr. ______________________ ________

8. In a manufacturing business, what three elements enter into the cost of a manufactured item?

....

9. In what period do period costs become an expense? ....

....

....

10. In what period do product costs become an expense? ....

....

....

11. One type of overhead rate makes use of the total direct labor costs and total production overhead costs for a period. Write a ratio that shows how this overhead rate is calculated.

Numerator
____
Denominator

12. A given finished item requires $50 of direct materials and 5 hours of direct labor at $8 per hour. The overhead rate is $4 per direct labor hour. At what amount would the finished item be shown in inventory? $______________ .

13. How is the inventory turnover ratio calculated?

Numerator
____
Denominator

14. An inventory turnover of 5 is generally . . . [better / worse] than an inventory turnover of 4. Why? ....

....

....

....

Answers for Post Test 7 are on page 35.

POST TEST 8

1. The amount at which a new plant asset is recorded in the accounts includes its purchase price plus what other elements of cost? ....

....

....

....

....

....

2. A plant asset is acquired in 19x1. It is expected to be worn out at the end of 10 years and to become obsolete in five years. What is its service life? ______________ years

3. Land is ordinarily not depreciated. Why not?

....

....

4. A plant asset is acquired in 19x1 at a cost of $20,000. Its estimated service life is 10 years, and its estimated residual value is $2,000.

(a) The estimated depreciable cost of the asset is $__________.

(b) If the straight-line depreciation method is used, the depreciation rate for this asset is __________.

(c) What amount will be recorded as depreciation expense in each year of the asset's life? $__________.

(d) What account will be debited and what account will be credited to record this depreciation expense?

Dr ....

Cr ....

(e) After five years have elapsed, how would this asset be reported on the balance sheet?

(1)* .... $__________

(2)* .... __________

(3)* .... __________

---

*Fill in the name below.

(1) ....

(2) ....

(3) ....

5. A machine is purchased on January 1, 19x1, for $20,000, and it has an expected life of five years and no estimated residual value.

(a) If the machine is still in use six years later, what amount of depreciaion expense will be reported for the sixth year? ....

(b) What amount, if any, will be reported on the balance sheet at the end of the sixth year?

Answer: (1) It will not be reported.

or

(2) It will be reported as follows:

__________ .... $ __________

__________ .... __________

__________ .... __________

6. A machine is purchased on January 1, 19x1, for $50,000. It has an expected service life of 10 years and no residual value. Eleven years later it is sold for $3,000 cash.

(a) There will be a . . . [loss / gain] of $__________.

(b) What account will be debited and what account credited to record this amount?

Dr. ....

Cr. ....

7. Give an example of each of the following types of assets, and give the name of the process used in writing off the cost of the second and third type.

Asset type	Example	Write-off process
Plant asset	__________	Depreciation
Wasting asset	__________	__________
Intangible asset	__________	__________

8. Conoil Company purchased a producing oil property for $10,000,000 on January 1, 19x1. It estimated that the property contained one million barrels of oil and that the property had a service life of 20 years. In 19x1, 40,000 barrels of oil were recovered from the property. What amount should be charged as an expense in 19x1? $__________.

9. Wasting assets and intangible assets are reported on the balance sheet in a different way than building, equipment, and similar plant assets. What is this difference? ....

....

....

....

10. In calculating its taxable income, a company tries to report its income as ________________ as it can. In calculating its financial accouting income, a company tries to report its income as ________________ as it can.

11. What is the "half-year convention" in calculating depreciation? ....

....

....

....

12. As compared with straight-line depreciation, accelerated depreciation writes off . . . [more / the same / less] depreciation in the early years of an asset's life and . . . [more / the same / less] in the later years. Over the whole life of the asset, accelerated depreciation writes off . . . [more / the same / less] total cost as straight-line depreciation.

13. Why do companies usually use accelerated depreciation in tax accounting? ....

....

....

....

14. Assume an income tax rate of 50%. If a company calculated its financial accounting income (before income taxes) in 19x1 as $6 million and its taxable income as $4 million, what amount would it report as income tax expense on its 19x1 income statement? $_______________ .

15. Fill in the missing name on the following table.

Income tax expense	$100,000
Income tax paid	− 60,000
....	$ 40,000

The $40,000 would be reported on the balance sheet as a(n) . . . [asset / liability].

Answers for Post Test 8 are on page 36.

POST TEST 9

1. The term *working capital* means ....

....

....

....

2. The two principal sources of a company's permanent capital are: ....

.... and

....

3. Bonds obligate the company to ....

.... and also

....

Bonds are . . . [never / sometimes / always] current liabilities.

4. The two principal sources of equity capital are

....

and ....

5. A corporation issues 1,000 shares of $1 par value common stock in exchange for $10,000 cash. Complete the journal entry for this transaction.

Dr. ___Cash___ ___10,000___

Cr.______________________ ______

______________________ ______

6. The equities section of a balance sheet is as follows:

Common stock (1,000 shares, no par value)	$10,000
Other paid-in capital	20,000
Retained earnings	40,000
Total equities	$70,000

Circle the correct answer to the following:

(a) The stated value per share is: $10, $30, $70, can't tell.

(b) The company received from its shareholder: $10,000, $30,000, $70,000, can't tell.

(c) The shareholders' equity is worth: $10,000, $30,000, $70,000, can't tell.

(d) The company has cash of at least: $20,000, $40,000, $70,000, can't tell.

(e) The company's income to date has totaled: $40,000, at least $40,000, can't tell.

(f) If the company is liquidated, the shareholders will receive at least: $10,000, $30,000, $70,000, can't tell.

7. The dollar amount reported for common stock on the balance sheet is the amount for the number of shares . . . [authorized / issued]. This amount is called the amount ____________________.

8. Kay Company had 200,000 shares of stock authorized. It issued 150,000 shares. It later bought back 10,000 shares. The 10,000 shares are called ____________________ stock. The total shareholder equity on the balance sheet would be the amount for ____________________ shares.

9. Preferred shareholders usually have preference as to .... and also as to

....

....

10. A cash dividend . . . [increases / decreases / does not change] shareholder equity. A stock dividend . . . [increases / decreases / does not change] shareholder equity. A stock dividend . . . [increases / decreases / does not change] the number of shares of stock outstanding.

11. Circle the correct words in the following table, which shows the principal differences between debt capital and equity capital.

	Bonds (Debt)	Stock (Equity)
Annual payments are required.	[Yes / No]	[Yes / No]
Principal payments are required.	[Yes / No]	[Yes / No]
Therefore, risk to the entity is	[High / Low]	[High / Low]
But its cost is relatively	[High / Low]	[High / Low]

12. Corcoran Company has the following permanent capital:

Debt capital	$ 80,000
Equity capital	20,000
Total	$100,000

(a) Its debt ratio is ____________________%

(b) The company is said to be highly ____________________.

13. Able Company owns 51 percent of the stock of Charlie Company, 50 percent of the stock of David Company, and 49 percent of the stock of Eastern Company. Able Company is the ______________ company. The accounts of ______________ Company and ______________ Company would be consolidated in consolidated financial statements. The equity of the shareholders who own 49 percent of the stock of Charlie Company would be reported as the item ______________ on the consolidated balance sheet.

14. Able Company's income statement reported revenue of $1,000,000, of which $10,000 was sales to Charlie Company. Charlie Company's income statement reported revenue of $500,000, of which $20,000 was sales to Able Company. Revenue on the consolidated income statement would be reported as $______________ .

Answers for Post Test 9 are on page 36–37.

POST TEST 10

The following financial statements are to be used in answering questions 1 through 9.

KAY COMPANY

Balance Sheet as of December 31, 19x1

Assets		Liabilities and Equities	
Current assets		Current liabilities	40
Cash	10	Noncurrent liabilities ..	80
Accounts receivable	30	Equities	100
Inventory	20		
Other	40		
Subtotal	100		
Noncurrent assets	120	Total liabilities	
Total assets	220	and equities	220

KAY COMPANY

Income Statement for 19x1

Sales revenue	100
Cost of sales	60
Gross margin	40
Operating expenses	10
Earnings before interest and taxes	30
Interest and income taxes	20
Net income	10

1. The current ratio was:

______________ = ______

2. The inventory turnover was:

______________ = ______ times

3. The profit margin percentage was:

______________ = ______ %

4. The debt ratio (to the nearest percent) was:

______________ = ______ %

5. The return on equity investment was:

______________ = ______ %

6. The EBIT margin was:

______________ = ______ %

7. The capital turnover (to one decimal place) was:

______________ = ______ times

8. The pretax return on permanent capital (to the nearest percent) was

______________ = ______ %

9. The pretax return on permanent capital can also be calculated as:

______________ x ______________ = ______ %

Note: This does not exactly check with Question 8 because of rounding.

10. A company can decrease its equities by:

(a) . . . [increasing / decreasing] its assets.

(b) . . . [increasing / decreasing] its liabilities.

11. Liquidity means ....

....

....

....

12. Solvency means ....

....

....

....

13. Following is a portion of a financial statement for Brim Company.

Sources of Cash:	
Net income	$100,000
Depreciation	20,000
(a)______________	(b)__________

(a) What name should be inserted on line (a)?

....

....

(b) What is the amount on line (b)? $________

(c) What is the name of the financial statement of which this is one portion? ....

....

14. Depreciation is not a source of Cash. Why, then, does it appear on the statement shown in question 13? ....

....

15. Give three reasons why accounting cannot provide a complete picture of the status or performance of an entity.

(a) ....

....

(b) ....

....

(c) ....

....

16. Three bases (i.e., standards) that are used in judging an entity's performance are comparisons with

(a) ....

....

(b) ....

....

(c) ....

....

Answers for Post Test 10 are on page 37–38.

Answers for Post Tests

ANSWERS FOR POST TEST 1

1. (a) assets
   (b) cash
   (c) liabilities
   (d) equities

2. liabilities
   equities

3. at a point in time

4. Assets = Liabilities + Equities

5. The dual-aspect concept

6. This is necessary so that amounts can be added together or subtracted from one another.

7. Money-measurement concept

8. no better or worse off; less; entity

9. accounts are kept for entities as distinguished from the persons who own these entities.

10. LEWIS CORPORATION

Balance Sheet as of December 31, 19x1

Assets		Liabilities and Equities	
Cash	$12,000	Liabilities	$10,000
Other assets	25,000	Equities	27,000
Total	$37,000	Total	$37,000

ANSWERS FOR POST TEST 2

1. Going-concern concept: Accounting assumes that an entity will continue to operate indefinitely.

2. Cost concept: Accounting focuses on the cost of assets, rather than on their market value.

3. (a) Market values are subjective.
   (b) Many assets are not likely to be sold, so there is no need to know their market value.

4. Yes: (a), (e), (f)
   No: (b), (c), (d)

5. (a) Test (f)
   (b) Test (a)
   (c) Test (e)

6. A favorable name or reputation purchased by the entity.

7. one year

8. one year

9. current; noncurrent

10. Shoes in a shoe store, groceries in a grocery store

11. Prepaid insurance, prepaid rent

12. A building, an item of equipment, automobiles

13. (b)

14. (a); [(b) is also correct, theoretically, but is not done in practice.]

15. Inventory; property and plant

16. receivable; payable

17. All the statements are false. Assets must have been acquired at a measurable cost. Neither the amount reported as paid-in capital nor the amount of total equities has any necessary relation to market value or what the entity is worth. Retained earnings is not cash; cash is an asset on the left-hand side of the balance sheet. Land is reported at its cost, which is not necessarily the same as what it is now worth.

18. $\frac{\text{Current assets}}{\text{Current liabilities}}$

ANSWERS FOR POST TEST 3

1. BROWN COMPANY

Balance Sheet as of January 31

Assets		Liabilities and Equities	
Cash	$11,500	Notes payable	$15,000
Accounts receivable	2,500	Paid-in capital	5,000
Inventory	2,000	Retained Earnings	3,000
Automobile	7,000		
Total	$23,000	Total	$23,000

BROWN COMPANY

Income Statement for January

Revenue	$6,000
Expense	2,000
Income	$4,000

2. The difference is the $1,000 that Brown withdrew.

3. The balance sheet should not be changed because assets are reported at their cost, not their "worth" or market value.

ANSWERS FOR POST TEST 4

1.

JOURNAL

1981	Transactions	Dr.	Cr.
March 5	Inventory	6,000	
	Cash		6,000
10	Cash	6,000	
	Accounts receivable	9,000	
	Revenues		15,000
10	Expenses	8,000	
	Inventories		8,000
31	Revenues	15,000	
	Income summary		15,000
31	Income summary	8,000	
	Expenses		8,000
31	Income summary	7,000	
	Retained earnings		7,000

2. and 3.

Cash

Dr.	Cr.
Bal. 25,000	6,000
6,000	
Bal. 25,000	

Accounts Receivable

Dr.	Cr.
Bal. 11,000	
9,000	
Bal. 20,000	

Inventory

Dr.	Cr.
Bal. 40,000	8,000
6,000	
Bal. 38,000	

Property and Plant

Dr.	Cr.
Bal. 30,000	

Accounts Payable

Dr.	Cr.
	16,000 Bal.

Paid-in Capital

Dr.	Cr.
	60,000 Bal.

Retained Earnings

Dr.	Cr.
	30,000 Bal.
	7,000
	37,000

Revenues

Dr.	Cr.
15,000	15,000

Expenses

Dr.	Cr.
8,000	8,000

Income Summary

Dr.	Cr.
8,000	15,000
7,000	

4.

KAY COMPANY

Balance Sheet as of March 31

Assets		Equities	
Cash	$25,000	Accounts payable	$16,000
Accounts receivable	20,000	Paid-in capital ..	60,000
Inventory	38,000	Retained earnings	37,000
Property and Plant	30,000		
Total	$113,000	Total	$113,000

KAY COMPANY

Income Statement for March

Revenues	$15,000
Expenses	8,000
Income	$7,000

5.

	Debits	Credits
Increases in asset accounts are	X	
Decreases in asset accounts are		X
Increases in liability accounts are		X
Decreases in liability accounts are	X	
Increases in equity accounts are		X
Decreases in equity accounts are	X	
Increases in revenue accounts are		X
Increases in expense accounts are	X	

6. Income is an increase in retained earnings, not necessarily cash. For example, the sales revenue was $15,000 even though only $9,000 was received in cash.

ANSWERS FOR POST TEST 5

1. (a) Recognize increases in equity only when they are reasonably certain.
   (b) Recognize decreases as soon as they are reasonably possible.

2. (a) Disregard trivial matters.
   (b) Disclose all important matters.

3. one year; interim

4. equity (or retained earnings)

5. revenues; expenses; income

6. delivered

7. November

8. (a) Advances from customers (a liability)
   (b) Revenue
   (c) Accounts receivable

9. (a) Accounts receivable
   (b) Cash
   (c) Advances from customers

10.

February	Cash	100	
	Advances from customers		100
March	Accounts receivable	500	
	Advances from customers	100	
	Revenue		600
March	Expenses	400	
	Inventory		400
April	Cash	500	
	Accounts receivable		500

11. (a) Revenue
    (b) Allowance for doubtful accounts
    (c) \$198,000
    (d) \$598,000

12. (a) Allowance for doubtful accounts
    (b) Accounts receivable

13. $\dfrac{\text{Accounts receivable}}{\text{Credit sales} \div 365}$

ANSWERS FOR POST TEST 6

1. acquired; consumed

2.

(a) March	May
(b) February	February
(c) February	April
(d) February	March

3. expenditure; asset; expense

4. unexpired; expired

5. Costs associated with the revenues of a period are expenses of that period.

6. (a) costs of the goods or services delivered during the period;
   (b) other expenditures that benefit operations of the period;
   (c) losses.

7. Prepaid; asset
Accrued; liability

8. $10,000

9. The difference between sales revenue and cost of sales

10. $\frac{\text{Gross margin}}{\text{Sales revenue}}$

11. The difference between revenues and expenses in an accounting period (*or* the amount by which equity [i.e., retained earnings] increased from operating activities during the period).

12. a distribution of earnings to shareholders.

13. (d) = (c) + (a) – (b)

ANSWERS FOR POST TEST 7

1.

Dr. Cash	800	
Cr. Revenue		800
Dr. Cost of Sales	600	
Cr. Inventory		600

2. A record is kept for each item, showing receipts, issues, and the amount on hand.

3. Cost of sales = beginning inventory + purchases – ending inventory.

4. (a) by taking a physical inventory
(b) same as the ending inventory of the prior period.

5.

	Cost of Sales	Inventory July 31
(a) FIFO	$300	$340
(b) LIFO	340	300
(c) Average cost	320	320

6. It gives a higher cost of sales and hence a lower taxable income.

7.

Dr. Cost of Sales	1,000	
Cr. Inventory		1,000

8. Direct materials, direct labor, and overhead

9. In the period in which they were incurred.

10. In the period in which the products were sold.

11. Overhead rate = $\frac{\text{total production overhead costs}}{\text{total direct labor costs}}$

12. $110 [= $50 + $40 + $20]

13. $\frac{\text{Cost of Sales}}{\text{Inventory}}$

14. Better, because it indicates that less capital is tied up in inventory, and there is less risk that the inventory will become obsolete.

ANSWERS FOR POST TEST 8

1. all costs incurred to make the asset ready for its intended use (such as transportation and installation)

2. five

3. Its service life is indefinitely long.

4. (a) \$18,000

(b) 10 percent

(c) \$1,800

(d) Dr. Depreciation expense

Cr. Accumulated depreciation

(e) (1) Plant \$20,000

(2) Less accumulated depreciation 9,000

(3) Book value \$11,000

5. (a) zero

(b) Machine (or plant) \$20,000

Accumulated depreciation ... 20,000

Book value 0

6. (a) gain; \$3,000

(b) Dr. Cash

Cr. Gain on disposition of plant

7.

	Example	Write-off process
Plant asset	machine, building	Depreciation
Wasting asset	coal, oil, minerals	Depletion
Intangible asset	goodwill, trademark	Amortization

8. \$400,000 (40,000 barrel @ \$10 per barrel) (*not* \$50,000)

9. Wasting assets and intangible assets are reported at the net amount only. Plant assets are reported at cost, less accumulated depreciation equals the net amount (i.e., book value).

10. low; fairly

11. It is assumed that the asset is purchased in the middle of the year, so half a year's depreciation is taken in the first year.

12. more; less; the same

13. It reduces taxable income and hence income tax in the early years, so the company has the use of more money in these years.

14. \$3 million

15. Deferred income tax; liability

ANSWERS FOR POST TEST 9

1. the difference between current assets and current liabilities.

2. debt (noncurrent liabilities); equity (shareholder equity)

3. make regular interest payments; repay principal when due.

sometimes (i.e., when due date is within the next year)

4. paid-in capital from shareholders; retained earnings (income not paid out as dividends)

5. Cash 10,000

Cash	10,000	
Common stock		1,000
Other paid-in capital		9,000

6. (a) $10
   (b) $30,000
   (c) can't tell (equity does not represent "worth")
   (d) can't tell (equity has no relation to cash)
   (e) at least $40,000 (it exceeds $40,000 by the amount of dividends)
   (f) can't tell (equity does not show liquidation value)

7. issued; outstanding

8. treasury; 140,000

9. dividends; par value in the event of liquidation

10. decreases; does not change; increases

11. Yes No
    Yes No
    High Low
    Low High

12. (a) 80 percent
    (b) leveraged

13. parent;
    Able Company, Charlie Company (not David Company);
    minority interest

14. $1,470,000

ANSWERS FOR POST TEST 10

1. $\frac{100}{40} = 2.5$

2. $\frac{60}{20} = 3$ times

3. $\frac{10}{100} = 10\%$

4. $\frac{80}{180} = 44\%$

5. $\frac{10}{100} = 10\%$

6. $\frac{30}{100} = 30\%$

7. $\frac{100}{180} = 0.6$ times

8. $\frac{30}{180} = 17\%$

9. $0.3 \times 0.6 = 18\%$

10. (a) decreasing
    (b) increasing

11. a company's ability to meet its current obligations.

12. a company's ability to meet its long-term obligations.

13. (a) Cash from operations
    (b) $120,000
    (c) Cash flow statement

14. Because it adjusts the amount of net income to show the amount of cash provided by operations.

15. Any three of the following.

- Accounting deals only with events that can be reported in monetary terms.
- Financial statements report only past events.
- Balance sheets do not shows the market value of assets.
- The accountant and management have some latitude in choosing among alternative ways of recording an event (e.g., LIFO, FIFO, or average cost).
- Accounting amounts are affected by estimates.

16. (a) its own performance in a previous period(s) (historical)

(b) other companies in the same industry (external)

(c) a judgmental standard

(Any order)

Glossary and Index

Note. The definitions here are brief. For a fuller discussion and examples, see the frames indicated. References are to parts and frames; e.g. 1:13–17 means part 1, frames 13–17.

Accelerated depreciation A method of depreciation that charges off more of the original cost of a plant asset in the earlier years than in the later years of the asset's service life. Used mainly in calculating taxable income. **(8:77–92)**

Account A record in which the changes for a balance sheet or income statement item are recorded. **(4:1–2)**

Account payable The amount that the entity owes to a supplier, not evidenced by a note. **(2:61)**

Account receivable An amount that is owed to the business, usually by one of its customers as a result of the ordinary extension of credit. **(2:41)**

Accounting income Income measured according to accounting principles. Contrast with **Taxable income. (8:72–76)**

Accounting period The period of time over which an income statement summarizes the changes in equity. Usually the *official* period is one year, but income statements are also prepared for a shorter, or *interim*, period. **(5:4–9)**

Accrual accounting Accounting for revenues in the period in which they are earned and for expenses in the period in which they were incurred. This is normal accounting practice. Cash accounting, which accounts only for cash receipts and payments, is usually not acceptable. **(5:10–20)**

Accrued expense Another term for **Accrued liability.** Note that this is a liability account, not an expense account. **(6:37–46)**

Accrued liability A liability that arises because an expense occurs in a period prior to the related cash payment. Example: accrued wages payable. **(6:37–46)**

Accumulated depreciation An account showing the total amount of depreciation of an asset that has been accumulated to date. It is subtracted from the cost of the asset, and the difference is the asset's **Book value. (8:41–46)**

Advances from customers A liability account showing the amount due customers who have paid for goods or services in advance of their delivery. Sometimes called **Deferred revenue** or **Precollected revenue. (5:50–57)**

Allowance for doubtful accounts The amount of estimated bad debts that is included in accounts receivable. This amount is subtracted from accounts receivable on the balance sheet. **(5:71–75)**

Amortization The process of writing off the cost of intangible assets. Sometimes used as a name for expensing the cost of all assets. **(8:68,71)**

Asset A valuable item that is owned or controlled by the entity and that was acquired at a measurable cost. **(2:25–32)**

Auditing A review of accounting records by independent, outside public accountants. **(10:13–18)**

Authorized stock The total number of shares of stock that a corportion is permitted to issue. (The total number actually issued is usually a smaller amount.) **(9:31)**

Available for sale The sum of beginning inventory and purchases during the period. **(7:12–15)**

Average-cost method Finding cost of sales by taking the average cost per unit of the beginning inventory plus purchases. **(7:36–37)**

Bad debt An account receivable that never will be collected. **(5:65–67)**

Bad debt expense The estimated amount of bad debts applicable to an accounting period. **(5:65–75)**

Balance The difference between the totals of the two sides of an account. An account has either a debit balance or a credit balance. (See **4:8,63** for procedure for balancing an account.)

Balance sheet A financial statement that reports the assets, liabilities, and equities of a company at one point in time. Assets are listed on the left and liabilities and equities on the right. (For balance sheet items, *see* **2:20–80.**)

Bond A written promise to repay money furnished the business, with interest, at some future date, usually more than one year hence. **(9:9,13)**

Book value The difference between the cost and the accumulated depreciation of a depreciable asset. **(8:45–46)**

Calendar year The year that ends on the last day of the calendar, December 31. The accounting period for many entities is the calendar year, but some use the **Natural business year. (5:5–8)**

Capital In general, the amount of funds supplied to an entity. **(9:17–18)** Also used as the name for *Paid-in capital* in a proprietorship or partnership.

Capital-intensive Characterizes a company that has a large capital investment in relation to its sales revenue. **(10:81)**

Capital lease An item the entity controls by a lease agreement that extends over almost the whole life of the item. A capital lease is an asset. **(8:9–12)**

Capital stock A balance sheet account showing the amount that the shareholder contributed in exchange for stock. This plus retained earnings equals equities in a corporation. **(9:17–42)**

Capital turnover A ratio obtained by dividing annual sales by the amount of permanent capital. **(10:80,81)**

Capital utilization, tests of (10:44–67)

Cash The name for money, whether in currency or in a bank account. **(2:35–37)**

Cash flow statement A financial statement reporting the sources and uses of cash during an accounting period. **(8:93–97)**

Cash–basis accounting An accounting system that does not use the accrual basis; it records only cash receipts and payments. Usually not an acceptable basis for accounting. **(5:17–18)**

Charge (verb) To debit an account.

Claim Amount owed to creditors or others who have provided money or have extended credit to a business. **(1:12,13)**

Closing entries Journal entries that transfer the balances in revenue and expense accounts for a period to retained earnings. **(4:55–62)**

Common stock Stock whose owners are not entitled to preferential treatment with regard to dividends or to the distribution of assets in the event of liquidation. **(9:25–34)** Its book value is not related to its market value. **(9:35–38)**

Comparisons, bases of Performance can be compared with past performance, with performance of other entities, or with a judgmental standard. (*See* **10:29–32**)

Concepts *See* **6:91–99** for a summary of accounting concepts.

Conservatism concept Recognize increases in equities only when they are reasonably certain; recognize decreases as soon as they are reasonably possible. **(5:21–26)**

Consolidated statements Financial statements prepared for a whole corporate family as an entity. The family consists of a **Parent** and its **Subsidiaries**. **(9:81–96)**

Conversion cost The labor and overhead costs of converting raw material into finished products. **(7:51)**

Cost A monetary measure of the amount of resources used for some purpose. (For product cost, *see* **7:52–65**. For acquisition cost, *see* **8:5–8**. *See also* **Period costs**.)

Cost accounting The process of identifying and accumulating manufacturing costs and assigning them to goods in the manufacturing process. **(7:56)**

Cost concept Accounting focuses on the cost of assets, rather than on their market value. **(2:6–18)**

Cost of goods sold Same as **Cost of sales.**

Cost of sales Cost of the same products whose revenues are included in sales revenue. **(Part 7)**

Credit (noun) The right–hand side of an account or an amount entered on the right–hand side of an account. Abbreviated as Cr. **(4:26–30)**

Credit (verb) To make an entry on the right–hand side of an account. Rules for debit and credit are summarized in **4:42.**

Creditor A person who lends money or extends credit to an entity. **(1:12–14)**

Current assets Cash and assets that are expected to be converted into cash or used up in the near future, usually within one year. **(2:34–49)**

Current liabilities Obligations that become due within a short period of time, usually one year. **(2:59–67)**

Current ratio The ratio obtained by dividing the total of the current assets by the total of the current liabilities. **(2:68–73)**

Days' receivables The number of days of sales that are tied up in accounts receivable as of the end of the accounting period. Sales per day is found by dividing annual credit sales by 365, and accounts receivable is divided by sales per days to find the days' receivables. **(5:79–81)**

Debit (noun) The left–hand side of an account or an amount entered on the left–hand side of an account. Abbreviated as Dr. **(4:26–30)**

Debit (verb) To make an entry on the left–hand side of an account. Rules for debit and credit are summarized in **4:42.**

Debt capital The capital raised by the issuance of debt securities, usually bonds. **(9:8–10)** For differences between debt capital and equity capital, *see* **9:66–80.**

Debt ratio The ratio of debt capital to total permanent capital. **(9:78–80;10:62–66)**

Deduction method Finding cost of sales by adding the beginning inventory and purchases and subtracting the ending inventory. **(7:10–19)**

Deferred income taxes The difference between the actual income tax for the period and income tax expense. **(8:33–97)**

Deferred revenue *See* **Advances from customers.**

Depletion The process of writing off the cost of a wasting asset, such as natural gas, coal, oil, or other minerals. **(8:61–65)**

Depreciable cost The difference between the cost of a plant asset and its estimated residual value. **(8:28)**

Depreciation expense The portion of the estimated net cost of plant assets (e.g., buildings, equipment) that becomes an expense in a given accounting period. **(8:13–53)** (For accounting entries, *see* **8:43–51.** For depreciation in calculating taxable income, *see* **8:77–97.**)

Depreciation rate The percentage of the cost of an asset that is an expense each year. In the straight–line method, the rate is 1 divided by the service life. **(8:32–34)**

Direct labor or materials The labor or material that is used directly on a product. **(7:52–53)**

Disposition of plant, gain or loss on The difference between book value and the amount actually realized from a sale of a plant asset. **(8:55)**

Dividend The funds generated by profitable operations that are distributed to shareholders. Dividends are *not* an expense. **(6:75;9:43–60)**

Double-entry system A characteristic of accounting in which each transaction recorded causes at least two changes in the accounts.

Dual-aspect concept The total assets of an entity always are equal to its total liabilities and equities. **(1:26–29)**

Earnings Another term for **Net income. (9:44)**

Earnings before interest and taxes (EBIT) An amount used in calculating return on permanent capital. **(10:76–78)**

Earnings per share A ratio obtained by dividing the total earnings for a given period by the number of shares of common stock outstanding. **(10:71)**

Entity A business or other organization for which a set of accounts is kept. **(1:2)**

Entity concept Accounts are kept for entities, rather than for the persons who own, operate, or are otherwise associated with those entities. **(1:50–58)**

Entry The accounting record made for a single transaction. **(4:44)**

Equation, fundamental accounting Assets = Liabilities + Equities. **(1:28,29)**

Equities Capital supplied by (1) equity investors and (2) the entity's retained earnings. Also, claims against the entity by equity investors. **(2:74–84;9:17–52)**

Equity capital The capital supplied by owners, who are called equity investors. **(9:18–22)** For differences between debt capital and equity capital, *see* **9:66–78.**

Expenditure The decrease in an asset or increase in a liability associated with the acquisition of goods or services. Do not confuse with **Expense,** which represents the use of goods and services and which may occur after the expediture. **(6:3–19)**

Expense A decrease in equities resulting from operations during an accounting period; that is, resources used up or consumed during an accounting period. Example: wage expense. **(6:3–19)** For assets that will become expenses, *see* **6:20–35**; for expenses that create liabilities, *see* **6:36–46.**

Expensing The process of charging the cost of an asset to expense.

Expired cost Another name for **Expense. (6:16–19)**

External basis of comparison Comparing an entity's performance with the performance of other entities. **(10:30)**

Extraordinary gain (loss) A large, unusual, and nonrecurring gain or loss. **(6:74)**

Face amount The total amount of a loan that must be repaid, specified on the face of a bond. **(9:10)**

FIFO (first-in, first-out) method Finding cost of sales on the assumption that the oldest goods (those first in) were the first to be sold (first out). **(7:28–32)**

Financial accounting income Income as measured according to accounting principles. **(8:74)**

Financial statements *See* the three required financial statements: balance sheet, income statement, cash flow statement.

Fixed assets Tangible, noncurrent assets **(8:3)**

Gain (or loss) on disposition of plant, *see* **8:55.**

Going-concern concept Accounting assumes that an entity will continue to operate indefinitely. **(2:1–5)**

Goods available for sale The sum of the beginning inventory plus purchases during the period. **(7:12–15)**

Goodwill An intangible asset; an amount paid for a favorable location or reputation. Goodwill is an asset only if it was purchased. **(2:57–58)**

Gross margin The difference between sales revenue and cost of sales. **(6:69)**

Gross margin percentage Gross margin as a percentage of sales revenue. **(6:86,87)**

Half year convention Taking half a year's depreciation in the first year an asset was acquired. **(8:78—81)**

Historical basis of comparison Comparing an entity's performance with its own performance in the past. **(10:29)**

Income The amount by which equities increased as a result of operations during a period of time. **(3:39–45)**

Income statement A statement of revenues and expenses, and the difference between them, for an accounting period; a flow report. It explains the changes in equities associated with operations of the period. **(3:44–58;6:65–77)**

Income summary A temporary ledger account used to calculate net income. **(4:56–62)**

Income tax A tax levied as a percentage of taxable income. *See* **Taxable income.**

Intangible asset An asset that has no physical substance, such as the protection provided by an insurance policy or goodwill. **(8:67–69)**

Intercompany transactions Transactions between the corporations in a consolidated family. These transactions are eliminated in preparing consolidated financial statements. **(9:86–89)**

Interest The amount paid for the use of money. A loan requires payment of both interest and **Principal. (9:13–16)**

Interest expense The entity's cost of using borrowed funds during an accounting period. **(9:13–16)**

Interest revenue Revenue earned from permitting someone to use the entity's money. Revenue from the "rental" of money. Often but erroneously called interest income. **(5:60–61)**

Interim statements Financial statements prepared for a period shorter than one year, such as a month or a quarter. **(5:5)**

Inventory (noun) Goods being held for sale, and material and partially finished products that will be sold upon completion. **(2:44–45)** For inventory valuation methods, *see* **Part 7.**

Inventory (verb) To conduct a physical inventory.

Inventory turnover A ratio that shows how many times inventory was totally replaced during the year; calculated by dividing the average inventory into cost of sales. **(7:71–75)**

Investments Securities that are held for a relatively long period of time and are purchased for reasons other than the temporary use of excess cash. They are noncurrent assets. **(2:55)**

Issued stock The shares of stock that have been issued. Issued stock less **Treasury stock** equals **Outstanding stock. (9:31)**

Journal A record in which transactions are recorded in chronological order. It shows the accounts to be debited or credited and the amount of each debit and credit. Transactions are **Posted** to the ledger. **(4:44–46)**

Judgmental basis of comparison Comparing an entity's performance with our personal judgment. **(10:31)**

Land, life of see **8:13**

Lease An agreement under which the owner of property permits someone else to use it. The owner is the *lessor*. The user is the *lessee*. **(8:9)**

Ledger A group of accounts. Entries are posted to the ledger from the journal. **(4:43)**

Leverage A company that obtains a high proportion of its permanent capital from debt is said to be *highly leveraged*. **(9:76,77)**

Liability The equity or claim of a creditor. **(2:59–73)**

LIFO (last-in, first-out) method Finding cost of sales on the assumption that the goods most recently purchased (last in) were the first to be sold (first out). **(9:33–35)**

Limitations on financial statement analysis (10:19–24)

Liquidity An entity's ability to meet its current obligations. Often measured by the current ratio. **(10:90)**

Losses Expenses resulting from assets whose future benefit has expired during a period, for example, from fire or theft, and liabilities occurring in a period, for example, from lawsuits. **(6:47–54)** *See also* **Gain** (or loss).

Manufacturing company A company that converts raw materials into finished, salable products and then sells these products. **(7:50–52)** For accounting for inventory in a manufacturing company, *see* **7:49–70.**

Manufacturing overhead *See* **Production overhead cost.**

Market value The amount for which an asset can be sold in the marketplace. **(2:11–13)**

Marketable securities Securities that are expected to be converted into cash within a year; a current asset. **(2:39)**

Matching concept Costs that are associated with the revenues of a period are expenses of that period. **(6:20–24)** For matching of income tax expense, *see* **8:93–97.**

Materiality concept Disregard trivial matters, but disclose all important matters. **(5:27–35)**

Merchandising company A company that sells goods that it has acquired from other businesses; a retail store, a wholesaler. **(7:49,50)**

Minority interest The equity of those shareholders in a subsidiary other than the equity of the parent. Reported as an equity item on the consolidated balance sheet. **(9:91–93)**

Monetary assets Cash and promises by an outside party to pay the entity a specified amount of money. **(5:76,77)**

Money-measurement concept Accounting records report only facts that can be expressed in monetary amounts. Accounting therefore does not give a complete record of an entity. **(1:45–48)**

Mortgage A pledge of real estate as security for a loan. **(3:31)**

Mortgage payable The liability for a loan that is secured by a mortgage. **(3:31)**

Natural business year A year that ends on the day that actitivities are at a relatively low level. For some entities, the accounting period is the natural business year, rather than the calendar year. **(5:7)**

Net The amount remaining after something has been subtracted from a gross amount. Example: accounts receivable, net. **(5:73)**

Net income The amount by which total revenues exceed total expenses for an account period; the "bottom line." **(6:75)**

Net income percentage Net income expressed as a percentage of sales revenue. **(6:88, 89)**

Net loss The amount by which total expenses exceed total revenues in an accounting period; negative net income. **(6:73)**

Net worth Another (but misleading) name for equity. **(9:51)**

Nonbusiness organizations Municipalities, hospitals, religious organizations, and other organizations that are not operated for the purpose of earning a profit. **(1:58)**

Noncurrent asset An asset that is expected to be of use to the entity for longer than one year. **(2:50–58)**

Noncurrent liability A claim that does not fall due within one year. Similar to **Debt capital. (2:70–73)**

No-par-value stock Common stock that does not have a par value. It is recorded at its **Stated value. (9:29,30)**

Note A written promise to pay. **(3:10)**

Note payable A liability evidenced by a written promise to pay. **(3:11)**

Note receivable An amount owed to the entity that is evidenced by a promissary note. **(2:43)**

Obsolescence A loss in the usefulness of an asset because of the development of improved equipment, changes in style, or other causes not related to the physical condition of the asset. It is one cause of depreciation; the other cause is wearing out. **(8:21)**

Opinion letter The letter in which the auditor gives his or her opinion as to the fairness of the financial statements. **(10:14–18)**

Other paid-in capital The amount paid by investors in excess of the par or stated value of the stock. **(9:27,28)**

Outstanding stock Shares of stock held by investors. Consists of **Issued stock** less **Treasury stock. (9:32)**

Overhead *See* **Production overhead cost.**

Overhead rate A rate used to allocate overhead costs to products. **(7:66–70)**

Owners' equity The claims of owners against the assets of a business. In a corporation, owners' equity consists of capital stock plus retained earnings. **(2:74–79)**

Package of accounting reports A balance sheet at the beginning of an accounting period, another at the end, and an income statement for the period. **(6:78–85)**

Paid-in capital The amount paid by investors in exchange for stock. The amount in excess of the stock's par or stated value is called **Other paid-in capital. (2:75–79;9:27,28)**

Par value The specific amount printed on the face of some stock certificates. No longer significant in accounting **(9:25,26)**

Parent A corporation that controls one or more other corporations because it owns more than 50 percent of their stock. The controlled corporations are its **Subsidiaries. (9:81,82)**

Partnership An unincorporated business with two or more owners. **(1:56)**

Patent A grant that gives an inventor the exclusive right, for 17 years, to produce and sell an invention. **(2:56)**

Percentage A number obtained by dividing one number by another (which is the base, or 100 percent), and multiplying by 100. Income statement items are often expressed as percentages of sales revenue.

Performance, measures of For overall measures of performance, *see* **10:25–31**; for tests of capital utilization, *see* **10:44–67**; for other measures, see **10:68–83.**

Period costs Costs associated with general sales and adminstrative activities. Contrast with **Product costs. (7:57–65)**

Permanent account An account for a balance sheet item, so called because it is not closed at the end of the accounting period. Contrast with **Temporary account. (4:67)**

Permanent capital The sum of noncurrent liabiltiies and equities. **(9:6–9,17–24)**

Perpetual inventory A record of the cost of each item in inventory showing the quantity and the cost of receipts, issues, and the amount on hand. **(7:5–6)**

Physical inventory The amount of inventory currently on hand, obtained by making a physical count. **(7:16–17)**

Plant assets All tangible, noncurrent assets except land. **(2:52)** For acquisition of plant assets, *see* **8:5–8.** For sale of plant assets, *see* **8:54,55.**

Posting The process of transferring transactions from the journal to the ledger. **(4:50–52)**

Precollected revenue See **Advances from customers.**

Preferred stock Stock whose owners have a preferential claim over common stockholders for dividends and for assets in the event of liquidation. **(9:39–42)**

Prepaid expenses The general name for intangible assets that will become expenses in future periods when the services they represent are used up. Example: prepaid insurance. **(2:47–48)**

Price-earnings ratio A ratio obtained by dividing the average market price of the stock by the earnings per share. **(10:71–73)**

Principal The amount that must be repaid on a loan. The total repayment consists of principal plus **Interest. (9:13)**

Product Goods or services sold or to be sold. (Sometimes refers only to tangible goods.)

Product costs The direct materials, direct labor, and production overhead costs of a product. Contrast with **Period costs. (7:57–65)**

Production overhead cost Product costs other than direct materials and direct labor. Includes, for example, supervision, building maintenance, and power. **(7:54)** *See also* **Overhead rate.**

Profit Another name for **Income. (3:57)**

Profit and loss statement Another name for **Income statement. (6:66)**

Promissory note A written acknowledgement of the amount that a borrower owes a creditor. A note receivable on the books of the lender and a note payable on the books of the borrower. **(2:43)**

Proprietorship An unincorporated business with a single owner. **(3:6)**

Ratio The result of dividing one number by another. *See*, for example, **Current ratio. (10:58,59)**

Realization concept Revenue is recognized when goods or services are delivered, in an amount that is reasonably certain to be realized. **(5:36–43)**

Recognition The act of recording a revenue or expense item as being applicable to a given accounting period. Revenue recognition is governed by the realization concept. **(5:36–63)**

Rental revenue Revenue earned from permitting someone to use a building or other property. **(5:58–60)**

Report package Consists of a balance sheet for the beginning and end of the accounting period and an income statement for the accounting period. **(6:78–85)**

Residual claim The claim of equity investors. **(1:18)**

Residual value The amount for which a company expects to be able to sell a plant asset for at the end of its service life. **(8:26,27)**

Retained earnings The increase in equities that has resulted from the operations of the entity. It is an equity item, not an asset. **(2:80–83;6:81–85)**

Return on equity (ROE) A ratio obtained by dividing net income by the amount of equity. **(10:26–28,36–43)**

Return on investment (ROI) Earnings before interest and taxes divided by noncurrent liabilities plus equities. (Some people calculate it in other ways.) **(10:74–83)**

Return on permanent capital Another name for return on investment. **(10:74–83)**

Revenue The increase in owners' equity resulting from operations during a period of time, usually from the sale of goods or services. **(3:47–48)** For measuring the amount of revenue, *see* **5:64–75**.

Sales income Sometimes used to mean **Sales revenue**; a misleading term because income is supposed to be the difference between sales revenue and expenses.

Sales revenue Revenue from the delivery of goods or services. **(5:42)**

Security An instrument such as a stock or bond. Securities give the entity that owns them valuable rights from the entity that issued them. **(2:38–40)**

Service An intangible product. Examples are personal services, rent, interest, insurance protection. **(5:58–63)**

Service life The period of time over which an asset is estimated to be of service to the entity. **(8:15–17,22)**

Service revenue Revenue from the performance of services. **(5:58–63)**

Shareholder equity The equities section of a corporation's balance sheet. **(9:23,24)**

Shareholders The owners of a corporation. Also referred to as stockholders. **(9:23)**

Shrinkages Goods that have been stolen or spoiled and hence are no longer in inventory. **(7:19)**

Solvency An entity's ability to meet its long–term obligations. Often measured by the **Debt ratio**. **(10:91)**

Stated value The amount at which no–par–value stock is reported on the balance sheet, as voted by the directors. **(9:29,30)**

Statement of financial position Another name for a **Balance sheet**.

Stock *see* **Capital stock, common stock, preferred stock.**

Stock dividend A dividend consisting of shares of stock in the corporation. **(9:55–60)**

Stock split An exchange of the number of shares of stock outstanding for a substantially larger number. **(9:61–65)**

Stockholders The equity investors in a corporation. Also referred to as shareholders. **(9:23)**

Straight–line depreciation A depreciation method that charges off an equal fraction of the estimated net cost of a plant asset over each year of its service life. **(8:30–31)**

Subsidiary A corporation that is controlled by another corporation, the parent, which owns more than 50 percent of its stock. **(9:82,83)**

T account The simplest version of an account. **(4:2–4)**

Tangible assets Assets that can be seen or touched; they have physical substance. Noncurrent tangible assets are often referred to as property, plant and equipment. **(2:51–54)**

Tax depreciation The depreciation used in calculating taxable income. **(8:77–92)**

Taxable income The amount of income subject to income tax, computed according to the rules of the Internal Revenue Service. For difference between taxable income and accounting income, *see* **8:72–76**. For treatment of depreciation, *see* **8:77–92.**

Temporary account A revenue or expense account. A temporary account is closed at the end of each accounting period. **(4:67)**

Trademark A distinctive name for a manufactured good or a service. **(2:56)**

Transaction An event that is recorded in the accounting records; it always has at least two elements. **(3:15–19)**

Treasury stock Previously issued stock that has been bought back by the corporation. **(9:32)**

Unexpired cost The cost of assets on hand now that will be consumed in future accounting periods. **(6:16–19)**

Wasting assets Natural resources, such as coal, oil, and other minerals. The process of charging wasting asset to expense is called **depletion. (8:61–66)**

Working capital The difference between current assets and current liabilities. **(9:4)**

Write down To reduce the cost of an item, especially inventory, to its market value. **(7:45–48)**

Write–off of bad debt To remove a bad debt from Accounts Receivable. **(5:71–75)**